Dear Tom & Lorraine,

Truly great neighbors &
friends,

Nash & Sonia
2/4/21

A PURSUIT of HAPPINESS

Memories, Dreams, and Mortality

NAUSHERWAN HASAN

ARCHWAY
PUBLISHING

Archway Publishing books may be ordered through booksellers or by contacting:

Archway Publishing
1663 Liberty Drive
Bloomington, IN 47403
www.archwaypublishing.com
844-669-3957

Because of the dynamic nature of the Internet, any web addresses or links contained in
this book may have changed since publication and may no longer be valid. The views
expressed in this work are solely those of the author and do not necessarily reflect the
views of the publisher, and the publisher hereby disclaims any responsibility for them.

Any people depicted in stock imagery provided by Getty Images are
models, and such images are being used for illustrative purposes only.
Certain stock imagery © Getty Images.

ISBN: 978-1-4808-9904-9 (sc)
ISBN: 978-1-4808-9961-2 (hc)
ISBN: 978-1-4808-9905-6 (e)

Library of Congress Control Number: 2020921657

Print information available on the last page.

Archway Publishing rev. date: 12/08/2020

Dedication

This Book is dedicated to my parents, Shaikh Mohammad Hasan and Begum Rashida Hasan as well as all the third generation of great-grandchildren, including Hannah and Adam.

This book is dedicated to my parents Abdul Suleiman and Kobra Oram, and Turson who have ever supported me through good moods and bad moods.

Preface

The inspiration of writing this personal story came from my elders, including (Late) Prof. K. K. Aziz and Dr. Parvez Hasan. The former was a first cousin of my father, who was a political science teacher, and a noted historian, having contributed several books on Pakistan Independence Movement and biographies, including a personal memoir. He wrote about a Portrait of a Punabi Family[1]. It is a detailed account of the family, with roots in Batala and Amritsar, India, that included an opportunity for his grandfather, Dr. Ghulam Nabi, to become the personal physician of the King of Afghanistan, Amir Habibullah (105-1917). This book also became a good source of historical information about my paternal side of the family.

The latter, Dr. Parvez Hasan, is my eldest brother. He was trained as an economist and served in responsible positions at the Pakistan Government and later at the World Bank. He wrote his memoir[2] upon retiring from the World Bank in 1995. His story is of an economist belonging to the first generation of the profession in Pakistan. He memoir narrates the unexpected turns in his life, while focusing on the history and economic development of Pakistan.

This is a story of a survivor- a survivor of two World Trade Center bombings and the tragedy that ensued. But more than that, it is a

---

[1] K.K. Aziz, "Portrait of a Punjabi Family 1800-1970- A Journey into the Past", Vanguard (PVT) Books, Lahore, 2006
[2] Dr. Parvez Hasan, "My Life My Country- A Pakistani Remembers", Ferozsons (PVT) Ltd. Lahore, 2011.

personal story of an immigrant's journey from the East to the West in pursuit of a better life with equality, fairness and happiness.

The long journey has taught me valuable lessons though the years-as a child, growing up and finally raising a family. Of course, there have been disruptions and challenges that came unexpectedly in the form of illness, death, loss of possessions, or dislocations. One of the early disruptions in our lives came when our family was forced to migrate to Pakistan following the partition of India in 1947. My father had to adjust to the new reality of raising a large family. He rose to the challenge and met it with hard work and faith.

It is a story of a middleclass family that persevered.

It is also a story of powerful dreams. The dream of an inventor who harnessed electrical energy. He was Thomas Edison. The dream gave birth to a Company, called Ebasco, formed by General Electric in 1905. That fruits of that energy dream would last for 100 years. As a civil engineer, I have been a small part in realization of this dream, of building nuclear and hydro-based electrical generating plants in USA and Overseas, for over forty-four years.

However, some of the dreams remained unfulfilled. It is a story of several such dreams.

Contents

Chapter 1

9/11

September 11, 2001

Sonia woke up due to loud voices coming from the apartment below. Jill, our tenant, sounded frantic and hysterical. She shouted at her husband, "War has begun! Go to the bank and get cash immediately!"

Jill had just heard about the attack on the World Trade Center. She thought it was an act of war. If war had begun, they would need cash for their immediate needs.

Sonia dressed quickly. The doorbell rang. She hurried downstairs. She opened the door. Jay and Fauzia, our neighbors, were there with horrified looks.

"We are here to support and comfort you." Jay spoke in a soft voice. Sonia was perplexed not knowing there had been an attack on the World Trade Center, (WTC), where I worked.

Their daughter, Amina, was on a bus commuting to work in Manhattan from Staten Island. She saw the North Tower of the World Trade Center ablaze from the Verrazano-Narrows Bridge and had called her parents. She knew I worked at the WTC. The news of the attack spread quickly through the media. Soon thereafter, Shanaz and Saadia, our friends and neighbors, came to our home. Their presence and support should have eased Sonia's fear about my safety, but she felt anxious and thought the worst had happened to me.

The doorbell rang again. It was Kathy. Vincent and Helen stood behind her on the porch. The family lived next door and had settled on the island long before we had moved there. Vincent worked in the bakery while Kathy was a RN at the Staten Island Hospital. Helen was Kathy's mother, well in her eighties, and lived with them.

"Sonia, a second plane has crashed into the WTC," Kathy said in an alarmed voice. "The entire plane including the cockpit is inside the building. The South Tower is in flames. Did you hear from Nash?"

"No, but he will be fine," Sonia replied. She was crying inside but strong on the outside.

"Nobody could have survived the impact." Kathy was emphatic.

The phone was ringing every few minutes. Friends and relatives were calling from around the world. Saad, calling from Alexandria, Virginia, asked, "Mom, have you heard from Dad?" He sounded worried. When Sonia answered in the negative, he was supportive and talked about the good times and happy memories. He said he was on the road bound for Staten Island. It would take him at least four hours to reach Staten Island.

A few minutes later, the phone rang again. Parveen Apa was calling from Bethesda, Maryland. "Sonia, which tower was Sheri in? North or South?"

Sonia replied, "The South Tower."

Parveen Apa was my eldest brother's wife. My eldest brother, Parvez, was in Islamabad, Pakistan, that day. It was early evening there (nine hours ahead of EST). As he was packing to catch a plane to London and then to the US that night, his phone rang. Ambareen, my niece, told him what she had seen of the North Tower being attacked on CNN news. My brother was shocked. Both knew I worked at the WTC but were not sure in which tower. He called his wife, Parveen, in Bethesda to find out. Parveen in turn called Sonia for the details. She was able to get through as the landlines were still working. Sonia confirmed that I worked in the South Tower. Shortly thereafter, the South Tower had been attacked and would fall. The Hasan family feared the worst had happened to me.

A Beautiful Day Turned Ugly

September 11, 2011, was a beautiful fall morning in NYC. The sky was clear with no clouds, the air was crisp, and the temperature was sixty-five. Low humidity. Visibility of ten miles or more. The winds were from the northwest blowing gently at eight mph. My ferry commute from Staten Island to downtown Manhattan was uneventful, and I was in my office on the ninety-first floor of 2 WTC by 8:00 a.m. My office faced City Hall, the East River, and the Brooklyn Bridge. The rising sun reflected off glass and metal facades; the WTC was a shining and glowing object for a few minutes only.

I got to my office with a coffee and a bagel I bought from a vendor next to the fire station on Liberty Street. I took the express elevator and was alone in it for the forty-five-second ride. As was my routine, I recited some verses from the Qur'an as the elevator rose to the seventy-eighth floor, where I took the local elevator to the ninety-first floor.

I was at my desk on the east side. That morning, the curtains were drawn, so I did not see the sun rise. I was working on a large dam and hydroelectric project in Philippines. After my bagel and coffee, I reviewed the shop drawings for the supply and erection of the hoists and cranes received via fax from Manila the night before (Manila was twelve hours ahead of EST). I sent my comments via fax around 8:30. By that time, Shiam Goyal was in the office, and we were discussing the intake structure under construction at San Roque.[3] We were unaware that the North

---

[3] The hydroelectric project was in San Roque in Luzon Province, 320 miles from Manila. It was a design-build services contract valued at $720 million for Raytheon Engineers and Contractors. The 345 MW project was one of the largest hydroelectric, flood-control projects in Asian history at that time. Its major feature included a 650-foot-high rock-filled dam, intake, power tunnel, and penstocks, an underground powerhouse, and a controlled spillway with gates. The various cranes and hoists for the project were being purchased from Demag.

Tower had been hit and that the 96th to the 103rd floors were engulfed in fire, that burning bodies were jumping out of the inferno some 1,000 feet to the plaza. I did not hear any explosion but did witness a brief flickering of the overhead lights. If the curtains were open, charred pieces of paper floating in the air around the tower would have been visible. At that time, there was no announcement on the PA system.

Suddenly, an ashen-faced Rita Meloy approached us and ordered us to leave immediately. Rita was the deputy warden on our floor, and during our quarterly fire drills, we had been accustomed to such orders and compliance. Her tone had an urgency that could not be ignored. There were others behind Rita. I grabbed my jacket and briefcase and followed my colleagues to the elevators that took us to the seventy-eighth floor lobby.

The lobby had a large crowd already. Nobody spoke, but facial expressions exhibited fear and anxiety. I hugged a sobbing Florence, a secretary from the typing pool whose sister was in the burning North Tower. I consoled her with positive thoughts that her sister would be fine. I was in front of the express elevator I had taken up an hour or so earlier. Two other elevators there served the floors between the forty-forth and seventy-eighth floors. Some of my colleagues including Rashil Levent and Hasu Patel rushed to them. Perhaps they were reluctant to ride the express elevators directly to the lobby. That thought did not enter my mind. Sometimes, decisions are made instinctively and with little rationality.

After a few minutes, the express elevator opened. During the short ride down, I asked Bill Heffernan, a colleague, what had happened in the North Tower. He said, "A small plane has hit the building."

We were in the lobby in less than a minute. There was absolutely no panic as we exited the elevator. The WTC security staff directed everybody to stay away from the revolving doors facing Liberty Street; we were directed to leave the WTC complex via the concourse connecting the two towers and exit on the Church Street side.

I was curious as to what had happened. Before exiting the building, I raced up the escalator to the mezzanine floor that opened to the plaza between the North and South Towers. A quick glance was enough to curb my curiosity. The plaza's revolving doors were closed, but through the glass, I saw debris falling from the North Tower. I instinctively took the escalator back to the lobby.

As I walked in the concourse toward the Church Street exit, I ran into another colleague, who asked me if he should hang around. I told him, "Go home. I am."

At that time, there was no rationale for my statement. There was no formal announcement from the Port Authority to leave the WTC or of an impending threat to the South Tower at that time. Actually, the PA system in the South Tower was advising people to return to their offices. There was no apparent panic since most people were unaware of the inferno in the North Tower at that time. My subconscious was calling the shots and perhaps knew the danger at hand.

It was 9:02 according to my watch when I was standing on the east side of Church Street across from the Burger King.[4] The air was full of debris—glass and charred paper. I saw a gaping hole in the east face of the North Tower some eight to ten stories in height approximately above the eighty-sixth floor with little smoke or fire evident. I looked around and saw hundreds of eyes focused on the North Tower gazing at the dramatic view but without apprehension. I almost wished I had a camera to record the event. Such a thought was quickly turned into fear as we heard the roar of the engines of a jet that crashed into the South Tower. The explosion caused a thunderous and ear-shattering sound that made me and others watching run for cover. Within seconds, the plaza was empty. I ran across the plaza and then down Broadway until I was breathless. I needed a restroom badly and tried entering a building on Broadway, but the security guard would not let me in. I walked past Wall Street, Trinity Church, banks, and other buildings and past the bronze bull and Custom House toward the ferry terminal.

---

[4] At that spot now exists a statue of a serene man sitting and working on his computer oblivious to the upheaval of that day.

Returning Home to Staten Island

I was one of the first arrivals at the ramp leading to the ferry entrance doors, which were closed. I thought of calling home, but there were huge lines at the public phones in the terminal. I met Faisal and Farooq Abbasi, who had left their offices at the Merrill Lynch Building after they witnessed the attack on 1 WTC. Faisal lent me his cell to call home, but there was no service.

Smoke continued to rise from the WTC. There was little wind. Skies around Battery Park were blue and clear. There was not a single plane in the air. The subways had stopped running. Police sirens were blowing around Battery Park. People were walking on the streets. Vehicular traffic was barely existent.

The South Tower was hit between the seventy-third and eighty-seventh floors at 9:06 a.m., exactly eighteen minutes after the North Tower had been hit between the eighty-sixth and the hundredth floors. I was lucky to have left the ninety-first floor immediately after the first plane struck the North Tower and to have been outside the WTC complex barely a few minutes before the South Tower was struck.

At 9:50 a.m., the entrance doors at the ramp were closed. A woman with a transistor radio heard that a plane had crashed into the Pentagon. I heard a woman say that she had seen the second plane as it turned around and aimed at the South Tower. As we anxiously waited for the ferry doors to open, we saw heavy smoke spewing from the towers. I was safe and away from the attack scene. I was grateful to be alive and shared my thoughts with Faisal and Farooq; I told them to offer special prayers of thanks upon reaching home.

At 10:00, there was no room on the ferry ramp; more than six thousand people waited anxiously to board. We heard another thunderous, roaring sound similar to jet planes breaking the sound barrier. I ducked instinctively for cover, yet there was none. People started pounding on the ferry doors in panic and desperation. It was like doomsday.

I found out later that the roaring sound was associated with the collapse of the South Tower at 9:59 a.m. The building collapse was attributed to the burning of thousands of gallons of jet fuel; the heat generated softened the exterior steel columns and led to their failure. The floors collapsed on each other creating a domino effect down to the lower floors.

Another plane crashed somewhere in Pennsylvania by 10:10 a.m. It was becoming clear that this had been a terrorist attack. The crowd at the terminal was getting larger and more restless, jittery, and nervous.[5]

Immediately after the collapse of the South Tower, the ferry ramp doors opened and a stampede followed into the new boat, *Newhouse*, with a capacity of approximately 5,200. Everybody grabbed orange life jackets until there were none left. I grabbed a seat on the middle level; the thought of donning a life jacket crossed my mind but was rejected quickly. All the seats were taken. The boat wobbled as the large crowd moved to the front or sides shifting the weight.

I was a somewhat patient and calm observer of the panic around me. A scared young fellow wearing a life jacket sat next to me. He was perhaps concerned that the boat would sink under the extra load but thought wearing a life jacket could save him. I may have remarked about our situation perhaps humorously that if the boat capsized, we would all drown and that wearing a life jacket might not be enough. That made him more agitated and nervous. We had no more conversation.

I was at peace with myself and ready for any outcome. Staying calm was dictated by the situation at hand. We were all lucky to have escaped unhurt. We would be safe once the boat left Manhattan. I had complete trust in God. Perhaps it was the morning prayers that strengthened my

---

[5] We learned later that the two planes that struck the towers had flown from Logan (Boston) airport bound for LA. Both planes were Boeing 767s with approximately 24,000 gallons of jet fuel. American Airlines Flight 11 departed at 7:45 am; Flight 175 departed at 7:58 am. It is apparent that the attacks were carefully coordinated. The terrorists planned to crash the two jets into the WTC complex almost simultaneously. If they had been successful, the death toll would have been perhaps ten to fifteen times higher than it was. The fifteen-to-eighteen-minute delay between the two attacks allowed most of the occupants, estimated at 20,000 to 30,000, of the South Tower to evacuate the complex.

faith. I reminded myself to offer *Nafal* (thanks) prayer upon reaching home.

The boat did not leave right away; there was a continuous rush of new, anxious passengers. While docked, the boat was engulfed in thick smoke and a cloud of fine dust from the fall of the South Tower. The beautiful day had been turned into an ugly, grey day.

That day, this would be the first boat that would leave lower Manhattan after the attack.[6]

As the boat moved out of the slip, I was relieved to leave Manhattan. Reality was sinking in. I was a lucky survivor. I was lucky to leave on that boat; otherwise, I would have had to probably walk home or go to my sister's home in Linden, New Jersey. Most of the people who came downtown that day faced undue delay and hardship returning home.

There had been a great tragedy. Many loved ones were lost. I was thirsty, and I had the continuous urge to relieve myself, but that would wait for another hour or so.

The boat raced across Hudson Bay leaving the chaotic Manhattan scene and the dust cloud. The smoke rose into the sky where the buildings burned. The towers were no longer visible.[7] On the Staten Island side, a Staten Island Rapid Transit (SIRT) train, a local train, was waiting. I ran into Fred Hassel, a colleague from the ninety-first floor, who was visibly moved by what had happened at the WTC. I tried to talk to him, but he was quite blunt and said, "I don't want to talk about it." I was puzzled by his response. Ten years later, I ran into him in Manhattan and told him I was still puzzled by his response to me that day. He said he had seen burning bodies jumping from the North Tower and was overcome with trauma. Recalling that Rita had seen burning, falling bodies, I understood his trauma.

---

[6] The Department of Transportation has operated the Staten Island Ferry since 1905. The ferry carries over 22 million passengers annually on a 5.2-mile run between the St. George Terminal in Staten Island and the Whitehall Terminal in lower Manhattan. The ferry runs twenty-four hours a day, 365 days a year.
[7] The North Tower collapsed at 10:28 a.m., an hour and forty minutes after it was struck.

Nash Is Safe! Nash Is Home!

It took over thirty minutes and fifteen stops for the train to reach the Huguenot Station. I walked up the thirty steps from the station and rushed across Huguenot Avenue to Ciro Pizzeria's restroom. I had had the desperate need to relieve myself for over two hours.

I told the waitress there had been an attack at the WTC; she had not yet heard about it.

I hurried home to Edgegrove Avenue, a ten-minute walk, and I heard my next-door neighbor, Kathy, shouting with joy and relief, "Nash is safe! Nash is home!" She hugged me. Before long, she was ringing the doorbell of our home. Sonia opened the door; she was crying. Tears rolled down my cheeks as well, but they were happy tears.

I was unaware of what Sonia had been going through. While I was relieved after leaving the chaotic scene following the attack on WTC, she had been quite shaken up at seeing the collapse of the South Tower and not having heard from me for over two hours. She had been continuously badgered by phone calls, visits from friends, and neighbors to console her. Finally, she stopped answering the phone fearing the worst had happened to me. Phone messages were piling up; we had over two hundred missed calls. Unable to meet the call volume, the landlines died too. The agony she went through during those hours is still fresh and will not fade.

Aamir, Sonia's brother, was in Chicago. He was able to get through. "Where's Sheri?" he asked. When Sonia replied that she hadn't heard from me, he comforted her: "He'll be fine."

We did not have cell phones, and the landlines were not restored until about 1:00 that afternoon. I listened to messages from family and friends as far away as Pakistan.

One of the messages was from the Human Resources Department (HR) of my firm, Washington Group International (WGI). The caller asked me to call back confirming that I was safe. I called HR the next morning at six and reported to an operator on duty that I was safe. I asked, "Why are you working at this early hour?"

"We've been manning the phones for the last twenty-four hours," he said.

The response elated me. Somebody cared about me.

Other calls were from relatives and friends who knew I worked in the WTC complex. There was genuine concern from them all about my safety.

My sister Mona and her family lived in Linden, New Jersey. She had been stopped from crossing the Goethals Bridge to Staten Island. Yasmin and her husband, Perwaiz, lived on Staten Island. He was stopped from returning home via the Outer Bridge Crossing and had slept in Linden. All other bridge crossings including the Verrazano-Narrows Bridge, which connected Staten Island to New York/New Jersey, were closed immediately after the attacks. Traffic was allowed in the late afternoon that day. Also, train service was suspended in downtown Manhattan. Some of my colleagues reached home late in the afternoon after walking several miles.

Some did not make it home at all including thirteen from our firm.

My brother, Pervez, in Islamabad, spent many anxious hours until the news of my safety reached him and relieved his worst fears. His plans to return to the US were jeopardized by the 9/11 event. He could not fly back to the US for several days since all the international flights to the US were canceled for a week.

It was a long day that I spent catching up with the developing news of the disaster and rescue operations and thanking all my friends, relatives, and community members for their well-wishes.

I went to bed early and had the best sleep that I remember.

Stories of the Survivors

September 11 was indeed a day of great human tragedy, but it was also a day of great human courage, heroism, and kindness.

A week after 9/11, the WTC survivors of WGI group (listed below) got together in midtown Manhattan to pay homage to our thirteen colleagues and offer prayers of gratitude to the Almighty. Every survivor had a story. It was an emotional prayer meeting that brought some closure, and it was followed by much hugging and sharing the chronology of that day. I share some of the stories that provide glimpses of hope and gratitude that come our way in adversity.

Susan worked in mailroom on the ninety-first floor. She suffered from high blood pressure. She decided to walk down the stairs instead of taking the elevators. Her physical condition slowed her descent, and colleagues and others walked past her on the way down. She was nearly halfway down when the plane struck the building. She fell down and hurt her shoulder. She could not continue her descent. A stranger (she called him an angel) persuaded her to get up and led her slowly down. She had no idea that the building was burning and would collapse soon. As they reached the lobby, she was then taken into an ambulance parked on Vesey Street. Soon thereafter, as the South Tower collapsed, a fireball and dust cloud descended with such force that it launched some parked into the air. The angel and Susan quickly got out of the ambulance and ran from the dust cloud. They were fighting to stay alive and holding hands to support each other. When they made it to safety, the angel disappeared. He was a real unsung hero who saved Susan's life that day.

Katherine Ilachinski, an architect, decided to take the stairs after disembarking from the forty-fourth floor. She said, "The whole stairs was shaking, and I started praying. I thought I was a goner." Her prayers were answered. She made it to safety.

Bob Keilbach, an engineer, had an office on the ninety-first floor. On the morning of September 11, he drove from his Queens home to a meeting at WGI's offices in Princeton, New Jersey. At the prayer meeting, he told me, "I'm having nightmares since 9/11 even though I wasn't at the accident site."

WGI responded to its employees' post-accident depression and trauma issues and offered them psychiatric help. Bob Keilbach and some others elected to avail themselves of the help. A psychiatrist told him that the nightmares were due to survivors' guilt. Bob gradually overcame the nightmares.

Rashil and Hasu were in the office on the ninety-first floor having finished egg sandwich breakfasts. Rashil heard a coworker who sat in a cubicle facing the North Tower yell that they should leave immediately. He also heard Kula shouting to leave. He and Hasu took the elevator to the seventy-eighth-floor lobby and saw Ed O'Connor, Bill Gesztes, and

Florence. Ed had a frightened look Rashil had never seen. He and others took the elevator to the forty-fourth floor and then followed a crowd to a stairway leading to the ground floor. While descending, they heard on the intercom that the emergency was related to 1 WTC only, that everything was okay in 2 WTC, and that people should await further instructions.

A group of WGI employees including Kula Hrisovolous, Maureen Cunningham, Verna Clark, Hasu, and Rashil was slowly descending the well-lit staircase B somewhere below the twentieth floor when they heard an explosion and felt an earthquake-like jolt from the impact of the plane hitting the South Tower. The lights flickered; it was dark for a few seconds before the generators kicked in. It was light again. At that point, their calm gave way to panic, and there was a mad rush going down several flights of stairs to the lobby, which was dark and smoky. Some windows were completely shattered. Rashil thought it was Armageddon.

The WTC security staff warned the shaken evacuees not to exit on Liberty Street, but Rashil ignored the warning and exited onto Liberty Street. It was like a war zone outside; cars were burning on Liberty Street, and debris was on the ground. He was separated from Hasu. Being athletic and fit, he ran south on Greenwich Street. He reached Rector Street and saw Hasu; he was amazed that Hasu, being smaller built and less athletic, had managed to beat him to safety.

Through a good Samaritan, Rashil was able to send a message to his wife, Fazile, that he was safe. Fazile worked in Midtown for Finnair. Rashil walked Uptown to meet her, at which time she realized he had survived. They were very happy to be reunited. Rashil was covered with dust from the collapse of the South Tower.

Shiam Goyal left me and walked to the north side of the building to view the burning North Tower. He saw the inferno. Then he decided to take the staircase to the seventy-eighth-floor lobby accompanied by Alan Bonderanko and others. Shiam left the stairs there and waited for the express elevators; Alan continued downstairs to the forty-fourth-floor lobby. The Port Authority announced that the South Tower was safe. Alan never made it to safety.

Shiam took the express elevator and was safely out on Church Street when the second jet struck. He was able to take the last train going Uptown that morning. Since the Port Authority Bus Terminal buses to New Jersey were not running, he took a ferry to Hoboken, New Jersey, and reached home in South Brunswick, New Jersey, after 4:00 p.m. He was able to call home through a stranger's cell about his safety prior to reaching home.

Dave Hunter took the express elevator to the lobby and went out on Church Street and to Broadway. He saw the explosion when the plane hit the South Tower. He was able to take the last train to Grand Central Station for his return to Connecticut. The Metro North trains were shut down. He went to Central Park and sat there for several hours until his wife called him that the trains were running. He reached home in the late afternoon.

Rita was in the small park on Broadway near the bull sculpture when she was fully engulfed in the debris from the South Tower collapse.

Ed O'Connor wanted to be as far from the WTC as he could get. His destination was the George Washington Bridge, where he could ride a bus to his New Jersey home. He kept walking and resting until he could walk no more. He took a cab, which was not allowed on the GW Bridge. After paying the cab, he walked up to Van Courtland Park and then to Manhattan College. As an alumnus, he was allowed to spend the night in the residences. He did not reach home until the next day.

Sunil Rajani saw the impact of the first plane crashing into the North Tower as he was making coffee. He told others to leave the building. He was one of the last to leave the ninety-first floor, and he escorted Christina. He escaped the South Tower just before it was hit. He did not reach home until late evening.

Shah Habibullah also escaped the South Tower before it was hit. He ran south as the crash occurred. He wife also worked downtown. His cell phone was not working, but he was able to call her from a pay phone. They were able take a ferry to Staten Island. Later that afternoon, they were able to cross the Verrazano-Narrows Bridge via a special bus to Brooklyn. They reached their Queens home around 6:00 p.m.

Dr. Salman Zafar, a friend from Staten Island, escaped the WTC attack. He was at the concourse level in the Citibank to transact some business, but the line was too long, so he left for Uptown by subway minutes before the first plane struck.

His intuition guided him to safety.

Colleagues Who Perished

The thirteen who perished that day could not tell their stories. Their spouses waited desperately for days to hear from them hoping they had survived. There was Vassillos Haramis, a Greek-American, who was on loan from the Princeton office. He was supposed to return there within a few days. His wife kept on calling his friends and colleagues for news about him, but there was none. Most of the people who died that day were identified through dental records, pieces of jewelry, or DNA.

A story of valor was Bob DeAngelis's. He was working on the San Roque Project at the time, and he was a voluntary fireman in his town on Long Island. As people started to evacuate the building, Bob went up again to our offices, where two secretaries had left their purses. He escorted them to the sky lobby and went back to his ninety-first-floor office to talk to his wife. As he was speaking with her, the second plane struck. His wife, who also saw the plane hitting the South Tower, told Bob to get out. Bob's body was never found.

Fred Kuo, a Chinese-American and a devout Catholic, also went back to his office that morning. A few months before 9/11, he had been in an express elevator that malfunctioned. While others were seriously hurt during this incident and were hospitalized, Fred escaped without injury.

Anthony Portillo, an architect and father of two young children, took the elevator going down to the lobby. He was presumably on the train platform trying to go home when the tower fell. He was never seen again.

Ming Liu was using the toilets on the ninety-first floor when the plane struck. It cost him his life.

Alan Bondarenko's story was unusual. He had been on the ninety-first floor of the South Tower for a job interview on February 26, 1993, when a bomb went off in the WTC parking garage during the lunch hour.

The smoke quickly filled the three stairwells in the South Tower making the exit from the upper floors impossible. The stairs were also dark since there were no emergency lights. It took the fire department several hours to install fans to clear the smoky staircase. As he walked down the stairs with Shiam that morning of 9/11, the 1993 episode was obviously on his mind. Somebody heard him say that he was not coming back. Alan's body was never found.

The thirteen colleagues who perished were these.

First Row	Second Row	Third Row
Ulf R. Ericson	Robert DeAngelis Jr.	Frederick Kuo Jr.
Oleh Wengerchuk	Frank Moccia	Carlos Cortes
Luis C. Revilla	Emelda Perry	Peter Gyulavary
Alan Bondarenko	Ming-Hao Liu	Vassilios G. Haramis
Anthony Portillo		

Heroes of the Day

In addition to Bob DeAngelis, who showed unusual courage in escorting the secretaries from the ninety-first floor to safety, other heroes were these.

Sue Sisk: Sue was the IT technician responsible for backing up the project drawings and documents weekly. That day, she showed a tremendous sense of responsibility by retrieving the backed-up computer discs. She became one of the heroes that day since the saved documents assured the continued engineering and design of the San Roque Project without interruption.

Peter Totten: Peter, the engineering manager, was our floor's warden. He and our deputy wardens conducted regular fire safety drills. He went around the floor and advised the engineers, who were unaware of the attack, to leave immediately, and he was perhaps the last person to evacuate the floor. His persistence saved lives of the reluctant evacuees, who would otherwise have perished in the second plane attack.

Disruptions and Rescue Operations

The towers were perhaps half-filled at the time of the attacks (estimated to be 25,000 people for the two towers). Just before 9:00 a.m., many commuters were still approaching the WTC from the Path trains from New Jersey or subway stations below the concourse level. One was Sam Martinovich, an electrical engineer. He had just bought coffee from a street vendor when the north tower was hit. His life was spared.

While nearly 3,000 people lost their lives on 9/11, a greater number of lives were spared. Many of those who survived were traumatized by the loss of friends and loved ones. The physical, emotional, and psychological wounds from this tragedy have left scars that would require a long time to heal.

NYC Transit suspended all subway service downtown at 10:30 a.m. Partial subway service was restored in the late afternoon on select trains only.

The Federal Aviation Administration shut down the Newark, Kennedy, and La Guardia airports immediately after the attack. Commercial air traffic was halted in the entire space over the US, and Canadian officials quickly followed suit. International flights en route to the US were diverted to other countries or returned to their points of origin. The airlines announced that the families of the victims would receive $25,000 to meet their immediate needs.

The explosions in Manhattan prompted significant disruption of telephone service in the morning, but it was restored in the late afternoon. Wireless service was particularly disrupted due to overload in the morning hours. Pay phones at the ferry terminal were working, but the lines were very long. The loss of the antenna at the North Tower disrupted television service also, which had to resort to backups at the Empire State Building antenna.

In Washington, DC, the White House and the Capitol buildings were evacuated by 10:00 a.m., after the assault on the Pentagon.

Since there were no trains or buses running in downtown Manhattan, thousands of people took to the streets and streamed across the Brooklyn and Manhattan Bridges and the 59th Street Bridge to Queens and as far as Staten Island. They walked in bewilderment and perhaps fear. Many were covered with ash and dust from head to toe; some were wearing masks or holding handkerchiefs or wet cloths over their mouths. Some walked while others ran. Some commanded their fellow citizens to calm down as they tried to assess the sudden disruption. Roads and highways were empty of vehicular traffic, a scene seldom experienced in NYC. It was reminiscent of the NYC transit strikes in 1966.

Rudolph Giuliani, the mayor of New York then, took control immediately after the attack at the command center in lower Manhattan. As the towers collapsed, he exercised effective leadership that reassured the public and restored calm.

Ferries offered a more reliable service to connect Manhattan and New Jersey, Brooklyn, and Queens. As the towers fell, dust clouds enveloped Manhattan and hundreds of thousands of people were panicked and stranded due to the nonexistence of all road transportation in lower

Manhattan. The US Coast Guard issued a distress call to all ferry and other boat operators in the vicinity for help. Before long, hundreds of boats converged on lower Manhattan and rescued the stranded people. It was later estimated that over 500,000 people were rescued via ferries and boats that day from Manhattan, the operation lasting over nine hours. Perhaps this evacuation was larger than the Dunkirk evacuation in 1940.[8]

Death Toll

The official death toll for the 9/11 attacks at WTC was 2,966 including the 19 hijackers.

In addition to the two planeloads of people who lost their lives at the WTC attacks, Flight 77, which had taken off from Dulles Airport, crashed into the Pentagon, while Flight 93, which had taken off from Newark, crashed in Shanksville, near Pittsburgh. A total of 266 were on board the four airplanes that were hijacked and crashed that day.

Among the missing and presumably dead were several thousands of people from over eighty-five countries and included Americans, Chinese, Japanese, Indians, and others—innocent people who had failed to escape the attacks. Many others who survived the event will be telling their stories to their children and grandchildren for years to come.

---

[8] The Dunkirk evacuation, also known as the Miracle of Dunkirk, was the evacuation of Allied soldiers during World War II from the beaches and harbor of Dunkirk, in the north of France, between May 26 and June 4, 1940. The operation commenced after large numbers of Belgian, British, and French troops were cut off and surrounded by German troops during the six-week Battle of France. In a speech to the House of Commons, British Prime Minister Winston Churchill called this "a colossal military disaster," saying "the whole root and core and brain of the British Army" had been stranded at Dunkirk and seemed about to perish or be captured. In his "we shall fight on the beaches" speech on 4 June, he hailed their rescue as a "miracle of deliverance." It involved the evacuation of some 340,000 Allied troops from the French port of Dunkirk during World War II. Refer to https://en.Wikipedia.org/wiki/Dunkirk_evacuation.

February 26, 1993 WTC Bombing (refer to https://www.fbi.gov/ history/famous cases-world trade center-bombing-1993)

The 1993 World Trade Center bombing was a terrorist attack on the World Trade Center carried out on February 26, 1993, when a truck bomb detonated below the North Tower of the World Trade Center in New York City. The bomb was laden with explosives and left in the underground garage at the Complex. It went off at 12:17 pm. It left a 100-ft crater, several stories high Six people were killed immediately and more than 1000 people were injured from the bombing that resulted in evacuating 50,000 people from the Complex.

It was lunch hour at the WTC. The express elevators were carrying people down to the lobby. Both towers shook from a blast in the base-ment of the complex. The six-floor-deep basement garage was between the Twin Towers known as WTC 1 and WTC 2.

I was in my office on the ninety-first floor facing the east side. I was not planning to go down since I was fasting, it being Ramadan, the month of fasting for Muslims between dawn and sunset. Looking down, I noticed unusual activity—NYC fire engines enveloping the WTC complex on the Church Street side. Since I could hear no sound, I went to the south side of the building and looked down on Liberty Street, where I saw the same fire engine activity.

Somebody informed us that there was no elevator service. A few minutes later, the PA announced that there was some fire in the base-ment, which was being investigated. We were told to remain on our floors. The PA explanation caused more anxiety. Somebody on the floor had a transistor radio, which was broadcasting additional information on the incident and instructions for the occupants to remain calm. Hearing this, Ed O'Connor decided to walk down. The smoke from the blast was rising slowly in all three staircases. He walked the entire ninety-one flights to the lobby and safety.

He told us later the staircase was dark and full of heavy smoke on the lower floors. He had to hold his hand on the railings as he ventured down. Some colleagues abandoned their escape and came back; they were too scared to walk down through the smoke-filled stairs below the forty-fourth floor. The staircases had no emergency lights then. But Ed made it through.

While stranded on the ninety-first floor, we heard radio instructions: "Keep the office doors closed and use wet handkerchiefs to avoid inhaling smoke." I went to the restroom to wet a paper towel, but there was no water due to the power outage.

Since it was midday, there was plenty of sunlight on the floor. We got together in George Kanakaris's corner office; being the farthest from the staircases, it was relatively free of smoke.

I was able to call home and let Sonia know I was fine and would not be coming home soon. The PA informed us that the fire was under control and that the firefighters had set up fans to blow the smoke from the lobby areas but that we should wait for approximately two hours before the smoke cleared the staircases for safe exit.

There were some anxious moments. The extent of the fire (the word *bomb* was not even mentioned over the PA or radio) was unknown. Helicopters buzzing near the roof gave us hope of an escape via helicopters in case the fire got out of control. Having seen the movie *Towering Inferno,* I could imagine that scenario of escaping that way.

Some of my colleagues were thirsty, but the water fountains were dry. Also, we had no beverages, tea, or coffee service on our floor.

Around 2:30 p.m., two firefighters showed up on our floor via a staircase and told us how to exit in an orderly fashion—no running; we were to stay in line and hold the handrails to avoid tripping. A few flashlights that some thoughtful colleagues came in handy; the WTC designers had failed to recognize the need for battery-operated lights and luminous paint on the steps and landings for emergency evacuation.

I counted the steps as we descended; our spirits lifted as we counted the landings and floors, ninety, eighty-nine, eighty-eight, and so on until we reached the forty-fourth floor, where we exited one staircase and took another. It was a big relief. We felt safer every step down. It took us over forty minutes to descend all the way to the lobby. I was indeed happy to have made it to safety. People were cheering each other, hugging each other, and thanking the firefighters for the rescue.

I rushed to catch the ferry to Staten Island. I was home well before sunset. As I ended my fast that eventful day, I felt truly grateful for my safe exit from the towers and Allah's blessings.

The bomb had gone off just after noon two floors below the Vista Hotel on the west side of the Trade Center, a complex of six buildings that were the city's crown jewels. The explosion was so powerful that it tore a 180-foot wide crater through four levels of the subterranean transportation, food, and mechanical complex that stretched beneath the center's two 110-story towers.

Thousands more were trapped for several panicky hours in stalled elevators, darkened hallways, and smoke-choked stairways as legions of emergency personnel rushed to cope with the first terrorist act on the WTC. The death toll from the fire was limited to six; there were quite a few injuries, but it could have been much worse.

The effect of the bombing and associated damage on the furnishings was massive. The South Tower Complex was shut down for repairs and refurbishing. We would not return to the WTC for another month.

Temporary Offices

We became refugees. Our company had a satellite office in Rutherford, New Jersey, where we reported. I was working on a water main tunnel for the Washington, DC, area. At that time, we did not have desktop computers and had paper files only. In order to work, I had to retrieve the working files from the WTC offices. However, I needed an authorized escort.

A week later, I returned to the ninety-first floor. The burned smell was everywhere, and soot was on the desks, ducts, curtains, and floors. There were no lights. We carried our files in large dumpsters on wheels and were out of the building in less than an hour.

During the month, our productivity was low, but I was grateful in a way since I was able to fast with little office stress.

Numerous improvements to evacuation facilities and procedures were made in the Twin Towers after the attack including the battery-operated light fixtures in the stairwells, luminous paint on the handrails and a centerline down the stairs, and a PA system. Perhaps even more important was the change in attitude of the buildings' occupants, who reportedly took the fire drills much more seriously after the bombing. These improvements saved many lives during the 9/11 evacuation eight years later.

Welcome Back

A month later, the WTC interior was clean and ready to receive its tenants. We were welcomed with a generous breakfast on each floor and were given "Welcome Back to WTC" coffee mugs. It was good to be back and see the gleaming Manhattan skyline as the sun rose over the East River and see the Empire State Building illuminated at sunset.

WTC Memorial (Refer to https://twintravelconcepts. com/911-memorial)

The 9/11 Memorial is located at the site of the former World Trade Center complex and occupies approximately half of the 16-acre site. It includes a museum as well two enormous waterfalls and reflecting pools, each about an acre in size, set within the footprints of the original Twin Towers. The Memorial Plaza is one of the eco-friendliest plazas ever constructed. More than 400 trees surround the reflecting pools. Its design conveys a spirit of hope and renewal and creates a contemplative space separate from the usual sights and sounds of a bustling metropolis.

Architect Michael Arad and landscape architect Peter Walker created the Memorial design selected from a global design competition that included more than 5,200 entries from 63 nations (https://www.nyc.arts. org/organization/2640/national-september-11-memorial-9-11-memorial)

The memorial was opened to public in 2011 and became a big tourist attraction. The memorial has a visual and emotional impact on visitors. The 2,977 names of the men, women, and children killed in the attacks of September 11, 2001 and February 26, 1993 are inscribed on bronze parapets surrounding the twin memorial pools. The display of these names is the very heart of the memorial. The serene and soft sounds of the water cascading beneath the names of the dead some seventy feet below the original foundations of the tower offer a subtle feeling of quiet reverence for our mortality.

9/11 Survivors' Health

Each time the anniversary approaches, it is always hardest for 9/11 survivors. The survivors are faced with disturbing thoughts and memories of their lost colleagues and loved ones; they are also the victims in a sense as many suffer from mental health problems common to soldiers returning from Iraq and Afghanistan. They grieve over their lost colleagues and find it painful to think about the anniversary of the attack. (Refer to https://www.newsscientist.com/artricle/2105581-deaths-from-911-related-illness-are-set to exceed-initial-toll/)

World Trade Center Health Program was set up in 2010 to offer healthcare to those still in ill health as a result of the 2001 attacks. It revealed a sharp rise in the number of people diagnosed with cancers that have been linked to dust generated when New York's Twin Towers collapsed. Those directly exposed to WTC Disaster, including the rescue officials from police, fire and other and related agencies, and those who worked and lived in the downtown Manhattan area were affected by the environmental pollution caused by the accident. In December 2015, Congress reauthorized federal resources to provide free medical services and treatment to responders and survivors of September 11 for the rest of their lives.

The data shows that 50,000 people have been certified sick as a probable consequence of the attacks and 1140 have died – which is more than a third of the 2977 deaths on 9/11 itself. As of June 2016, the respiratory and digestive disorders account for the highest number of cases, which reached 32,291. But cancer cases were rising fastest, tripling from 1822 in January 2014 to 5441 in June 2016.

(Refer to https://www.newsweek.com/2016/09/16/9-11-death-tol l-rising-496214.html)

The number of people who continue to die from 9/11-related illnesses is being tallied. As of July 2016, 1,140 people have died since the attacks, the majority of whom worked or lived at or near the site, according to data from the World Trade Center Health Program. But that's only based on unsolicited reports, since the program does not seek out mortality data, nor analyze it for things like cause of death. The program says it is focused solely on health monitoring and treatment. The number of fatalities is likely to be far greater than that tally. Fewer than 10,000 people deemed eligible for the survivor program have enrolled. It is estimated that nearly half a million people are probably at risk, to what doctors are now calling "the World Trade Center disaster area". The amount of care this population will need over the next decade is expected to be monumental, since the incubation periods for cancer can be up to 15 to 20 years—a time window patients are hitting now.

Parallels with the Pearl Harbor Attack

Another day of infamy in US history is the December 7, 1941 attack on Pearl Harbor by Japan. Over 3,000 American sailors, soldiers, and airmen were killed in the attack in addition to nearly 1,000 wounded. It led President Franklin D. Roosevelt to declare war on Japan the next day.

A comparison of two attacks on US soil shows similar death tolls in addition to loss of property. Both attacks had responses by the US presidents. The 9/11 attack led President George Bush to declare war not on a country but on an individual, Osama bin Laden, who was eventually caught and killed in a CIA-led operation during a raid in Abbottabad, Pakistan, on May 2, 2011.

The Twin Towers

The Twin Towers Aerial View (Courtesy of Port Authority NYNJ)

**WASHINGTON GROUP INTERNATIONAL EMPLOYEES AND
CONTRACTORS ASSIGNED TO THE WORLD TRADE CENTER
On September 11, 2001**

As of September 14th, the following 13 employees are still missing. We are continuing to do everything possible to locate them. Anyone with information that may be helpful, please contact WGI's Princeton Crisis Management Center at (609) 720-3050. We are also providing assistance to their families.

Bondarenko, Alan
Cortes, Carlos
DeAngelis, Robert J.
Ericson, Ulf R.
Gyulavary, Peter
Haramis, Vassilios G.
Kuo, Jr., Frederick
Liu, Ming Hao
Moccia, Frank V.
Perry, Emelda
Portillo, Anthony
Revilla, Luis C.
Wengerchuk, Oloh D.

The following 177 employees and contractors assigned to the WTC, or believed to have been in the area, were located and confirmed to be safe. We are extending counseling services to help them cope with Tuesday's tragedy.

Ahmed, Osman	Chattergoon, Lonny	Eng, Weyland K.
Alvear, Jorge A.	Chon, Francisco A.	Farnen, Gerard E.
Anderson, Rosemary R.	Chin, Neville W.	Favorite, Peter M.
Anolin, Melvin P.	Chiu, Yuk M.	Flola, Peter
Armand, Harry R.	Chiusano, Donato J.	Finavia, Bhanukumar R.
Bageac, Sylvia V.	Chizhik, Vladimir	Flore Jr, John
Baglino, Ralph J.	Chokshi, Vasant B.	Fralol Jr, John
Baig, Anis A.	Cipriano, James F.	Gallagher, Christopher
Baird, Rudolph M.	Clarke, Verna	Gallegos, Leonardo A.
Balarezo, Michael	Cooper, Daniel	Gazilo, Stephen A.
Barsky, Ann	Corredor, Sonia	Gennaro, Nicholas D.
Batheja, Lekh	Cristobal, Cielito	Gerter, Leopold
Bendersky, Evalena	Cunningham, Maureen L.	Gesztes, Vilmos
Benitez, Diana L.	Dandigar, Ruzena	Goddard, Kurt A.
Bhasathiti, Nabha	Davis, Robert E.	Goyal, Shiam N.
Blaslakierski, Lukasz	De Maio III, Ralph J.	Gray, Susan
Binsingl, Rudolf	Decoursey, Maureen E.	Greene, Charles
Boucher, Paul A.	Decresenzo, Angela	Habibullah, Shah
Bounse, Habib A.	Djurasovic, Milenko	Hamilton, Florence G.
Brennan, Anne M.	Doctor, Lynne L.	Harper, David W.
Brisbin, Deborah F.	Dunn, Michael T.	Hart, Janet L.
Brown, Magdalene	Eisenbarth, Roger L.	Hasan, Nausherwan
Chao, Chih C.	Emmerich, Robert F.	Hassel, Frederick 7.

List WGI Employees (Sheet 1)

Hauser, George K.
Haywood, Kathryn C.
Hernandez, Romulo M.
Hildebrand, Howard G.
Hilliard, Sheridell
Hrisovulos, Vasiliki K.
Hunter, David S.
Iftode, Itisoara
Ilachinski, Katherine
Iqbal, Muhammad S.
Jalil, M.
Jones, Duane A.
Kanakaris, George A.
Katen, Ronald N.
Keilbach, Robert A.
Kelleher, Moira Eavan
Kenna, William E.
Kim, Hahn
Lacqua, Mary Ann
Levent, Rashil
Linz, Paula D.
Liquet, Regino
Liu, Patrick
Loney, Michael
Longworth, Geoffrey
Loule, Kam M.
Majerovsky, William J.
Malik, Julie S.
Martin, Michael J.
Martinez, Susan Elizabeth
Martinovich, Sam
McManus, Edward
McPhail, Jon-Henry
Meloy, Rita
Mendez, Juanita
Minerva, Victor Robert
Miranda, German

Moss, Evelyn M.
Moul, William F.
Mulligan, George A.
Murphy, Daren
Nelson, Donald N.
O' Connor, Edward J.
Oganov, Yurly
Olidort, Joseph Z.
Ostrow, Stephen L.
Parikh, Bhanuvadan K.
Passiglia, Peter
Patel, Hasmukh
Patel, Ishverlal J.
Patti, Jean M.
Podolak, Robert
Poonawala, Tayeb G.
Pragdat, Harry
Pusateri, Victor J.
Rajani, Sunil H.
Resch, Robert H.
Reyes, Artemio R.
Reynolds, Bernard F.
Romeo, James G.
Sandiford, Paula T.
Santos, Aurora M.
Sardar, Aditi K.
Sasson, Selim
Schimmenti, James R.
Schlick, John C.
Schoenewaldt III, Arthur C.
Scragg, William
Sequeira, Mario F.
Shields, Kenneth C.
Sierpnisk, Christina E.
Slibejoris, Paul
Simon, Lois A.
Sisk, Susan

Smith, Jaime
Solimando, Nicholas
Stephan, Joan T.
Strauss, Steven R.
Stuckey, William L.
Swe, Khin T.
Switala, Keith A.
Tassoulas, Nicholas
Taylor, Walt R.
Totha, Steven
Tottan, Peter A.
Trombetta, Peter
Telforas, William V.
Ungureanu, Andrei
Van Name, John N.
Velkos, John N.
Vesprey, Frankie D.
Wagner, Paul F.
Wang, Chang W.
Weiss, Ellen J.
Wong, Edward Y.
Wong, Jorge
Worchel, Herbert
Wynne, William E.
Yee, James W.
Zerbouis, Jerry

Others

Girard, Michel
Grande, Joseph
Lepine, Reginald
Manis, Glykeria
Perikh, Hasmukh
Rahman, Hamudur
Ram, Ravi
Vargas, Elvin

List of WGI Employees on 91st Floor of South Tower (sheet 2)

Eiichi Yamamoto, a colleague of mine from Northwestern University, wrote a sympathy letter dated December 10, 2001, to me from Tokyo following the WTC disaster. He was sixty-six and working for a consulting firm in Tokyo. He wrote, "I guess your life has greatly changed since September 11."

The Japan economy had continued to drift in a 1990–2000 decade-long recession that caused economic hardship to the older population to the point of depression and hopelessness. According to

Yamamoto, the 9/11 disaster caused a "fatal sickness" to the Japanese economy. His consulting firm had gone into bankruptcy in July 2001. He continued, "I would like to make use of my five senses which I am going to lose sooner or later."

That was the last communication from Eiichi. He had never married and died soon thereafter becoming a victim of the economic recession in Japan.

Twin Towers Features

The World Trade Center with approximately 9 million square feet of rentable office space was constructed in 1970 but was not fully rented for the next ten years. New York State agencies occupied a large portion of the office space. The South Tower was 1,362 feet tall and a little shorter than its companion North Tower. Each floor had 40,000 square feet measuring 200 feet on each side. The identical floor layout facilitated the construction since it was replicated 220 times for the two towers resulting in cost savings. When construction was completed in 1970, the Twin Towers became the tallest building in New York.

Designed by Yamasaki, the 110-story gleaming Twin Towers were unique and lifted the lower Manhattan skyline into the clouds. Since its dedication in 1973, it became a gateway to New York City and became an added tourist attraction and unofficial trademark that stood for nearly three decades.

The towers were designed with a new approach to skyscrapers in that they consisted of lightweight, resilient, modular construction to accelerate construction schedules and costs. The structural design of the towers consisted of 244 perimeter steel, box-shaped columns that served as main supports with a group of interior columns forming the central core. The core structure, measuring 85 feet by 120 feet, housed express and local elevators, three stairwells, mechanical systems, and utilities. Steel web joists, which connected the core structure and the perimeter columns using clip angles, supported the individual floors. The building floors are thus free of columns. To assure safety, the tempered glass was designed for a wind load of forty-five pounds per square foot.

One significant feature in the fire code that the WTC followed was the provision of fire safety teams on each floor. Tenants on each floor were selected as the floor warden, deputy warden, warden alternates, and male and female searchers. Though unusual, this worked well since regular fire drills were performed and the responsible fire safety team ensured compliance.

The WTC had approximately 50,000 employees mostly commuting via the subways or path trains. In addition, there were 80,000 visitors daily. The subway systems had sufficient capacity to handle the traffic. The observation deck was on the 107th floor of the South Tower and was accessible by an express elevator.

Each tower was served by ten high-speed express elevators to the two lobbies on the forty-fourth and seventy-eighth floors as well as several banks of local and freight elevators. The whole system was computer controlled to provide the best possible service. In addition, in case of fire, three sets of staircases provided each tower emergency evacuation routes.

The North Tower housed the Windows of the World restaurant on the 107th floor and offered spectacular views. It was served by express elevators that were damaged by the plane and cut off the evacuation of the restaurant workers and diners. The entire restaurant staff perished that day.

There were several restaurants at the concourse level including the Big Kitchen. Dean Witter had a cafeteria on the forty-third floor in the South Tower. I used to frequent that café, which served soup, sandwiches, and hot food. I loved the lentil vegetable soup. One day, I asked the chef if the soup was vegetarian or if it contained any meat stock. When the chef confirmed that the vegetable soup did contain meat broth (probably ham), that ended my love of the lentil soup. At my request, a sign at the soup counter was then added to clarify that the soup was made with meat stock.

It is estimated that over a million tons of rubble resulted from the sixteen-acre WTC site—300,000 tons of steel and 700,000 tons of concrete, stone, glass, paint solvents, and insulating materials. It is estimated that the steel was enough to build twenty Eiffel towers. The debris required some 20,000 to 30,000 truckloads for its removal. The debris included hazardous material from the incineration of the PCBs contained in glass, fixtures, and building materials. The debris ended in the Fresh Kills Landfill on Staten Island. Part of the steel from the wreckage was used to make a US navy ship, the *New York*.

> You and I
> Every day, A long, falling, restive shadow
> Says to the wall, "Come with me!"
> Time is a friend, neither to the wall, nor to the shadow,
> And now under the debris, of stones, sand and dust
> The pride of that wall lies shattered.
> The sun shines, but who knows where the shadow is?
> (from a poem by Ahmed Faraz)

Author at his office on 91st Floor of South Tower

WTC and Ferry Terminal in Manhattan

South View from South Tower- Statue of Liberty and Staten Island

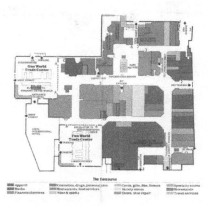

WTC- The Concourse (Courtesy of Port Authority NYNJ)

13 WGI Colleagues lost on Nine Eleven

Rita at WTC Memorial (2011)

Author with Wife at WTC Memorial (2011)

View of Brooklyn Bridge from WTC

Eiichi Yamamoto and Sonia in Tokyo-2000

Lessons Learned

The WTC attack robbed me of my professional library and memorabilia including books, awards, published papers, project files, documents, and reference literature that could never be replenished. I stored some of my personal papers including my US naturalization documents at my office. The WTC was designed to withstand the forces of nature including earthquakes and hurricanes but was unable to withstand the impacts of jets filled with fuel. For some time, it was painful to recall the loss of my material assets, which were a significant part of my professional life.

The event is a reminder of our mortality and the stark reality that evil and good coexist. Due to the evil deeds of some, nearly 3,000 innocent persons never returned home to their families and loved ones. They became victims of an ugly, unforeseen attack. Since death is inevitable, the 9/11 tragedy imparts an important lesson—Our worldly lives are short and should be spent in a meaningful way with faith, love, and goodwill for humanity.

The good came from hundreds of firefighters, policemen, personnel of the Port Authority, and good Samaritans who rescued people stranded in the towers and brought them to safety. In the process, some of them died valiantly.

Although the WTC exists no more, it lives in our hearts. The quarter-mile-high view of New York's skyline, breathtaking sunrises and sunsets, fogs, and the historic Manhattan and Brooklyn Bridges will always be in my memory. One a clear day, one could see over fifty miles and beyond. I used to take a few moments to admire the breathtaking views, which was always refreshing.

Here's an important lesson about the power of prayer. That morning, I recited the verses of the Qur'an, which surely helped me survive with calm and patience. These verses from Sura Al-Hashr (59), verses 22 to 24, are reproduced with an English translation below.

Verse 22: God is He beside whom there is no God Knower of the unforeseen and the Seen, He is Most Gracious, Most Merciful.

Verse 23: God is He besides whom there is no other God. The King, the Holy, Source of Peace, Guardian of Faith, Watcher of His Creation, the Exalted in Might, the Compeller, the Supreme, Glory to God, above the Partners, they attribute to Him.

Verse 24: He is God, the Creator, the Elevator, The Bestower of Forms, to him belong the Best Names, Whatever is in the Hereafter and on Earth, Glorify Him, He is Almighty, All Wise.

The grief of the survivors of 9/11 is reflected in a poem (English translation) by Ahmed Faraz, a Pakistani poet.

> God, countless names
> In this graveyard of names
> Anguished fathers, frenzied mothers
> Grief stricken widows and
> Beloveds in mourning
> Look for faces of their ones
> On their name plates
> Thousands of Names.

Chapter 2

MY EARLY YEARS

Our Parents

We called our father Abba ji and our mother Apa ji. Abba ji was five-eight and stocky with curly hair and a fair complexion. He was a self-made, adaptable person who worked as a banker, excise /taxation officer, and finally a businessman. He was a principled, performance and result oriented, hard-working, and far-sighted individual. His full name was Shaikh Mohammad Hasan, but family members referred to him as Shaikh Sahib out of respect. My *dada* (grandfather) was Shaikh Khairuddin, a religious person. He died before any of his sons married.

Our father was the fourth child following two girls, Habeeb (1890–1900) and Iqbal (1891–1914), and Ahmed Hasan 1 (1893–1900). He was born in Batala, India. By the time my father was born, two elder siblings, Habeeb and Ahmed Hasan, had died. Three other siblings followed.

Our father (1900–1968) must have been traumatized by the deaths of a sister when he was barely fourteen and later by the loss of his mother, Fatima (1874–1922), when he was twenty-two. Being the eldest with three younger siblings, he matured early and shouldered the responsibilities well. He started to work soon after his graduation from high school and held several jobs including as a bank accountant. By the time he was twenty-eight, he had lost his parents and became the de facto head of the household responsible for his younger siblings especially Ghulam Hasan, who was barely sixteen.

Our father's parents were Kakezai Pathans. Marrying within your sect including first cousins was the norm. Our father and his two younger brothers were married in 1930 with one day between each wedding. I was told that the decision for the joint weddings was made by my father. It was a pragmatic decision that minimized expenses by combining the three events. While my father chose his wife, Rashida, outside the immediate family, Ahmed Hasan married his first cousin Akhtar, daughter of Abdul Aziz, and Jamil Hasan married Hanifa, daughter of Amir and Zuhurul Haq. Amir was another granddaughter of Dr. Ghulam Nabi from daughter Barkat (married to Muhammed Husain).

Our mother, Rashida Begum (1913–79), was the oldest daughter of Sheikh Mohammad Sadiq, a respected member of the Amritsar Kakezai community. She was raised in Amritsar, and she studied up to the eighth grade. She did not like math and therefore did not finish high school. She married when she was barely seventeen.

My dada died in 1928 leaving behind no assets except the house they lived in. My father took over the financial responsibilities at his death. My father suffered from a rheumatic heart and angina, and he had a heart attack in 1931. After that, he followed a rigorous diet of raw food, fiber, and tub baths recommended by German doctor Louis Kuhne.[9] He was fully recovered after the first episode and enjoyed a very good and active life as an excise and tax officer until the partition of India and Pakistan in 1947.

His second heart attack would come when he was fifty-seven, when we were residing at the State Bank Flats, No. 13A, in a third-floor walk-up apartment. After that incident, his strong frame and muscular body steadily declined.

---

[9] Louis Kuhne (1835–1901) was a German naturopath primarily known for his cold-water hydrotherapy methods that were meant to improve the detoxification functions of the body by stimulation of the lower abdomen.

Between 1930 and 1948, the family had grown to eight children, arriving in roughly two-year intervals. My father's job in the excise and tax department forced the family to move frequently in Punjab Province from Narowal to Sialkot to Amritsar to Delhi.

My father was very close to his maternal uncle, Abdul Hamid (1889–1943), who was eleven years his senior and a successful civil servant in the British government. My father wrote a letter to him in August 1943 asking for the hand of his daughter, Shamim, for his youngest brother, Ghulam Hasan (G. H.). Abdul Hameed agreed resulting in a marriage of the two first cousins. The letter was shown to the eldest son before it was mailed. My eldest brother, barely thirteen, remembered asking that if the contents were shared with Chacha G. H. Abba ji confidently replied, "Yes. I left the open letter on the staircase for Ghulam Hasan to read it. I assume he read it." He was referring to the staircase that led to the second floor of our Daryagunj home occupied by Chacha G. H. It was a discreet way to obtain the acquiescence of a younger sibling.

My father was only twelve years older than Chacha G. H., but the relationship was like father and son since my father was the head of the household. It was understood that his wish was a like a command for the youngest sibling.

Abdul Hamid died of a heart attack on September 13, 1943, after agreeing to the marriage between Ghulam Hasan and Shamim; he left behind a very young widow with seven young children ranging in age from five to eighteen. The marriage took place exactly a year later— September 13, 1944.

My Earliest Years

I was born in Sialkot, the fifth child following three brothers and a sister. The eldest sibling, Parvez, given the title of *Bhaijan (It is a sign of respect for an elder)*, was born in October 1931 in Amritsar. He was followed by a sister, Parveen (1938–1945), Jamshed (1936–1979), and Behram (1938–2019), who was born in Narowal. Four siblings came after me—three sisters and a brother. I ended up exactly in the middle.

In some respects, it was a blessing while growing up since I was not the focus of my parents. The primary focus was either on the Bhaijan or my younger sisters. The boys went unnoticed most of the time except when the school was open.

During World War II (1939–1945), the Indian subcontinent was a colony of the United Kingdom; the British held territories in India including over five hundred autonomous princely states. British India officially declared war on Nazi Germany in September 1939, a time when the Indian Army numbered just under 200,000. By the end of the war, it had become the largest volunteer army in history rising to over 2.5 million men by August 1945.

The year 1940 was a remarkable milestone in the history of India. On March 23, the Pakistan Resolution was passed by the All-India Muslim League's annual session in Lahore. Pakistan's independence had originally been envisioned by Allama Mohammed Iqbal on March 23, 1930, who sought a separate homeland for Indian subcontinent Muslims.[10]

My father's work for the Excise and Taxation Department of Punjab under the British raj of the undivided Hindustan (India) was frequently transferred within Punjab Province. From 1943 to 1946, he was posted in Delhi, where the younger sister siblings were born and where my earliest childhood memories are.[11]

---

[10] Allama Iqbal, a great poet-philosopher and active political leader, was born at Sialkot, Punjab, in 1877. He descended from a family of Kashmiri Brahmins, who had embraced Islam about three hundred years earlier. He received his early education in the traditional *maktab*. Later, he joined the Sialkot Mission School, from where he passed his matriculation examination. In 1897, he obtained a bachelor of arts (B.A.) degree from Government College, Lahore. Two years later, he earned a master's degree and became a lecturer in the Oriental College, Lahore. He went to Europe for higher studies and obtained a degree from Cambridge and a doctorate in Munich and finally qualified as a barrister. He returned to India in 1908. Besides teaching and practicing law, Iqbal continued to write poetry.

[11] More family history about the 1930–46 period is described in *My Life My Country—Memoirs of a Pakistani Economist* written by my eldest brother, Dr. Parvez Hasan.

Delhi Memories

My earliest memories are of our home at 12 A Darya Ganj (River Place) near the Jumna River. It was large, two-story, six-room house in the shadow of the Mughal Red Fort. The old city wall with a *rajghat* (means King's court) which overlooked the Jumna River, was close by. A main road in front of our house gave us easy access to bazaars, cinemas, parks, and open grounds. It became famous landmark when the political leaders including Mahatama Ghandi were cremated there.

Daryaganj was a neighborhood of Delhi inside the walled city of Shahjahanabad (Old Delhi). The *darya*, or river, refers to the Jamuna River just outside the walled city. It was one of the three subdivisions of the Central Delhi District beginning at Delhi Gate and ended at Red Fort.

The upper floor of the two-story home was occupied by Chacha G. H. and his wife, Shamim, in 1945. Chacha was serving with the Indian air force and had privileges of special rations including biscuits, chocolates, and other goodies during the war. Since I was too young to attend school, I was tutored by my aunt Shamim in the morning. She would pamper me with the scarce wartime goodies including English biscuits and chocolates.

The house had an interior open courtyard and covered verandah facing it. The kitchen and the toilet facilities were away from the main building.

Our cook, Fakhruddin, made good food, both Indian and Western dishes. I remember relishing his rich layered *prathas*, which were always square.

I remember getting struck with the smallpox along with my siblings. It was a long and slow recovery. The large verandah facing the courtyard became our field hospital. Luckily, under the supervision of the local *hakim* (a doctor practicing traditional medicines in muslim culture), Hamdard Dawakhana, the treatment with *khamira marwarid* and neem tree leaves minimized the discomfort during this affliction. All of the five siblings spent considerable time lying in individual cots (*charpoys*) in a row during our slow recuperation.

An Early Death Memory

Just as the war ended, our family faced its first loss. My sister Parveen was struck with rheumatic fever in late 1945, when she was twelve. Her heart was weakened since there were no antibiotics available. She died in April 1946, a month after my youngest sister, Mahjabin, was born. I was too young to comprehend the tragedy. There was a large family gathering for the funeral. The kids were sent away to the nearby Purdah Bagh (park), which was reserved for ladies only, but boys under six were allowed. I remember playing there a long time.

The rajghat provided an opening in the walled city around the Jumna River and access (with steps perhaps fifty feet wide) to the river for people and goods traffic in the earlier days. There was a *dhobighat* (washing facility) where clothes were washed in the river. We played with other young cousins while the adults attended the funeral ceremonies.

In the early morning before sunrise following Parveen's death, my parents would go to the graveyard for prayers (*fatiha*). One morning, I got up and wanted to join them too. It was my first trip to my sister's grave and an unforgettable experience. We rode a *tonga* (horse carriage) past the India Gate and to the graveyard. The *mali (water carrier/gardener)* was there and brought some water for sprinkling on the fresh grave. It brought closure for me.

My father was responsible for collecting taxes from cinemas. Due to his position, we could watch any newly released Indian or foreign movie even if it was a full house; the cinema management would put additional chairs in the balcony to accommodate our family. One of the movies that I remember was *Adventures of Sabu*.

Being small, I often accompanied my mother when she visited her ancestral home in Amritsar. The family home where my widowed *nani* (grandmother) lived with the extended family in the old city was in one of the well-known streets (*galis*) known as Maashki wali Gali (Waterman Street). The street was so narrow that a tonga could not go down it. It was named after the residents who would bring water to individual homes in large leather pouches.

There was a large door at the entrance, and a well in the interior courtyard laid with stones had a hand pump. There was no plumbing or water faucets. To take a shower, you had to use the handpump to bring the water from the well and fill a bucket. The water was quite cold. One of my uncles (my mother's brother) would take an early morning bath regularly. He was a health freak.

One of my older cousins, Rabia, was old enough to do the house chores. The mosaic-tiled floors were laid in red-green chips embedded in concrete. While she would sweep the floor with a wet rag, we dare not walk around; if we did, we would be shouted at.

Such visits were fun as my mother, being the only sister, was pampered by her older and younger brothers. Three of my *mammos* (maternal uncles) were in their teens and were always having fun flying kites and playing physical games. One of them, Yusuf (nicknamed Pup), was quite athletic and well built; he was known to jump over the adjoining flat roofs of the detached townhomes in Amritsar.

My nana (maternal grandfather) who was head clerk in the local government, Amritsar, had died in 1933 of a brain hemorrhage leaving behind several teenage sons, Ihsan Elahi, Younas, and Yousaf. This loss must have traumatic for my nana, who became a young widow and had to raise the young children on her own. The teenagers were unable to complete high school. Upon being uprooted from Amritsar following the 1947 partition, they did not lead a normal life. Only Yousaf married and had children.

Partition of India

From 1858 to 1947, India was under the rule of the British crown. Muslims had coexisted with Hindus and Sikhs for a long time, but that changed when India was partitioned in 1947. The British left, and India split into two independent countries, India and Pakistan. That triggered a mass migration, at that time, the largest migration of people of the century based on religion. Nearly 10 million frightened people were displaced from their ancestral homes and fled across borders. Most of the

Muslim migration occurred from India to West Pakistan (now Pakistan), and most of the Hindus and Sikhs migrated to India from Pakistan. It is estimated that over a million people died in the conflict and that thousands of others were victims of murder, sex abuse, rape, and suicide.

Gujrat

Prior to the 1947 partition, our family had moved to Gujrat. My father, being Muslim, was transferred to the predominantly Muslim area to be later named Pakistan in anticipation of the breakup of India into Muslim and Hindu populations. Gujrat, in Punjab Province, is the eighteenth largest city in Pakistan. It was a blessing for our family since this occurred prior to the transmigration on both side of the borders of India and Pakistan. We lived on Kutchery Road, a relatively affluent area. We were unaffected by the atrocities and riots that were committed as several millions of people were forced to leave their homes and belongings following the partition. It was perhaps one of the largest voluntary migration in the history.

Our family, including six children, moved into a large mansion on the Grand Trunk Road. Bhaijan had joined the Government College, Lahore, as a freshman, and he lived in a hostel. My mother was always busy tending to household chores while my father worked.

Our next-door neighbor was a Hindu family who were concerned about their safety. They decided not to move to the local refugee camp and nervously waited for evacuation arrangements to India. Such were the times.

I was admitted to the second grade of the elementary school across the street, and Behram was in the third grade of that school. It was my first experience of formal education. It was eager to learn. On wintry days, the assembly was outside, where it was sunny and warm. My teacher liked me and was a source of encouragement. He found me thirsty for knowledge with an open mind. One day, he said to me, "You're like a frog in a large pond and unlike a frog in a well." He was perhaps referring to my curiosity and social behavior making an analogy between a confined well and a large pond. He had sensed my attitude toward life.

Gujrat is on the banks of River Chenab. Punjab (literally, the land of five rivers) Province is served by five rivers; the other tributaries of the Indus are Sutlej, Ravi, and Jhelum. During the spring, the Chenab experienced peak floods from snowmelt in the Himalayas. To save the town from flooding, the river dike and the Grant Trunk Road was breached to divert the rising waters. For several days and nights, the floodwaters ran by our house gushing out of the thirty- to forty-foot wide cut; it was a scary yet amusing sight for a seven-year-old. I watched with excitement at the failed attempts of people desperate to get across against the fast-moving water. The worst time was at night when I heard water hitting the foundations of our home and wondered if the house would collapse. Luckily, it was well built with apparently good foundations; it withstood the onslaught. That was my first interest in foundation engineering in which I later pursued a career.

On one of our first nights there, I went to a mosque and called *azaan*, the call for Muslim prayer. Somebody had told me that an azaan would seek divine help in mitigating an impending disaster.

The breach disrupted traffic for several days including caravans of refugees on buses and on foot moving from India to Pakistan. Some carried their limited belongings on their heads as they slowly moved down the road. They were all ages, young and old, determined to find new beginnings. It was one of the largest population migration events of the twentieth century.

The summer of 1948 was my first Ramadan. The fasting days were quite long, but I was able to keep a fast from dawn to sunset. On one of the days while fasting and playing outside, I became really thirsty. I went to a fountain to wash my face and mouth and accidently swallowed some water. I felt very guilty for my inadvertent behavior, but I continued fasting without telling anyone until today.

My father's thin orderly used to come at midday to fetch his *tiffin*, his lunch box, from our home. One day, he didn't show up, and a new face, a burly man, came to collect the lunch. I asked my mother, "Mota aya hai, kia baat hey?" "Why has the fat man come? What happened to the thin man?" My remark became a joke shared by older cousins who narrated this to me several years later.

While at Gujrat, the youngest sibling, Owais, was born.

Lahore

The family moved to Qila Gujar Singh in Lahore. It was a gated community for the Hindu families who had left the city after the partition. We lived in a huge, two-story mansion. The bathroom had a water tap but no shower. The small kitchen was in the courtyard with storage space for coal, which we used as cooking fuel.

I attended an elementary school in Lahore. Each student was provided with a low, wooden desk but no chair; we sat on *durries* (cotton mats) on the floor. Each student was required to develop handwriting skills using bamboo pens (*qalams*) with ink on clay painted wooden boards (*takhtis*).

One incident I remember well attests to my shyness. I had gone for a shower in the morning when I heard some noises. My aunt Shamim had come. Everybody joined her in the courtyard. I was embarrassed to come out of the shower with only a towel wrapped around my waist. Somehow, I managed to run out of the shower and hide in the adjoining coal storage bin for quite some time until my aunt moved away from the courtyard.

The family moved to Karachi in 1949. I stayed behind to finish the fourth grade with my uncle Jamil Hasan's family.

I received letters or news from Karachi from the family. I was told that Karachi was a modern and clean city. The major roads and streets were cleaned and washed every night. Unlike the tongas in Punjab, where the tonga driver shared the front seat with the passenger and the ride would be sometimes uneven, the horse carriages in Karachi provided a more comfortable and smoother ride. They were patterned after the European carriages and were named Victorias. Also, the coachman was seated separately; that allowed more room for the passengers. As a boy, I imagined that the streets of Karachi were as smooth as glass.

Bhaijan was pursuing a bachelor's degree at the Government College, Lahore. As soon as my exams were over, my brother took me to an Indian movie, *Mela* (*Fair*) starring Dilip Kumar. I forgot the love story, but there was a song in the movie sung by Dilip to his love: "Ye zindge kay Maley kum na ho gay, afsus hum na hongay," "Life is like a carnival in this world that one must leave one day." The song is a universal theme about our mortality. This song reverberated in my mind throughout the subsequent years as I went through good times and sad times leaving only memories of loved ones as they arrived and departed from this world.

The Karachi Years

Abba ji's decision to leave a stable government job and move to Karachi to do private business entailed risk; however, he did so to provide his children good educations and more opportunities than he had had.

Abba ji was almost fifty with seven children ranging in age from two to fourteen in Karachi besides the eldest one in college at perhaps considerable expense. Somehow, his sheer faith accompanied by hard work allowed him to meet his aspirations. He retired from government service and became the manager of a wholesale cloth business in partnership with his old business friend Azim Khan in Karachi. The establishment, Shahi Cloth House, imported silk, rayon, and cotton fabric for sale to retailers around the country. The Govardhan Das Market was a bustling place coming to life at 10:00 a.m., when hundreds of shops opened for business. The main street was so crowded that car traffic was nearly impossible except early in the morning and late in the afternoon. He was assisted by Umar, a salesman.

Jamshed Quarters

I joined the family at the government quarters on Jehangir Road. It was a complex of townhomes that were built to accommodate the migrant population from the partition of India. The walls were cinder block, and the homes had approximately 1,200 square feet. There were three rooms in each quarter with a veranda in front and a small courtyard, a small kitchen, a shower, and a lavatory fitted with a squatting-type toilet with an overhead water tank operated by a long chain for flushing it. It was an upgrade from the toilets in Punjab and Delhi.

Karachi was a big city even in 1949 with over 400,000 residents spread over several miles. The residential areas were scattered on the north and west; the commercial and business center were toward the east and close to the port facilities. The main artery was Bunder Road, over a hundred feet wide and six miles long from Jamshed Road to Keamari. The harbor was protected by a barrier sand bar, a sandspit, from the Arabian Sea.

Karachi was the southernmost city in Pakistan and its only port. Historically, it gained significance when the British became more focused on Afghanistan in the early part of the nineteenth century. The port city was expanded during 1850–1900 with critical roads and infrastructure. The early landmark buildings of Karachi were constructed of limestone and consisted of Holy Trinity Church, Frere Hall, Empress Market, Sind Madressah, D. J. College, and the Sind Club.

The post-partition migration to Karachi resulted in more than a twofold increase in the population, from 400,000 to more than a million, by 1950. The foresight in planning for the city infrastructure by the British government must be commended. The infrastructure including potable water, electricity, and roads proved to be adequate for the unforeseen burden of the exploding population. I do not recall any significant power outages or water main breaks in those early days. The city functioned well.

At the dawn of Pakistan's independence in 1947, Karachi was Sindh's largest city. Despite communal violence across India and Pakistan, Karachi remained relatively peaceful compared to cities farther north in Punjab. The city became the focus for the resettlement of Muslim Muhajirs migrating from India leading to a dramatic expansion of the city's population. This migration lasted until the 1960s and ultimately transformed the city's demographics and economy.

Due to school overcrowding, most schools had two shifts, 8:00 to 12:30 and 1:30 to 5:00. Initially, I was enrolled in the afternoon shift. I would travel alone on a bus both ways, a thirty-minute trip that cost one anna, a sixteenth of a rupee.

Moving to Pakistan Chowk

After a year at the Jehangir Quarters, the family was ready to move again. Residential accommodations were tight in Karachi. My father wanted to move closer to his business shop near the Bolton Market. He found a flat for rent at Pakistan Chowk; most rental flats in the city were rent controlled, and the cost was low, but to lease one involved making a goodwill payment (*pughree*) up front of 8,000 rupees, which my father did not possess. The payment was considered illegal, but the shortage of housing created by the flood of refugees from India made it the norm.

Being a retired excise/taxation officer, he thought of a clever scheme to bypass having to make the goodwill payment. He enlisted the help of a relative, a police officer, Inspector Rashid. On the day of the transaction, which was to be held at the location of the proposed flat in Bano Manzil, the family including my father, mother, and Inspector Rashid (who in disguise was wearing a *burqa*, a head-to-toe covering, and I took a Victoria to the Murar Street apartment. As the pughree transaction in the apartment was being completed, Rashid removed his disguise, charged the landlord with receiving an illegal payment, and threatened to arrest him. The landlord was completely taken aback and reluctantly agreed to hand over the rental apartment without the goodwill payment.

The Bano Manzil was a six-story, reinforced concrete, prewar building with twelve flats and a staircase with wood-top handrails. The building had electricity, running cold water only, a squatting toilet with a flushing system, and a balcony for each room facing the street. Our flat, on the second floor, had three bedrooms, a large dining/living area, and a small kitchen with storage for coal. The flat was quite airy and exposed to sunlight, and it had ceramic tile floors in all the rooms except the passage area. The passage area wall was also partly exposed to the atrium for additional natural light. This would be our residence for nearly six years.

My father was indeed an honest and fair person. He did not forget this episode. Six years later, when we vacated the Bano Manzil flat, it was returned to the original Landlord without receiving a goodwill payment in return.

The location was ideal. Meat and grocery shops were nearby, and an ice store occupied the corner of Out Tram Road and Murar Street.[12] Two blocks away was a major rotary intersection, Pakistan Chowk, where several streets merged—Kutchery Road, Strachan Road, Burns Road, and Out Ram Road.

My school was a mile away, within walking distance. A large, well-landscaped garden named Burnes Garden was also nearby. There were no laundromat facilities. Clothes were washed by professional washermen called *dhobis*; they picked up the clothes, hand-washed and ironed them, and delivered them weekly. A twenty-four-hour pharmacy, Akhtar Munir, was close by. Our family physician, Dr. Yahya, was few blocks away. A well-known wrestling gym owned by the Bholu brothers was a few blocks away.

Murar street in a recent (2020) Photo (The ice store is 70 years old)

---

[12] The ice store still exist today some seventy years later.

Pakistan Ckowk with British Council Building on left

Daily Routine

On weekdays, I would fetch fresh bread from a grocery around the corner on Out Ram Road. A bread factory, BP Industries, was new to the town; it was delivered throughout the city. One could buy either a half or full loaf of the sliced bread. The milkman would bring a cow to the entrance of the building and sell freshly squeezed milk.

After school, I would accompany my younger siblings including my three sisters to the nearby Burns Garden, which was well maintained with paved walkways, fountains, and flowers. A lot of children from the surrounding flats would enjoy the enormous open space and fresh air. I made the acquaintance of Javed Iqbal's children, who lived nearby. Javed Iqbal was the son of Allama Iqbal, the well-known poet and philosopher of Pakistan.

There were street gangs in the neighborhood who would rob and victimize the youth. A ruffian named Abdul Ghani always carried a switchblade. Luckily, I and my younger siblings were spared victimization.

Abba ji was focused on providing the best education he could to his children. Parvez, the firstborn, received special attention. My father did his best to stimulate his children to excel academically. He took direct interest in our homework through elementary and middle school; he helped us with reading, writing, and math. All his children followed this characteristic in turn teaching the next generation. He was focused on education and knowledge for all his children, especially the daughters. He consulted his friend, a headmaster at Sheldon High School, about the best schools in Karachi. It was his suggestion that I enroll at the Sind Madressah. Both Behram and I attended the school through eleventh grade, high school matriculation. Jamshed attended Sheldon High. Later, high school matriculation started after tenth grade, consistent with Punjab schools.

My sisters Shaheen and Yasmin attended Marie Colaco, an English medium of instruction school in the Saddar area. Its monthly tuition fee there was Rs. 15, or three to four times my school tuition, but that was what my father wanted to do for them. My father wanted the best education for the girls.

Evening Lessons at Home

We ate dinner usually around 8:00 p.m., after my father would return home. After dinner, my father would discuss the school activities and homework with all the children. Jamshed and I needed some tutoring in math, which was my father's strong suit. Even Jamshed's friends would come in the evening for such tutoring. Sometimes, the sessions would continue for several hours late into the night. He seemed to thrive on the challenge. He never complained.

He was a patient teacher and made sure we understood the basic concepts. My younger sisters were taught to read fairy tales and nursery rhymes in English daily. I learned most of the nursery rhymes secondhand from them.

Abbaji's Momentos

From his government and excise service, my father had a few momentos—a service revolver, a leather shoulder belt with bullets, and a classic bowler hat. He kept these items in his dressing table in the Bano

Manzil flat. The bowler hat, a hundred percent woolen felt also known as a derby, was worn by well-heeled businessmen and was ideal for cool weather.

I borrowed the hat for a month-long winter scouting excursion to Punjab. The rail excursion was led by our scout master, Niazi, and another teacher, Younas. Younas took fancy to my bowler hat and offered to exchange it for his light, summery straw hat. Out of respect, I accepted his uneven offer. When I returned from the trip, Abba ji inquired about the hat, but my response was less than truthful; he was obviously sad for the loss of his hat, but he did not reprimand me.

In 1958, with the imposition of martial law, all unlicensed arms and ammunition had to be surrendered. He reluctantly gave up his unlicensed revolver to Bhaijan for compliance. The revolver was stolen by one of his servants before he was able to return it.

Abba ji never took a vacation since moving to Karachi in 1948. The demands of his full-time, six-days-a-week job and the costs of maintaining a large family including education for the kids must have left him little money for vacations. His relaxation came from meeting relatives who would visit from Punjab to escape the summer heat. Our three-bedroom flat would become a mini motel for our visitors, who would enjoy our parents' hospitality. At night, the elders would sleep on cots while the younger ones would occupy mattresses spread on the tiled floors of the Bano Manzil apartment. The second-floor apartment was quite breezy with balconies on both sides—natural air conditioning.

Apa ji would visit Lahore often to visit her family, and one of the younger children would accompany her. I accompanied her on one trip and met my maternal grandmother and uncles who lived in the old residential area known as Gwal Mandi off Beadon Road in Lahore. The *haveli* (large building) was a three-story high, reinforced concrete building that housed the families of my two maternal uncles, Abdul Ahad and Nasir Malik, in addition to three unmarried uncles. Half of the haveli was occupied by my mother's maternal uncle, Sh. Jalal Din, who had a large family as well. Their family had modern baths and upgraded living and dining rooms.

Our parents were very loving. While our father exhibited firmness of character and strict discipline, our mother was malleable and easy to deal with. We young children would communicate more readily with our mother and often used her to convey our needs and desires to our father. Our parents were God fearing and had big hearts. Our doors were always open to receive family and friends any time of night or day.

Ours was a large, middle-class family though money was tight. Most of the budget went for rent, food, and clothing. Daily groceries cost about Rs. 10 and would include goat meat, vegetables, oil, yogurt, and so on. Wheat flour, rice, and lentils would be purchased monthly in bulk via a ration card.

We always had a full-time servant who would work in the kitchen from dawn to late at night. Breakfast would consist of toast and tea. Abdul helped our mother cook the other meals and wash dishes. We children would set the dining table for lunch and dinner and make afternoon high tea. The table would seat only eight, so the two youngest would not get regular chairs and would occupy stools instead.

Abdul must have been in his early twenties. He would be taken care of for his personal needs including clothing, medicine, and other perks in addition to his monthly salary of less than Rs. 50.

The kitchen was small and hot during the summer since there was little ventilation. Our mother was in the kitchen most of morning and afternoons. She would cook but would not make *chapattis*. Making fresh chapattis on a stove was the worst cooking chore and was left for Abdul, who also helped with cooking, washing utensils, cleaning, etc. My mother would take a siesta after lunch but would be back in the afternoon to prepare the evening dinner.

Bhaijan Joins the Family

At the Bano Manzil apartment, Bhaijan rejoined the family in 1953 after completing his master's degree in economics at the Government College, Lahore. He had excelled in his academic career and secured a gold medal. He was hired as a research bank officer at the State Bank of Pakistan; it was equivalent to the US Federal Reserve Bank.

Throughout his college years, Bhaijan had resided at the Government College hostel in Lahore. I am sure his hostel expenses were considerable, but my father focused on providing the best education to his children. He was perhaps motivated by his deceased uncle Abdul Hameed, who had distinguished himself in public service under the British before his untimely death at age fifty-five. When Bhaijan completed his education and started working in Karachi, it must have provided financial relief.

Bhaijan and his friend, Moinuddin Baqai, often came home for lunch. One day, my sister, Shaheen, who was barely ten, had an accident. She was heating a bottle containing dried nail polish to liquefy its contents. It exploded, and glass entered her left eye. Luckily, it happened when Bhaijan and Moin were there for lunch. She was quickly rushed to an eye specialist a few blocks away at Pakistan Chowk. She was lucky that the glass did not damage her pupil, but she wore a bandage for several days and learned a valuable lesson—don't play with fire.

Carrom Tournament

The summer of 1955 was memorable. Uncle Jamil Hasan and his family visited us. Our uncle GH was posted at Mauripur Station of the Pakistan air force. He had just returned from the UK after a long stay. Bhaijan Asif was residing with him too, and he commuted daily to Pakistan Insurance Corporation offices near the Merewether Tower Complex.

A carrom tournament was held. Carrom is a table-top game originated in India. It is similar to billiards and requires a table-top board with small game piece, with two or four players competing. The participants included all the children and adults. The younger players included beside me, Jamshed, Behram, Shaheen, Yasmin, and Naseema among others while the adults included Abba ji, Asif, and Auntie Shamim among others. It was a round-robin style tournament. The final tournament was held at our uncle's home in Mauripur. While I fully expected to win, my older brother Jamshed skillfully distracted my concentration with his subtle remarks, and I lost focus. Jamshed became the champion, and I was the runner-up.

We were served delicious food cooked by my uncle's longtime servant, Ramzan, and desserts including homemade ice cream. The evening culminated with singing *gazals (urdu poetry)*, where both Asif and her sister, Naseema, were the superstars. Asif was tall and handsome with a Dilip Kumar haircut that was fashionable those days. He voice was melodious and duplicated that of Talat Mahmood, the famous Indian singer at that time.

A Summer Visit to Quetta

One memorable summer vacation was visit to Quetta. The three younger siblings, Shaheen, Yasmin, and I, flew in a PAF freighter plane arranged through the courtesy of our Chacha G. H. We took off from the Mauripur air base. The group included the children of a naval officer, Khalid Jamil. As we were taxiing, a tire burst, and the plane failed to take off. We returned home but got to Quetta on a subsequent flight.

Chacha Ahmed Hasan (A. H.) was posted in Quetta. He lived in a large bungalow with spacious grounds lined with fruit trees at 400 Lytton Road in the cantonment. He was employed as a civilian officer in the Pakistan army. My aunt, Chachijan Akhtar, was the daughter of Abdul Aziz, who was educated in the UK having completed his bar at the Lincoln Inn. Chachijan was a literary person having read the Persian poetry of Iqbal, the great Indian poet and visionary of an independent homeland and statehood for Muslims of his time.

My uncle had five children—four sons, Javed, Asad, Naveed, and Najam, and a daughter, Nasreen. Nasreen was the second eldest; being older, she helped Chachijan in the kitchen. I became well acquainted with Asad and Naveed being about their age, and we were good friends for decades.

Chachijan ran a tight household. The children were given weekly rations of sugar in bottles. If you ran out earlier, too bad; you had to wait until the end of the week for replenishment. I am sure there was some stealing of sugar rations; all my cousins had sweet tooths.

Quetta, high in the Baluchistan Mountains, was like a summer resort. The days were warm, but the evenings were quite cool even in the summer. The climate was suitable for fruit trees, which all houses had; *khobani* (apricot) trees were everywhere, but the birds ate more fruit than humans did.

During Ramadan, all adults and kids fasted during the day. We got up after midnight for *suhur*. Asad, Naveed, and I would go to the Saddar bazaar by bike every night to buy *nan*, fresh-baked bread. The streets were dark and devoid of vehicular traffic then. One of our bicycles fitted with a light generator provided the necessary yet dim light.

The water source in Quetta came from a tube well and was quite cold. There was a hand pump to fill up pails for drinking, cooking, and washing. One could not take a bath with such cold water. To heat water for our infrequent baths, we used an electric rod. The toilets were in an outhouse fitted with an independent commode system that required manual disposal and cleaning daily. This was a novelty for us since we had had a shower and squatting-type toilets fitted with flushing systems in Karachi.

Elderly Mr. Hannah was the next-door neighbor of the Hasan family in Quetta. My cousins used to play pranks on him, which made him upset. He had no children of his own. We were quite childish in irritating him.

Javed, the eldest cousin, was in college those days. He would read the daily English paper from cover to cover for several hours while reclining in an easy chair. One day, I discovered that he was a smoker. He would hide his cigarette behind the newspaper. Smoking was probably forbidden for the children, and most of the elders in our paternal family did not smoke except for Abba ji. He was a heavy smoker perhaps having acquired this habit from his late maternal uncle, Abdul Hamid. On my maternal side, elders smoked *hookas*.

We returned home after a month-long trip with happy memories of our vacation in Quetta.

Sind Madressah-tul-Islam High School (SM)

Sind Madressah-tul-Islam

My formal education began at Sind Madressah, which was one of the oldest education institutions in the subcontinent established in 1885 by enlightened Muslims led by Khan Bahadur Hassanally Effendi (1830–1895), a Sindhi of Turkish origin. Those were perhaps the best years as I remember, and they inculcated certain qualities and behavior including truthfulness, punctuality, discipline, hard work, etc. Those were my formative years.

I had to take an entrance exam conducted by Abdul Jabbar. He was a distinguished-looking teacher who wore a *sherwani* and had a beard. The test covered reading and writing; I passed easily and entered fifth grade.

The classrooms had desks and chairs for each student; that was different from fourth grade in Lahore, where the students sat on the floor. I felt upgraded. I sat in the front row, a tradition I followed throughout my educational career.

The two-story school building was a quadrangle with covered verandas on both sides of the classrooms. It was constructed of sandstone and had a red-tiled roof. The foundation stone of the main building had been laid by the viceroy of India in 1887 and had been designed by James Strachan. The school complex spread over eight acres in the financial district consisted of several buildings including a hostel, an intermediate college, a large soccer and cricket grounds, and the principal's residence. The entrance was on Frere Road, a few blocks from Denso Hall on

Bunder Road. The entrance was inscribed with the school motto: Enter to Learn and Go forth to Serve.

The school staff had residences on the premises. The Talpur House, built in 1901, housed a wood workshop, a scout den, and a room for cricket equipment. It would later house a technical section and a boys' elementary section. Three more buildings that served as boarding houses (hostels) were added over time: Hassanally House (1909), Khairpur House (1912), and Sardar House (1919). A unique feature of the institution was its two mosques; a Sunni mosque was built in 1893, and a Shia mosque was built in 1894. They were available to students for midday prayer.

Since it was a public school, the tuition in 1949–50 was Rs. 30, but that increased to Rs. 70 or so by 1956. Over the next fifty years, the tuition rose to the Rs. 700–1,000 range based on the class level. The medium of instruction was Urdu, the national language.

The school had two shifts. The morning shift was for grades eight through eleven while the afternoon shift was for grades five through seven. It was a popular school for many Muslims from the interior, Sindh and Baluchistan, since it had boarding facilities. It was modeled after the British public schools and was supported by educators including Sir Syed Ahmed Khan.

Our Headmaster

Syed Nasir Hussein was a dedicated teacher and a strict disciplinarian. He was in his mid-fifties and had hair greying at the temples; he always wore a *karakul* cap. His rounds in the school corridors would terrify any loitering student. His cool, blue-green glare would freeze any pupil, but he was a compassionate family man. His nephew, Murtaza, was my classmate for a year having transferred from Lahore; he lived with his family at the headmaster's residence.

During the final high school year, he would conduct daily after-school class teaching us English with emphasis on its grammar, prepositions, idioms, and vocabulary. He would use *Martin's Handbook* as a reference. His dedication and hard work paid off; he helped me gain writing skills.

Our Teachers

Our teachers were dedicated educators. Most of them were graduates of the Aligarh University, India. Mr. Fauq introduced me to Urdu literature and poetry including the famous poets Ghalib, Anees, Mir Taqi Mir, and Iqbal. Haleem was our English teacher. Younas and Anwar Hussain taught us arithmetic. I studied Indian history for a couple of years. I was told that there were few Muslim historians though they ruled the subcontinent for over eight hundred years. Indian history books were mostly written by non-muslim historians, who had a bias toward the invaders from Central Asia.

Notable Alumni

The institution has produced several prominent Muslims including Pakistan's founder, Quaid-e-Azam Mohammed Ali Jinnah, who received his secondary education at Sind Madressah for five years (1887–1892). The school record showed his name on being first admitted on July 14, 1887 as Muhammadali Jinnahbuoy, and his birthdate was recorded as October 20, 1875. The father of the nation bequeathed a third of his estate to SMI in his will, which helped upgrade SMI to college level with the opening of Sind Madressah College on June 21, 1943.

Other notables included Sir Abdullah Haroon, Sir Shahnawaz Bhutto, Ghulam Hussain Hidayatullah, Dr. Daudputa, Muhammed Ayub Khuro, A. K. Brohi, Justice Sajjad Ali S., and many more like them.

Becoming a Boy Scout

The school offered several extracurricular activities including soccer, cricket, and scouting. I joined the Boy Scouts. Our scout master, MK Niazi, had a Baluch-Sindhi background. He was a full-time teacher and volunteer scout master. He was quite a literary figure with an interest in writing scripts for school dramas and plays.

The scout den was in the Talpur House. There were at least four patrols each headed by a patrol leader who reported to a troop leader. My patrol was called Kiwi. We met after school at the scout den. While we performed scouting activities, the school grounds were humming with cricket and soccer activities. Master Aziz was a dedicated cricket coach who later become famous after Hanif Mohammed became a world-renowned cricketer. My best memories of my childhood are associated with my scouting activities, which guided me as I grew older.

The Boy Scout motto is Be Prepared. Each scout took the scout oath: "On my honor, I will do my best To do my duty to God and my country and to obey the Scout Law; To help other people at all times; To keep myself physically strong, mentally awake, and morally straight." Scouts promised to live by the scout laws and be trustworthy, loyal, helpful, friendly, courteous, kind, obedient, cheerful, thrifty, brave, clean, and reverent.

Our scouting activities took us on day and night camps to the outskirts of Karachi including Malir and Korangi. On such trips, I learned how to pitch tents, cook, and be a team player. At the end of each day, the scouts sat around a campfire and told jokes, sang, and acted. At night, we took hourly turns as watchmen. There was a code word that changed every night.

We had our first weekend campout at Korangi Creek. We took a camel-driven cart there that was about eight feet wide and twenty feet long and rode on four tires. It was big enough for all the scouts and their tents, cooking needs, and other supplies. It was quite a smooth ride; it took two hours to reach Korangi, twelve or so miles away. The Korangi area was along a creek with saltwater marshes and strong breezes off the Arabian Sea.

We quickly set up our tents. At dinner, I felt crunchy sand particles in the *chapattis* that were freshly baked over the fire. At the end of the weekend, I came home with an award—a cup for my enthusiasm and behavior.

Liaquat Ali Funeral

In October 1951, the prime minister of Pakistan, Liaqat Ali, was assassinated while addressing a large crowd in Company Bagh, Rawalpindi. This came as a shock to the newly independent nation, another severe blow after the untimely death of its founder, Mohammad Ali Jinnah (Quaid-e-Azam). The entire country was in mourning; all offices, schools, and colleges were shut down.

Boy scouts from the schools gathered at the Victoria Road residence of the prime minister to pay homage. We were led by our troop leader, Khalid, and scout master, Niazi, to the funeral grounds about five miles away. The entire route was closed to all traffic except for the silent procession of the cortege and the rhythmic sounds of our boots hitting the pavement in unison. It was an unforgettable experience for a very young boy scout.

As a scout, I learned basic skills including, sewing, cooking, pathfinding, and map reading, which made me self-sufficient and came in handy in my later years living in the US.

Becoming an Eagle Scout

To become an eagle (Quaid-e-Azam) scout, I had to learn to swim. There were no public swimming pools in Karachi. An Olympic-sized swimming pool existed in a Pakistan navy facility, PNS Dilawar, but it was far from home with limited bus service. The swimming pool was filled with sea water, a lot of which I swallowed before I learned to swim.

By the time I was fifteen, I had completed my training and earned all the proficiency badges to become an eagle scout. Soon afterward, I became the youngest troop leader.

In 1955, I was selected for the World Boy Scouts Jamboree held in the US after an intense citywide competition. That was an opportunity of a lifetime. All I had to do was to pay for the roundtrip airfare. The school headmaster, Nasir Hussein, was unable to sponsor the fare, and my father could not afford the expensive Karachi-US airfare. I was disheartened, but Bhaijan consoled me that the month-long trip would disrupt my high school studies and possibly affect my final grades.

The scouts attended all important local events including the August 14 Independence Day celebration and political rallies. While in uniform, the boy scouts had easy access to the dais whereas the rest of the crowd was behind barricades. I was privileged to see political leaders and dignitaries up close. I admired the handsome face and the moustache of Sardar Sahib, who was always well dressed in a sherwani.

Apart from scouting, I took part in a school play concerning the Pakistan Freedom Movement. The main actor was one of our patrol leaders, Ibrahim, who acted as a Kashmiri freedom fighter captured and tortured by Indian troops. He won the best actor award for his role.

Merchant of Venice

An English drama troupe visited our school. It was quite an event watching the British actors particularly the one playing Shylock. The acting was superb, but I was a stranger to Shakespearean English.

School Friends

I developed friendships with some scouts that lasted beyond high school. One was Umar Munshi, whom I followed into NED Engineering College. Upon graduation, he went to Leeds, UK, for a master's degree. He formed a consulting firm in the 1960s and became a successful structural engineer. I believe his success came from his boy scout training. His mannerisms, hard work, professional acumen, and dedication to detail became his hallmarks. He will always be remembered. He died of heart ailment in 1970s at a young age right when everything seemed to be going his way.

Another friend was Taimoor Qureshi, who later became an air force pilot of F-16s and MiG-21 jets and rose to the rank of air commodore in the Pakistan air force before retiring.

Abdul Waheed was another contemporary who lived with his family in a flat above a twenty-four-hour pharmacy, Akhtar and Muneer. He studied at SMI as well. He attended D. J. Science College and later went to the University of Karachi. After receiving a master's in microbiology, he completed a PhD at the University of London. He and I became especially close after immigrating to the US in the 1970s. He worked for ICI and AstraZeneca, a biopharmaceutical company in Delaware, and then he established his own research laboratory.

A Summer Tour by Northwestern Railway

Pakistan Map

During the summer of 1956, our scout troop traveled in a reserved rail car to the northern cities of Lahore, Rawalpindi, and Havelian. My father paid for the excursion Rs. 150 for the three-week trip. Perhaps my parents appreciated my hard work on the high school examination. It was through these travels that I learned about the rich history of the Indus Valley civilization and places of interest including the resort hill stations of the Himalayas.

Mohenjo-Daro (https://en.wikipedia.com/wiki/Mohenjo-Daro)

Mohenjo-Daro is an archaeological site in the province of Sindh, Pakistan. Built around 2500 BCE, it was one of the largest settlements of the ancient Indus Valley civilization, and one of the world's earliest major cities, contemporaneous with the civilizations of ancient Egypt and Mesopotamia.

Mohenjo-Daro is west of the Indus River in Larkana District, Sindh, Pakistan. It is accessible via a local train station, Dokri, eleven kilometers from the site. After disembarking, we marched to the site and returned the same day. While returning, being afraid to miss the train, we had to jog most of the way. It was my first 5k run.

The ruins of the city remained undocumented for around 3,700 years until R. D. Banerji, an officer of the Archaeological Survey of India, visited the site in 1919–20 and identified the Buddhist *stupa* (150–500 CE) known to be there. A stupa is a mound-like structure containing relics, related to Bhuddist religion; he found a flint scraper that convinced him of the site's antiquity. This led to large-scale excavations of Mohenjo-Daro in the years 1930–45. Significant excavation has since been conducted at the site, which was designated a UNESCO World Heritage Site in 1980.

Hiking in the Foothills of the Himalayas

Hiking from Murree to Abbottabad through the hills remains a vivid memory. I walked twenty-two miles from Murree to Nathia Gali in one day, the longest walk I can remember.

Nathia Gali

Nathia Gali Mountains

Nathia Gali or Nathiagali is a mountainous resort town or hill station in Abbottabad District of Khyber Pakhtunkhwa, Pakistan. It is a part of the Galyat range, where several hill stations are situated close to each other and with their names mostly ending in *Gali*.

Nathia Gali is very picturesque hill station clad in pine, walnut, oak, and maple trees. The walking trail through the woods was mostly in the shade of tall evergreens. In addition to carrying a haversack, I was also the paramedic carrying a first-aid kit. We followed the trail through the hills resting every hour for water. Due to high altitude, 6,500–7,000 feet above sea level, the weather in the mountains was cool and comfortable, in the seventies with little humidity and air laced with pine freshness. We reached Nathiagali before sunset. At the day's end, I was exhausted after the march and had the most wonderful sleep in the cool night.

The next day, we marched to Abbottabad. The landscape changed from evergreens to barren hills with little vegetation, and the temperature soared into the eighties. I was thirsty more often than I had been the previous day.

Abbottabad

Abbottabad is in a valley in the foothills of the Himalayas four thousand feet above sea level and some sixty miles by winding mountainous roads north of Pakistan's capital. Abbottabad sits on the Karakoram Highway, an engineering marvel that links Pakistan with China through the Himalayas. Surrounded by green hills, it is renowned for its trees and parks. It's a popular retirement place for officers of the Pakistani army partly because of its military academy but also because of its agreeable climate.

During British rule, Abbottabad was named after Sir James Abbott, Commissioner Hazara (1845–1853). It was a garrison town with a population of 4,500 in 1868.

This small garrison town became known worldwide as the place where Osama bin Laden and his family hid; he was killed in a raid by US military in 2010.

The area to the north of Abbottabad saw a surge in Taliban activity two years ago as the Taliban sought to extend their influence from the tribal areas that border Afghanistan into what was North West Frontier Province, now called Khyber Pakhtunkhwa. The town of Buner, just thirty miles from Abbottabad and sixty miles from Islamabad, fell to the Taliban early in 2009. They also established a training camp close to the town of Mansehra, a few miles from Abbottabad. The Pakistani military has since gradually reasserted control over the area expelling the Taliban from the Swat Valley but at a bloody cost.

Havelian is a rail terminus in the north of Pakistan. That was the last place on our tour.

As I returned, Karachi Higher Secondary School Board announced the matriculation results. I was successful with a first division, an honor shared with only eight or ten other students from our school. I felt vindicated. I was really excited about my future.

Notable Contemporaries

One of the noteworthy cricketers produced by SMI was Hanif Mohammad. I watched Hanif and other cricketers practicing after school every day until sunset. Hanif was trained by Abdul Aziz, an Afghan cricket player who had earlier played in Ranji Trophy, and he made his first-class debut playing for Pakistan against the MCC in November 1951, when he was only sixteen.

Hanif Mohammed (1934–2016) was the most successful batsman of his time scoring marathon innings for days. He held the world record of 300 runs in a single test match against the West Indies in 1957–58. He was known as Little Master. In 1958–59, he surpassed Don Bradman's record for the highest individual first-class innings. Hanif made 499 for Karachi in a match against Bahawalpur before being run out attempting his five hundredth run; this mark stood for more than thirty-five years before being passed by Brian Lara in 1994. He died on August 11, 2016 at age eighty-one.

Another family, the Rizvis, with three sons, Ather, Saleem, and Naushad, and a daughter, Naushaba, lived across the street. They came from Gowaliar, India, after the partition. The eldest son was a gentleman student at NED Engineering College for a long term. Jamshed and I were friendly with them. In the evening, Mr. Rizvi would sit on the stoop outside their ground floor apartment while we played on the street. Saleem became a successful plastic surgeon in the US and settled in Michigan in the 1970s. Naushad became a successful test cricketer and a wicket keeper for the Pakistan cricket team in the 1960s.

Many years later, I ran into Dr. Saleem in Acapulco, Mexico. I saw him and shouted at him by his nickname, Atti, and he responded immediately calling me by my brother Jamshed's nickname. It was instant recall of the earlier memories of the Pakistan Chowk and pastime activities including family upgrades. Saleem was accompanied by her two loving daughters at that time.

It's a small world after all.

D. J. Science College, 1956–58

D.J. science College

I graduated from SMI with a first division and in the top 5 percent of the class of over two hundred students. I was good in math and science including biology. I had a difficult choice between opting for the pre-engineering or premedical courses. In the end, I opted for the pre-engineering curriculum; I was influenced in my decision by my first cousin, N. D. Yousaf, who was a botanist and dean of Agricultural University, Lyallpur (now Faisalabad) and a researcher on sugarcane. He was also a recipient of the president's Pride of Performance Medal in 1958.

I enrolled in the two-year, pre-engineering inter-science program at D. J. Science College. The college, a coed institution, offered pre-engineering and premedical courses as well as a four-year bachelor of science (B.S.) program. It was an elite institution in Karachi; it was established in 1887 and named after the Daryaram Jethmal, an Indian philanthropist. Admission was based on merit. The large building, facing Kutchery Road, was constructed with local limestone and was perhaps the same vintage as the SMI buildings. One of Sonia's aunts attended this college in the 1930s and graduated with a degree.

The walk from our apartment to the college took under five minutes; that was a luxury that lasted for a few months only as our family moved farther to the Saddar area a few miles away.

My courses included math, physics, chemistry, english, and islamic studies. My friends from SMI, Waheed and Mateen, joined the premedical program, which included zoology and botany.

First-year classes were held in the afternoon in a newer building adjacent to the main college building. There were new faces from other high schools. I became acquainted with Safdar Iqbal, Shahid, and Shezad, who had matriculated from Marie Colaco School. The initial acquaintance led to a lasting friendship through engineering college and continued during our diverse professional careers lasting for nearly fifty years until his untimely death during the 2005 earthquake in Islamabad.

Prof. Jamali taught advanced algebra, trigonometry, and calculus. He was a small-built, bearded person in his mid-fifties and wore traditional Pakistani dress—a sherwani, grey beard, and a Turkish cap. He had a quiet demeanor. I loved his classes.

Physics was taught by Anthony D'Souza, the principal of the college. He had a stern demeanor, but he was an enthusiastic teacher. His classes were held in an auditorium with long benches with desks. The first row was generally taken by a few girls and out of respect not shared by the boys. Organic and inorganic chemistry was taught by Prof. Sidhwa. His classes were held in the same room as were our physics classes, where laboratory practicals for physics and chemistry experiments were held. English literature was taught by Prof. Mahbub.

Possible Career in the Army

My father had a plan for me. He always wanted one of his children to join the military, which was considered an honorable profession that offered an improved quality of life as well. I was encouraged to take an entrance exam for the Commissioned Officers Program in the Pak Army. The entrance requirements for the program included a written test followed by several days of tests and interviews at the Inter-Services Selection Board (ISSB) at Kohat for candidates who passed the written test. While a freshman, I took the written test and qualified to appear at the ISSB at Kohat. The interview at Kohat required a reimbursable train ride to the north.

At Kohat, I was among approximately fifty candidates. We were housed in single rooms and provided with orderlies (servants). Each morning when the alarm went off, I was served bed tea, after which I shaved and showered and went to the dining room for breakfast with the other candidates. The food and service were excellent; we were pampered as potential officers.

We had several written and psychological tests during the first two days. The third day, we were assigned roles to test our behavior with others including cooperation and leadership qualities. The field exercises consisted of developing strategy/tactics as an army patrol to overcome obstacles and hurdles to overtaking enemy positions. Such exercises focused on scope and time. The exercises were to judge our behavior as individuals and as a team under simulated stressful situations. The army observers were continuously watching us as we made each decision, reacted, overcame the assumed hurdles, and dealt with the time constraints.

In addition to myself, my cousin Asad (who was studying at Government College, Lahore) and a friend Latif (who was a freshman at NED Engineering College) also qualified for commissions in the Pakistan army, but declined to join.

In 1957, we moved to the State Bank Officers Flats (SBF) in Saddar. It was quite an upgrade from the Bano Manzil flat. Abba ji ordered new furniture for the living, dining, and bedrooms including a new Persian rug. The bathrooms were modern with tiled floors, sinks, flush toilets, and showers. The three-bedroom flat had large windows with iron grills for safety.

The SBF adjoined the Regal Cinema. At night, the cinema auditorium doors would be open, and we heard the music of the movies being played.

Family Bonds

Chacha G. H. was in the administration directorate of PAF Headquarters in Mauripur until the headquarters was moved to Peshawar in the 1960s. Uncle and Aunt Shamim owned a Vauxhall and would visit us on weekends. Auntie would get gifts of silk and cotton fabrics she appreciated much.

Chacha and Auntie loved to travel abroad and especially to England. In 1955, they returned to Pakistan after a long stay. They told us stories of the young queen, Elizabeth, who was crowned in 1952, and how the British people loved the royalty. I received a book about Churchill, *The Man of the Century*, a pictorial biography edited by Neil Ferrier. I still possess the book.

Major (Ret.) Zaheeruddin Babar and his wife, Qamar, lived near the Cantt Station, at 6 Belgrave Terrace, near the Bristol Hotel. The family occupied one of the four large, airy apartments built in the 1930s of stone with mahogany staircases and red-tiled roofs. The windows were large and allowed ample sunlight and breezes. The Pakistan Western Railway tracks ran next door with a high wall separating the tracks from the premises. Qamar was the younger sister of Bobo, wife of (the late) Abdul Hamid, who was the maternal uncle of my father.

Babar Sahib, the son of Nawabzada Moizuddin Ahmed, took pride of belonging to a Loharo nawab family, Haryana, India. *(A Nawab is a royal title indicating a sovereign ruler of a state).* He was a WWII veteran and was employed with the Army Rangers based in Sind. An honest and pleasing personality, he was friendly to the children. Besides his military service, he served in civilian positions in the Sind government.

His wife, Qamar (fondly called Auntie Shako), was a calm, smart individual and a good listener. She came to live with her sister, Bobo, in Lahore. Through a mutual friend, a marriage proposal came from Zaheeruddin Babar, and they married and left for Simla, where he was posted. Aunty Shako was a great woman. She brought up her three children (Fauzia, Yawar, and Fizza) mostly alone as her husband was serving on the border police force. She was an excellent cook and hostess. Apa ji often looked for advice from her.

Our families became close, and we shared the weekends often. Nasriuddin Yawar Babar, known as Bogi, was always cheerful and somewhat mischievous. He played some pranks that sometimes upset his father. Once, Yawar was accidently hit by a plate thrown at him, damaging his elbow. He was taken to the hospital for stiches; he did not have full function of his elbow for years. He studied civil engineering at NED and Imperial College, London. He married Shahnaz and raised two children, Saam and Samia. He died in 2004.

Shahnaz's parents were Khawaja and Begum Najmunissa Nooruddin; they were in Calcutta before the partition. Her father was involved in politics and was member of Congress working with Quaid e Azam and others in the struggle for Pakistan movement. Nooruddin was secretary of the Mohammedon Sporting Club. While Khawaja Nazimuddin was president, they achieved their goal. After the partition, he published a newspaper in Calcutta that he continued in Dacca and Karachi, *The Morning News*.

Fauzia got married to Saeed Hai, the famous Pakistani tennis player. Fizza got married to Jilani, an executive with Pakistan Tobacco.

Another family was the MBK Malik working for the Pakistan Western Railway (PWR). His wife, Bilquis, was the oldest daughter of (the late) Abdul Hamid. Their children, Rehana, Azmat (Azzoo), and Afroze (Micchi), lived on Kutchery Road. Toward the end of his career, he became vice chairman of PWR. I visited him in his prestigious office, and he proudly showed me the Hall of Past Vice Chairmen behind his huge office at the Lahore Station.

Auntie Bilquis died in 1982, and MBK Malik passed away in 1996. Azmat joined the Pak army and later joined the police force and retired as Deputy Inspector General (DIG). He was married to Durdana in Karachi. He died in 2016. Reena (Rehana) married Zillur Rehman (Ducky), an officer in the Pak army. Ducky was a coursemate of Gen. Musharraf, who later became the president of Pakistan. Afroze was married to Aftab, who later became a chairman of Pakistan Steel Mills.

Another family, Afroze and Nazir, lived at 2 Bleak House Road near Clifton. Afroze was a daughter of Shaban Mirani, a prosperous landlord from Mirpur Khas. Their children were Tarik, Azra (Dodi), Salik, and Shahid. Azra attended Marie Colaco High School as did Shaheen. Nazir Ahmed was a civil servant and later became defense secretary during

Ayub Khan's regime. His son, Salik, joined the Pakistan Foreign Service while Shahid joined the Pak army. Tarik became a businessman.

Azim Khan, my father's business partner, had two wives. The senior wife lived in Karachi with sons Salim and Naeem and their families. Naeem graduated from SMI and went into the textile business following his father. Azim Khan, who lived in Bombay with his son, Naseem, owned textile mills in Bombay and Karachi. He was six feet tall and had broad shoulders that would barely squeeze through our Bano Manzil three-foot-wide door. He was a prosperous and shrewd businessman who respected the integrity of my father. When my father decided to leave the government and come to Karachi, it was Azim Khan who offered my father a business opportunity, which lasted more than fifteen years, when my father decided to retire for good.

Chacha J. H. used to relate stories about the hard way Azim Khan made his money—saving every penny on the way up. He told me that Azim Khan's pocket would be full of *channas* (gram) that he would make suffice as lunch—A penny saved is a penny earned. Many years later, when Dr. Farid Baqai was building his hospital in Karachi, he was similarly very frugal with finances and successfully negotiated contracts for the design and construction of the projects and kept a tight lid on the expenditures until the very end.

Celebrating Religious Festivals

Our family was moderately religious. Every eleventh of the lunar month, Ghiarween, sweets were made or bought and distributed to neighbors and friends out of respect for Islam's Sufi saint, Shaikh Abdul Qadir Jilani (1077–1166) of Iraq.

During the Islamic month of Rabiul Awwal, sometimes a *mowlood* would be held at the SBF, which required clearing the living room furniture to accommodate guests who would sit on carpets covered by white sheets. The attendees included religious figures, Iqbal Siddiqui, and Zawwar Hussain, Babar Sahib, and other relatives. The religious ceremony included *naats* and supplications and lasted up to two hours;

it was concluded with dinner. Our mother prepared the food for up to fifty guests at a time.

Every Ramadan, the adults and children over age twelve would fast beginning at dawn and abstain from food and drink until sunset. Breaking the fast at sunset brought joy and satisfaction in fulfilling Allah's commandment.

During fasts, Abba ji had to also abstain from smoking, a habit he acquired during his early years in the company of his maternal uncle. That was hard for him to do so, but he persevered through strong will. For Iftar, the treats included a sweet, delicious drink (*rooh-afza*) with rose fragrances, *pakoras*, *dehi-baras*, and *aloo-chat*.

The wake-up call for *suhur* was not by an alarm clock but a traditional one with professionals who walked the streets in the early hours beating drums and yelling, "Sehri Karo," "Wake up for suhur." For *suhur*, the usual recipe was *prathas* and yogurt. Our mother, with the help of the servant, would prepare the meals. The smell of the *parathas* served as a wake-up call. We would eat until the *Fajr Azan* was heard from the nearby mosque. During the night, the *Travih* prayers were held at Arambagh Park, where ice-cold water in large buckets was available as a treat for the devotees.

The entire family members observed fasting with devotion. At the end of Ramadan, Eid-ul-Fitr would be celebrated with great fervor and enthusiasm by the young. There was new clothing for all. The Eid prayers would be held at the Polo Grounds attended by tens of thousands in the open air. It was followed by a fancy lunch prepared by Apa ji that included special meat *pulao*, *kofta* curry, and *tandori prathas* followed by a dessert of *sheer khorma*. Relatives included Aunty Bilquis and Aunt Nasim, who would also visit us on Eid. They called my mother Bhabi with affection, and they loved our mother's cooking. After lunch, each child would receive Eidi as well from the aunties. The going rate those days was perhaps Rs. 2 per child.

Abba ji had a tough persona but a loving and kind heart. He discharged his religious obligations faithfully and distributed the *zakat* (the prescribed charity, 2.5 percent of wealth) annually in the month of Ramadan first to needy relatives and then to the deserving poor. He attended religious gatherings and met with Sufi saints from Pak Patten. He did not become a follower, but he respected such persons and met them for inspiration and guidance.

When Bhaijan had an opportunity to work in Saudi Arabia, Abba ji encouraged him to accept the assignment since it would afford him and his wife to perform pilgrimage.

Abba ji was active in social and cultural activities. He belonged to the Anjuman-Kakezai in Karachi and became an active member. He was the treasurer while Malik Bagh Ali was the president. He was well respected by the community due to his integrity and honesty. His friends included Sardar Mohammad and Tufail Elahi, who would visit often. When Sardar Mohammad sat for *aitekaf* during Ramadan, he visited him at the Saeed Manzil mosque.

He was a keen bridge player and taught us to play bridge using the Culbertson method of counting points for bidding. The foursome usually included Abba ji, Yasmin, Rikki, and me.

In early 1962, he had insomnia and had to be hospitalized in the civil hospital in Karachi for several days. I was taking my final BE exams at the time, and I visited him in the hospital to report my progress. I knew it gave him great satisfaction to hear any good news. He was praying for my success. During his stay in the hospital, he heard of the death of his old friend and successful businessman, Azim Khan, in Bombay. It must have been a great shock to him. My father and Azim Khan were like family with ties extending over several decades. As my civil engineering final exams ended, so did my father's insomnia. After he was discharged from the hospital, we went straight to the Azim Khan home in Karachi to give our condolences to his family.

Letters from Our Father

Abba ji wrote to his family and children, who were away, regularly. He wrote to Bhaijan when he was in the US and Saudi Arabia. He wrote to me weekly when I was in the US for two years. His letters, usually written on an aerogram, were limited to one page but included enough information about the family. Unfortunately, all the letters were lost over time except for the following three, which are reproduced in the appendix.

1. Letter from Abba ji to son, Sheri, dated September 8, 1964 congratulating him on his MSCE degree.
2. Letter from Abba ji to daughter Shaheen after her marriage to Maj. A. Y. Khan in 1967.
3. Letter from Abba ji to son, Behram, who was posted in East Pakistan in 1968. The letter talks of consulting a heart specialist and insomnia. Behram had a dream about Abba ji's illness/death during this time. Part of the letter is written by Yasmin.

Bilal, son of Chacha G. H., is the youngest cousin in our family. He remembers Chacha Mohammad Hasan.

"Even though I was very young at his untimely passing in 1968, I do have two memories of him. In one memory I remember him sitting on his bed at 17F, PECHS home wearing a white Kurta and white pajama. The other memory I have of him taking me and my sister for ice cream to nursery. We walked to the store and had to cross this very busy road. He was holding our hands to cross the road and half-way through I freed myself and ran the rest of the way. I was reprimanded but still got my ice cream. As we were the youngest we got away with a lot, basically we could do no wrong".

Abba ji passed away on September 15, 1968, at age sixty-eight. He fulfilled his dream of providing the best education available in Pakistan to all his children. He became a grandfather for the third time just before he died, and three of his eight sons and daughters were happily married.

His death transferred the task of marrying the four children fell to our mother, Apa ji, who was ably assisted by Bhaijan.

Apa ji lived for another twenty-one years and saw her children become successful in their careers, and the number of grandchildren went up to seventeen. She often visited all her children in various parts of Pakistan and the US. She proudly talked of her sons as five diamonds.

One of her last joyous act was attending the marriage of the oldest granddaughter, Samia, in the US. Despite being diabetic and in failing health, her strong will enabled her to complete the 10,000-mile hazardous journey. She died soon after the wedding, on October 17, 1989, and was buried in Maryland.

It is now over fifty years since our father passed away. The Hasan family has spread their wings far and wide. If he were alive today, he would be surprised at its growth. The grandchildren are following the paths of their parents and perhaps exceeding them in their careers in engineering, technology, finance, banking, medicine, biotechnology, and research at prestigious institutions around the world. Abba ji's hard work and investment in his children's education paid off handsomely.

The third generation of great-grandchildren, three to twenty-four years of age, is also in various stages of education and development. The oldest great-grandchild has recently graduated from the University of Chicago and is determined to help disadvantaged families in the US. By the grace of God, the family has realized the dreams of our parents including the moral values that they treasured. The torch has been passed on, and a bright future lies ahead for the next generation.

Abba ji in Delhi, India (1946)

Sister Parveen wearing the Air Force Cap (1945)

Brothers Ahmad Hasan and Mohammad Hasan- 1952

Abba ji with Farida (1950's)

Quaid-e-Azam with MM Ispahani and Noorudin

Chapter 3

BECOMING AN ENGINEER

NED Engineering College, 1958–62

After graduating from the pre-engineering D.J. college with a first division in the top 5 percent of the class, I was accepted into NED Engineering College on the merit basis. Most of my friends, including Safdar, Shahid, and Shehzad, joined me there. These three S's were very close. Initially, I was particularly close to Safdar, who was a quiet and serious student who lived in Saddar. Shahid and I became quite close during our NED years as we were fond of movies and hung out together particularly on weekends.

Of my friends, Shehzad came roaring in on his Triumph motorbike to the engineering college while Shahid drove his father's VW. Most of the students walked from the nearby hostels or came via bus.

The intermediate science curriculum was a two-year course with annual examinations. There were approximately twenty-two students, out of a class of two hundred pre-engineering students who were awarded the first division based on the combined scores of the yearly exams, and I was lucky to be one. All twenty-two were accepted based on merit into the first year of NED Engineering College curriculum in 1958.

NED Government College was founded by and named after its benefactor donor and philanthropist Nadirshaw Edulj Dinshaw family in 1921. It is one of the oldest institutions of higher learning in Pakistan. Originally founded to provide training for civil engineers working on building the Sukkur Barrage, the university came to its modern form after being established by the British government. *A barrage is a dam like structure in a watercourse to increase the depth of water fo to divert it to into an irrigation channel.* The undergraduate engineering college was a four-year program leading to degrees in civil, mechanical, and electrical engineering. It also offered a diploma program for overseers supporting the public works program.

The construction of the engineering college building was financed by donations including Rs. 150,000 from Nadirshaw Edulji Dinshaw. The new college was originally the Prince of Wales Engineering College but was later renamed in memory of Nadirshaw Edulji Dinshaw. NED College was provisionally granted affiliation in 1923 by the University of Bombay for the first- and second-year courses in civil engineering, and seventy-eight students were provisionally admitted into first-year classes in 1922. The original NED Engineering College was housed in several blocks of buildings and two sheds. The first-full time principal of NED Engineering College was G. N. Gokhale, who joined the faculty in 1923. The first professor (and vice principal) was S. B. Jannarkar.

Additions were made to provide accommodation for the machine shop on the ground floor and a mechanical drawing hall on the first floor. The fourth block, completed in 1945, contained a classroom and clerk's office on the ground floor and a civil drawing hall on the first floor. Two sheds were built later to house the carpentry and smithy shops and to train technicians. The total cost of the buildings was just over Rs. 265,000, and the cost of equipment, books and furniture was just under Rs. 400,000.

In 1947, it was taken over by the government of Sindh and re-named NED Government Engineering College and affiliated with the University of Sindh. After the establishment of the University of Karachi in 1951, the affiliation of the college was transferred to that university.

NED Government Engineering College became NED University of Engineering and Technology in 1977. From an enrollment of fifty students in 1923, the student population undergraduate and graduate is now nearly 7,000. NED University of Engineering and Technology was established in March 1977 under an act of the provincial assembly of Sindh after the upgrading of the former NED Government Engineering College, which was set up in 1922.

The admission to NED, the only engineering institution serving the city of Karachi, was very competitive. The college accepted approximately a hundred freshmen yearly. Many students unable to qualify for admission to NED after the two-year intermediate college would complete a four-year curriculum and earn bachelor of science degrees before being admitted. Acceptance to the freshman engineering was based on the candidates securing first division in inter-science and BSc and then those securing second division in BSc. A few seats were reserved for students from outside Karachi, those domiciled in Sind Province and other underdeveloped areas. This process allowed for a diversity of students from various backgrounds. Some of the students were nominated by the trustees of the school.

Ali Baqai sought to enter through the quota system reserved for the Sindh province but did not possess the domicile. My father timely intervened and arranged a Sind domicile for him so he could join NED based on the Sind quota. My father never mentioned this to those at home. I came to know this from Ali many years later. This was not an isolated incident; he was always there to lend a helping hand to those in need and especially family and friends.

NED College was behind the D. J. Science College on the Strachan Road and Burns Road intersection. It was a two-story, stone building with limited classroom space. The facilities including workshops and laboratory facilities were dated. The college landmark was a stone chimney that rose above the landscape. The college library was only twenty by twenty feet and had limited capacity. The technical books were few and dated. The library did not contain new research, technical magazines, or engineering literature.

There was no common room for students awaiting classes. There were squatting toilets only. Mostly, the students sat outdoors on a few benches with a single tree for shade. The lack of amenities such as a cafeteria did not provide an incentive to hang out; as soon as classes were over, I headed home.

The faculty consisted of professors and lecturers who had filled the vacuum left by the original faculty, mostly Hindus, who left for India after the 1947 partition. Most of the teachers had basic engineering degrees, but it would take another decade before more-qualified faculty would take over. A partial list of the faculty, 1958–62, is below.

Name of Professor	Civil Engineering Curriculum	Remarks
R E Mirza	Water Supply and Sanitary Engineering (FY)	Principal
Sirajuddin Ahmed	Hydraulics and Power Engineering (FY/SY/FY)	Professor
Ganatra	Strength of Materials (FY) Structures (SY/FY), town Planning (FY)	Professor
S M Haider	Building Materials	Professor
Abdul Hameed	Electrical Engineering (FY/SY)	Professor
Ibrahim	Heat Engines FY	Professor
F G Khan	Metallurgy (FY)	First year
A T Khan	Survey (SY), Pavements (FY), Harbor Engineering (FY), Foundations (FY)	Professor
Zialul Islam	Advanced Geometry (FY), Rails and Bridges(FY)	Lecturer
Azizul Hasan	Strength of Materials (FY)	Lecturer
Anwar Chaudhry	Mechanical Drawings	Professor
Khatri	Machine Shop and Carpentry Workshops (FY)	Lecturer

In the late 1950s, the college was visited by some educational foundations including the Ford Foundation. The principal, Kewalramani, took the delegation for a tour around the small campus. After the tour, he waited for their remarks about the facilities. He was told, "Scrap it." It was a true statement about the antiquated facilities and equipment of the college that would ring in the ears of its alumnus, Yayha Bengali, for many decades.

Textbooks for the engineering courses were written by Indian authors and imported from India except for the Ports and Harbors course, a small booklet written by Prof. A. T. Khan that was available locally. Since the imported books were expensive, most of the students relied on class notes and used the college library for technical books and related material. The British Council library at Pakistan Chowk was also an additional source. The United States Information Services library on Bunder Road Extension was another valuable source for technical books. I used all the libraries and borrowed the books as needed.

For engineering calculations, slide rules were required, and those cost several hundred rupees since they were imported. Bhaijan brought me a six-inch slide rule from the US after completing a PhD at Yale University. I used it extensively for many years. A decade later, the slide had become obsolete and was replaced by battery-operated, handheld calculators. The expensive ones were made by Texas Instruments, but cheaper Japanese models were available.

The engineering curriculum was based on the requirements of the Public Works Department to produce engineers with broad backgrounds and was diverse. The first-year (FY) engineering courses were compulsory for all engineering students. In addition, there were carpentry and smith workshops prerequisites for all students. In the second-year engineering, civil and mechanical and electrical students were split into their respective majors. In the late sixties, the broad curriculum was modified to focus on the individual disciplines from the FY engineering.

None of the family children got any allowance or pocket money. We were given money for our actual expenses including transportation, tuition, etc., as needed. We always ate at home and rarely would indulge in a snack or drink outside home.

The FY engineering was like a boot camp. There were over a hundred students in a class, and the classrooms were old and dimly lit. The teachers never smiled as if it were a prison. Lectures from the faculty were given rather robotically with prepared notes, which was less than inspirational. There was little encouragement to communicate or have enlightening discussion. A few were really bullies with little tolerance for anyone raising a question.

The classes were held in the morning, while the workshops, including smithy, carpentry, and mechanical drawings were conducted in the afternoon. The lunch break was generally forty-five minutes, which barely allowed me to eat lunch at home. In 1957, we had moved to SBF at Preedy Street. During the break, I used public transport from Burns Road to Preedy Street. At home, I had only fifteen or so minutes to change, eat, and rush back to the college for science labs.

In the evenings, SBF presented an active social scene. The residences included several four-story buildings each housing eight spacious apartments measuring over 2,200 square feet including two bedrooms with attached bathrooms, living and dining areas, a kitchen, and a store room. In addition, there was a bedroom and bath outside the main apartment intended for a servant. Some buildings included a garage at the ground level. The entire residential complex was gated with a boundary wall and had twenty-four-hour security.

The kids from the apartments would hang out and play in the compound. Our dinner was usually after sunset, around 7:00 p.m., when my father would return. His routine was flexible; it allowed him to return for lunch followed by a siesta. His working hours were from ten to six Monday to Thursday while Fridays and Saturdays were half days. His commute by bus to the market was about thirty minutes each way, resulting in two hours spent on the two round trips each day.

The first year gave little time to relax. However, we did manage some picnics with friends. One was a boat trip to Manora with some old and new friends. Our party included Safdar, Shahid, Shehzad, Matlub (all from NED), Shamsuddin, Sajid, and another friend whose father was surveyor general of Pakistan.

I had befriended Saifuddin Bengali, a very bright student from BVS Technical High School, who joined us on the picnic. Despite his proficiency in machine drawing, he was struggling in the FY engineering classes as were others. He was a quiet individual and kept to himself. On a visit to Manora Beach near Keamari, he drew a picture on the wet sand. The image, seen by the group, represented his struggle at NED. Saifuddin dropped out of college and died before completing his education. A bright student had succumbed to the rigorous imprisonment of the NED curriculum.

His older brother, Yayha, was a third-year mechanical engineering student at that time. I ran into Yayha and his family some twenty years later when we settled in the US, and we became close friends. His wife, Sakina, a psychiatrist, became a close friend of my wife.

The 1958 Revolution

On October 8, Iskander Mirza, the president of Pakistan, abrogated the constitution and proclaimed martial law throughout Pakistan; he handed over power to Ayub Khan, the commander in chief of Pakistan since 1951. General Khan had taken over the position from General Gracey, who was the first commander in chief upon the independence of Pakistan. It was one of several declarations of martial law that would follow in the newly independent country, which lacked political stability and failed to establish democratic rule during the next five decades.

Martial law brought relief to everybody and reforms that produced immediate efficiency in the government and the private sector. The rapid economic development and growth and political stability continued for the next decade (1958–68).

The FY results bore bad news for Safdar and me; we failed to pass the machine drawing and/or heat engines courses and had to take a supplementary exam before being promoted to second-year engineering. Safdar Iqbal Bhatti was the eldest son with four younger siblings who lived in an apartment across Abdul Khaliq, Sweet Merchants, in Saddar. His father was a civil servant and headed the General Post Office.

It was the first academic failure for us. It really hurt. I sat with Safdar in his building stairwell and sulked at night. But then suddenly, we felt positive. A voice within told us that the bad news could have been worse. It was perhaps a harbinger of good news. We must be patient and persevere. We immediately thanked the Almighty and felt better.

We studied hard that summer for the supplementary exam. My father, being action oriented, made sure I improved my drawing skills. I was happy that for the civil engineering curriculum, the courses on heat engines and machine drawing were not prerequisites in the second year; they were part of the mechanical degree curriculum in the subsequent years.

I excelled in the remaining years with a focus on civil engineering. I remained nearly at the top of the class of a hundred. Prof. Abdul Tawwab Khan had returned with an MS from the Massachusetts Institute of Technology (MIT). He taught surveying and soil mechanics courses. He also became my benefactor and guided me throughout the remaining years of college. Later on, his recommendations were quite helpful in my securing admission to prestigious US universities.

During my final year, my father met our principal, R. E. Mirza. He was a devoted father with high expectations for his children, but he also wanted an independent assessment and help for us if needed. Apparently, he was reassured about my academic progress. He was a trusting father but also an independent verifier based on his background in government service.

Union Elections

During the third year, I found time to run for the debating secretary position in the college union. The campaign required canvassing the entire college body including the students residing in the local Metharam and Shevakunj hostels. I was ably assisted by my friend, Ijaz Asghar, when I visited the hostels. I had a very tight budget of Rs. 100 or so, but I was able to print few hundred leaflets for distribution as we went around soliciting votes.

There were two candidates who sought the position. I was able to secure exactly a hundred votes, but that was not enough. My classmate, Mubarik, who lived in the Shevakunj hostel, was able to obtain the loyalty of all the hostelers and beat me by twelve votes. That was my first and last attempt to run for any elected office. Muzaffar Ali Shah, who was in the mechanical engineering curriculum, was elected as president of the union.

My older brother Jamshed also contested the union elections while studying at the University of Karachi. He ran for general secretary and lost by one vote. Many years later, my son, Saad, also ran for student body election while he was a freshman at Rensselaer Polytechnic Institute (RPI). He also lost by a narrow margin. It appears that those in our family are not attuned politically.

The basic democracy concept was promoted by the Ayub Khan government. Its concept recognized a grassroots approach with representatives from the electorate (48 million adult population in 1960) at the ward level (8,000), union/town committees (8,863), *tehsil*, municipal, and cantonment boards (754), district councils (790), and divisional councils (16).

One memorable trip was to visit with the class of 1962 via rail the dams and barrages in Pakistan. We visited Sukkur Barrage, newly constructed Warsak Dam, old hydroelectric stations at Dargai, and even Lundi Kotal and Torkhum on the border with Afghanistan. Such vivid examples of turning water energy into electric power made a favorable impression on me.

Engineering Graduation

When the bachelor of engineering results were announced, I was successful with a second position in the order of merit. Bhaijan was in Saudi Arabia as economic advisor to the Saudi Arabian Monetary Agency (SAMA) in Jeddah. My parents had gone to Saudi Arabia to perform Hajj. While they were there, the bachelor of civil engineering results were declared. I sent a telegram announcing my results, which my father eagerly awaited. In addition to my hard work, my father's prayers contributed to my success. I was really happy and grateful for achieving my academic goals.

Safdar Iqbal had also secured the second position in bachelor of mechanical engineering behind Muzaffar Ali Shah.

It was time to move on and pursue our dreams in the real world. Safdar and I left Karachi soon thereafter to pursue our careers. Safdar joined Pakistan Tobacco, a large corporation making cigarettes, and was posted at the Mardan factory. I joined the Water and Power Development Authority (WAPDA) as an assistant engineer to work on the Mangla Dam, some 1,000 miles north of Karachi.

Mangla Dam, 1962–1963

Pakistan has the largest contiguous irrigation system of the world fed by the Indus River and its five tributaries. The partition of 1947 placed portions of the Indus and its tributaries under Indian control. The division produced prolonged disputes between the two riparian nations. In 1960, assisted by the World Bank, the Indus waters dispute was resolved by a treaty between India and Pakistan.

Under the Indus Basin Treaty, Pakistan was awarded the use of waters of the Indus and its two western tributaries, the Jhelum and Chenab Rivers, while India received the use of the remaining three eastern tributaries of the Indus River, the Ravi, Sutlej, and Beas Rivers.

As a result of this treaty, funds contributed by various nations and administered by the World Bank provided for an initial rapid construction program. It consisted of several linked canals to transfer the water from the western rivers to the eastern Punjab to replace the flows in the eastern tributaries that India began to divert per the treaty terms supplemented by new construction of dams on the Jhelum and Indus Rivers. The construction of a 300-foot high earthen dam on Jhelum River at Mangla would generate 800 MW of hydroelectric power, while the construction of a 470-foot high earth and rock-filled dam on the Indus at Tarbela would provide 1400 MW of generating capacity in addition to increased water availability for irrigation. The construction of the multipurpose Tarbela Dam was started in 1968 when an additional $1.2 billion fund was established and administrated by the World Bank.

Mangla Dam Highlights

The construction of the multipurpose dam began in the summer of 1962 with a development fund of $800 million. The Mangla Dam is twelve miles from the Grand Trunk Road at Dina and about twelve miles north of Jhelum City. The dam was designed by Binnie and Partners, Consultants, UK, while the construction was awarded to Guy F. Atkins, a US contracting firm. It was the largest project under construction at that time involving several hundred engineers.

I was hired by WAPDA and assigned to Binnie and Partners. The consultants included a large expatriate staff of engineers and geologists from England and the US. I was assigned to the Foundation Department headed by SC Sargent from the US; it included Earnst Ringle and P. G. Fookes. The Pakistani group included geologists Maqsood, Salim, Shirazi, Iftikhar, Qureshi, etc. The engineers included besides me, Iqbal Chaudhry and Siddiq Dawood. We worked on the foundation exploratory program for the subsidiary dam at Jari, some fifteen miles from the main dam.

The consultants including the expatriate and Pakistani engineers lived in a residential colony built by WAPDA on the east bank. The contractor offices were on the west bank of the Jhelum River in Baral, where an entire residential colony complete with a commissary, bowling alleys, and a drive-in cinema was built for the engineers and laborers. There were also some senior engineers employed by WAPDA with whom we had little interaction.

The accommodations were tight. After staying at the Dina Rest House for a month, I relocated to the site and shared a two-bedroom officers' quarters at Mangla with Iqbal Chaudhry, which eliminated the daily commute from Dina. Zubair Hamid, my father's first cousin, showed up there and stayed with me one weekend.

On weekends, we had access to the project jeeps for paid private use. It included visits to Jhelum, Mirpur, and nearby attractions. I saw Rhotas Fort, which was constructed during the Moghul period; it was in a neglected state. One memorable trip was to Saidu Sharif and Kalam in Swat, where we stayed at a rest house for a weekend.

I visited Rawalpindi on weekends, where my maternal uncle Malik Siddique Hasan lived with his family. Rawalpindi was some seventy miles from Mangla and was at least a two-hour trip. I would catch a public transport from Dina on the Grand Trunk (GT) Road. He was employed as senior food inspector with the Punjab government and lived in a two-story home in the inner city, Said Puri Gate. It was always fun to visit his family. Both Mama (maternal uncle) and Mami (maternal aunt) Ashraf were fond of good food, fruits, and desserts. The family had six children, three boys and three girls. The eldest son, Suhail, was my age, and he was a good cricketer, whose mentor was the famous cricketer Maqsood (nicknamed Merry Max). Like me, Suhail was fond of Hollywood movies, and we went together to the Plaza Cinema, where Westerns were shown. A famous movie that we saw together was *The Bridge on the River Kwai* starring Alec Guinness. Our favorite actor in those days was Jack Lemmon. At night, we slept on cots on the roof, a unique experience.

Uncle Siddique, a health nut, would do sit-ups and push-ups every day. He would rise early for the *Fajr* prayers and read the Qur'an loudly each morning before breakfast. It was an unforgettable experience listening to his recitation in the early morning. Uncle Siddique remained active holding various jobs after he retired from the government. Due to his regular habits, he stayed healthy into the late nineties.

Asad and Naveed, my cousins from Lahore, also visited me at Mangla. All of us went to Murree for a long weekend. I had bought a carton of Pall Mall cigarettes from the Boral commissary that we consumed during the weekend between us, fifty cigarettes per person. Movie celebrities made it quite fashionable to smoke those days. We indulged in high tea at the famous Lintott Restaurant on the mall and watched the fashionable pedestrian crowd walking by.

In the fall, I applied to various universities for postgraduate studies including MIT, the University of Illinois, and the University of Michigan to mention a few. I wanted a scholarship to pay for tuition and living expenses. One day, I applied to Northwestern University also.

Bhaijan Marriage

In December 1962, my eldest brother, Parvez, married Parveen, the daughter of the(late) Shaikh Nazir Ahmed, in Jeddah, Saudi Arabia. The formal proposal was made earlier in June when my parents were in Saudi Arabia for Hajj. Parveen lived with her oldest sister, Saeeda, who was married to Anwar Ali, a Pakistani economist. He was the head of SAMA, a position similar to that of the chairman of the Federal Reserve Bank in the US. The marriage (*nikah*) ceremony was attended by my father only. It was the first wedding in our family. The *valima* reception was held in Karachi on December 26 *(A valima is the second traditional part of an Islamic wedding, following the nikah)*.

I took leave from work for a week and flew to Karachi from Mangla in a Fokker plane. Chacha G. H. came from Peshawar to help with the valima dinner arrangements that included setting up tents and furniture for some three hundred guests including dining facilities in the grounds adjacent to our rented home in Sindhi Muslim Society. By default, being the only driver in the family, I was assigned chauffer responsibilities. Food was catered by the Kali Delhi Muslim Hotel at Rs. 11 per head excluding condiments and spices (turmeric, red peppers, cloves, cardamom, etc.), which were purchased from Jodia Bazaar. The tents came from Rooldu and Sons at a cost of Rs. 2,200 after a discount.

The bridal party was received by the entire family. The *dulhan* (bride), who we later called Bhabi, was introduced to the large siblings and the extended family. Mama Yusuf and Khurrum and other families came from Lahore.

By midnight, everybody was thirsty for a warm cup of tea. It was then discovered there was no sugar in the house. There was panic in the kitchen. I dashed to Saddar, four miles away, where an Iranian hotel was still open and returned quickly with the sugar. None of the guests realized that a crisis had been averted. All enjoyed sweet tea.

As the celebrations ended, I told my brother of my plans for higher studies in the US for which I had already submitted applications to various universities. On New Year's Eve, Bhaijan wished that my plans for the next year would bear fruit. That was a good omen.

Bhaijan and Abba ji at Nikah Ceremony in Jeddah, Saudi Arabia 1962

Apa ji at Mina, SA (1962)

Abba ji and Apa ji in Jeddah (1962) after Hajj

Family Photo (1962)

Chapter 4

COMING TO THE US

A Dream Comes True

In the spring of 1963, I heard from the schools I had applied to; all had accepted me, and some had offered partial scholarships. Northwestern University, however, offered me a $4,200 per-year research assistantship that would more than cover the $2,400 tuition and leave me $1,800 for living expenses. I was exhilarated with the news except that I did not know how well NU was ranked academically. I tossed this thought to my boss, Sam Sargent, who told me it was good institution and a part of the Big Ten. Only later did I learn that Big Ten referred to the university football league of the Midwest. I accepted the Northwestern University offer for the 1963–64 year.

I left Mangla Dam in June and headed to Karachi to make travel arrangements. I was really excited and grateful that finally my dream of visiting the US was coming true. I thought of the day when I was selected to visit the US as a boy scout representing Pakistan but couldn't go because of the cost.

In 1959, I had been selected as an alternate for a full scholarship to study engineering at the American University in Beirut. Then, in 1962, soon after graduating from NED, I was offered a full scholarship at

SEATO School, Bangkok, Thailand. I declined the offer since my dream was to attend an American university. My dream had come true.

As I was leaving, I heard that an expatriate staffer, Mr. Henderson, was also traveling to Karachi in his Mercedes-Benz. When I mentioned my plans, he offered me a ride for the 1,000-mile trip. I would his guide and good company for two days.

Henderson was probably in his fifties with greying hair, and he wore glasses. We passed through Lahore cruising at high speed on the Grand Trunk Road, a historic route established during the days of Sher Shah Suri, emperor of India in the mid-sixteenth century. The road was essentially a single lane connecting the port city of Karachi to the Sind, Punjab, and the frontier provinces in the hinterland. We went through Punjab on this road without incident.

The monsoon rains occur in May and June when the moist winds from the Arabian Sea move northeast. With the rains and subsequent flooding, there is widespread destruction of roads and disruption of life including washouts of embankments at major bridges.

Near Bahawalpur, we encountered a diversion in the Grand Trunk Road, known as the GT road. The five major rivers meet near the town of Panjnad. While taking the detour, our right rear tire was damaged from the washout road. We had a spare we put on, but we would then had to drive four hundred miles without a spare. We had some good luck. We found an owner of another Mercedes who would sell a tire to us. We stayed in Bahawalpur overnight and arrived in Karachi the next day. The remaining trip was uneventful. It was my first road trip in Pakistan, and it exposed me to scenes of small town in Punjab and Sind Provinces, an unforgettable experience. I would be soon leaving my familiar surroundings for the unknown. It would be some years later that I would take a similar road trip driving from Karachi to Abbottabad in a Toyota Corona to attend the graduation of my brother, Owais, from the Kakul Military Academy (similar to West Point in US).

In Karachi, our family was renting a three-bedroom house in the Sindhi Muslim Housing Society. My father was still managing the Shahi Cloth House, a wholesale cloth business, in Govardhan Das Market.

He was in his early sixties and ready for retirement. Bhaijan was still in Saudi Arabia as advisor to SAMA.

Travel Loan

I had to make travel arrangements. My father suggested to contact Dawood Foundations, which offered interest-free loans for educational purposes. I signed the documents while my father provided the guarantee for the Rs. 3,000 loan. The money had to returned in easy instalments (Rs. 50 per month) upon my return to Pakistan.

Bidding Farewell

Armed with a J-1 Exchange Student Visa from the US Embassy and a one-way Karachi-Chicago Pakistan Air Lines (PIA) ticket and with US$80, I was ready to travel. In early August, I left for the US in a Boeing 707. My itinerary included Rome, Geneva, and Paris with a stop in New York for a connecting flight to Chicago. I had arranged to meet with Bhaijan and Bhabi in Geneva. All international communications were made generally via mail or wire and were quite reliable. Telephones calls were very expensive, so I mailed my itinerary to my brother.

My entire family was at the Karachi airport for the emotional farewell. My mother pinned the *imam zaman* (an Islamic tradition of prayers/sadaqah money wrapped in a piece of cloth for a safe journey) on my arm. With a copy of the Qur'an in my suitcase and a heavy heart, I said goodbye to my family and left Pakistan for the first time.

I arrived in Rome in the morning and took a shuttle bus to the city. I stayed at a *pensione*, an inexpensive room with breakfast. It was an early version of Airbnb that became popular some fifty years later. I ate pizza and spaghetti for lunch and dinner for the first time and found them tasty. Rome is a historical city with its famous Colosseum built nearly two thousand years ago. The Colosseum hosted violent gladiator games for the amusement of the emperor. This was like revisiting the movie *Quo*

Vadis starring Peter Ustinov as the despotic emperor. I walked around the city after seeing the Colosseum.

Early the next morning, I took the bus to the airport and left for Geneva.

Rendezvous in Europe

I was supposed to meet with Bhaijan in Switzerland. Bhaijan had written to me to contact American Express upon my arrival. When the agent pulled out the address of the hotel where my brother and his wife were, I was happy to learn that it was within walking distance. Those days, suitcases did not have wheels, so I left mine at American Express and went to the hotel.

Bhaijan and his wife were on kind of a second honeymoon having married nine months earlier. He had purchased a Mercedes in Frankfurt that he wanted shipped to Saudi Arabia. Bhabi was in the second trimester of her pregnancy.

We left Geneva for Dijon, a city in southeast France. Bhabi knew Italian, so we relied on her when we needed help getting directions or finding a hotel. The French are very nationalistic; they are reluctant to speak English even to help foreigners in need.

We traveled from Geneva to Paris through the Dejon Province. The day was sunny and warm. I saw plenty of flowers and fields as we drove. We arrived in Paris after staying overnight in a small town. Paris was full of lights and people walking. Not knowing French, we found it difficult to communicate with the locals. My brother knew some French he had learned as part of a PhD language course requirement while my sister-in-law knew fluent Italian, which helped during our travels through France. The lights of the city were dazzling, and I commented on that to my brother. My brother did not forget it and mentioned it in his memoirs.

I was given some French francs to sightsee on my own. I took the quiet and efficient underground to the Moulin Rouge in the Pigalle

District.[13] The admission price was high, but it was an unusual show with girls barely dressed, covered with feathers, and entertaining the audience with dance, songs, and jokes. I took the metro back to the hotel having survived an evening in Paris on my own. I also ate french fries and roast chicken.

The next day, after being together for forty-eight hours, it was time to say farewell to the City of Lights. My brother dropped me off at the Paris Orly Airport. I embarked on the nonstop flight to Idlewild Airport in New York.[14]

The PIA flight had originated in Karachi. The plane was full of Pakistanis including some students traveling to the US for higher studies. One was going to Buffalo University in New York. He refused to disclose the name of the university. Later, I found that out that he was embarrassed by its name, buffalo being a "cow" in Urdu. The name Cow University did not sound prestigious.

Arriving in the US

I arrived in New York around 7:00 p.m. I had notified via a letter the International Students Forum, and someone from there met me at the airport. After going through customs, I collected my baggage, he led me to the counter for my flight to Chicago. It was 8:00 p.m. My flight was leaving in an hour. I was tired after the transatlantic flight of over eight hours, but I was really excited at the lights of the airport, the blue-uniformed cops, and the large crowds creating an international, festive atmosphere.

By the time I arrived at O'Hare in Chicago, it was almost midnight. The airport was quiet and empty. A janitor was mopping the floors. I asked for directions to the city. The helpful janitor in a typical American accent pointed to the exit and told me to take a bus to the Palmer House.

---

[13] Pigalle is an area in Paris around the Place Pigalle. It is named after the sculptor Jean-Baptiste Pigalle (1714–1785).
[14] The airport would be later renamed as John F. Kennedy (JFK), after President Kennedy's assassination that year.

I followed his instructions and took the shuttle bus to Chicago's downtown. The bus ride was very comfortable with few people on board. I saw a US expressway for the first time. I traveled down a wide highway during the fifty-minute ride. The streetlights made it as bright as day, a sign of economic strength and quite a contrast with Pakistani roads with inadequate streetlights. I got to the Palmer House at 2:00 a.m., where I asked for directions to Evanston. I was told to take the El (short for "Elevated") train to the Howard Street Station, the Chicago city limits to the north, and take another train to Evanston. The El station was a block away.

As I boarded the El, I was struck by the strange environment on board. The train was well lit, but due to the lateness of the hour, there were few passengers. Its occupants appeared to be shabbily attired and appeared to be junkies or drunks. Being well-dressed with a jacket and a tie and carrying a large suitcase, I felt scared in that environment. I had not realized the hazards of my late-night journey through Chicago. I had traveled all day from Paris to New York through several time zones, had flown to Chicago, and then taken bus and El rides. *What if I get mugged?* I wondered, but I discarded the thought and focused on the positive—reaching the YMCA.

I was supposed to change to the Evanston local train at the Howard Street Station. The YMCA was not near a train stop. Imagine a well-dressed Asian on the streets of Evanston dragging a suitcase to the YMCA after getting off the train in the wee hours of the morning. Divine help was needed, and it came in the form of someone who boarded at the next stop. He wore a business suit and looked decent. I moved to a seat next to him and introduced myself. He asked where I was headed. "I want to go to the YMCA in Evanston," I replied. I had the YMCA address in my diary.

Sensing my situation, seeing my large suitcase, and considering the late hour, he suggested that we get off at the Howard Street Station and share a cab to our destinations. He would drop me off at the YMCA. I happily agreed.

Upon reaching the YMCA, he refused to accept my share of the cab fare. "We'll settle it later," he said as he handed me his business card. He was an associate editor at the *Christian Science Monitor* and was returning home to Evanston after proofreading the newspaper. I was really touched by his kindness during my first few hours in the US. I had received a warm welcome in New York followed by a goodwill gesture from a stranger in Chicago when I needed it most.

I had traveled for nearly fourteen hours through several time zones. I checked in and paid $3 for a room. It was 4:00 a.m. when I hit the bed. I slept for twelve hours, one of the best sleeps I ever had.

Northwestern University

Northwestern University.

Northwestern University, Evanston, ILL. (courtesy of NU)

Northwestern University Evanston Campus
(Courtesy of NU)

Northwestern was founded in 1851 by John Evans, for whom the city of Evanston was named, and eight other lawyers, businessmen, and Methodist leaders. Its founding purpose was to serve the former Northwest Territory, an area that today includes Ohio, Indiana, Illinois, Michigan, Wisconsin, and parts of Minnesota. Instruction began in 1855, and women were admitted in 1869.

The university is a founding member of the Big Ten Conference and remains the only private university in the conference. The Northwestern Wildcats compete in nineteen intercollegiate sports in the NCAA's Division I Big Ten Conference.

Refer to https: //en.Wikipedia.org/wiki/Northwestern-University

Northwestern's Evanston campus, where the undergraduate schools, the Graduate School, and the Kellogg School of Management are located, runs north-south from Lincoln Avenue to Clark Street west of Lake Michigan along Sheridan Road. North and South Campuses have noticeably different atmospheres, owing to the predominance of Science and Athletics in the one and Humanities and Arts in the other. North Campus is home to the fraternity quads, the Henry Crown Sports Pavilion and Norris Aquatics Center and other athletic facilities, the Technological Institute, Dearborn Observatory, and other science-related buildings, and the sorority quads.

The four-year, full-time undergraduate program comprises the majority of students at the university and emphasizes instruction in the arts and sciences plus the professions of engineering, journalism, communication, music, and education. Although a foundation in the liberal arts and sciences is required in all majors, there is no required common core curriculum; individual degree requirements are set by the faculty of each school. Northwestern's full-time undergraduate and graduate programs operate on an approximately ten-week academic quarter system with the academic year beginning in late September and ending in early June. Northwestern University Technological Institute was still closed for the summer; I was perhaps a week or so early.

The next day, I walked the streets of Evanston to become familiar with the university surroundings. My scouting training helped me in my reconnaissance. The early fall weather was perfect. The tall oaks and pines that lined the streets were indicative of the fall foliage. The streets were quiet except for light vehicular and pedestrian traffic with mostly foreign students searching for accommodations. After an initial search, I found a two-story building near the Technological Institute Building with a sign that read, Rooms for Rent. The building, 2024 Sherman Avenue, was a private house only six blocks from the institute.

The building had four rooms on the second floor that were sparingly furnished with one common bathroom. The two smaller rooms were $10 a week while the larger rooms went for $15. The first-floor apartment cost $60 per month and was equipped with a kitchen and a black and white TV, but it was already rented. The landlady would provide weekly maid service and cleaning of the rooms that included supply of crisply ironed linen every Friday.

Evanston Home

Prudential Building, Chicago Frank Nusbaum, Math Major at NU (1963)

Frank Nusbaum

I settled for the small room in the back and paid a week's rent in advance. It was cheaper than the Y. Since no refrigerator was provided, I could store only dry snacks in my room. My favorite drink was Tang, which added to water would be a good substitute for orange juice. The other small room was taken by a graduate student from Iraq. One of the larger rooms was taken by a graduate student, Jean Marie Nolf, from Belgium, who was majoring in electrical engineering. The last room was rented by Frank Nusbaum, a US-born student majoring in math.

In the spring of 1963, Martin Luther King Jr. led a civil rights march in Selma, Alabama. There was a growing recognition of discrimination against blacks in the south. At NU, while I was readily accepted for renting an apartment, some African students from Africa were discriminated against when they tried to rent places in the predominantly white Evanston.

I met my civil engineering professor and advisor, Dr. Kondner, and I was assigned to Dr. Krizek, who had just completed a PhD in civil engineering at NU and had been hired as an assistant professor in the Civil Engineering Department of the Technological Institute there. Eiichi Yamamoto, who hailed from Osaka, Japan, and I share the honor of being the first graduate assistants to work for Dr. Krizek. Currently, Dr. Krizek is a professor at the Management Institute at NU.

Eiichi and I shared a large office with two desks adjacent to Dr. Krizek's office. NU's Civil Engineering Department had received a research grant from American Association of State Highway and Transportation Officials (AASHTO) to assess the performance and serviceability of flexible pavements' experimental test data from Illinois pavements. Both Eiichi and I were to work on that research project for the next twelve months as research assistants. We were told to devote a minimum of twelve hours per week to the research project; our work would be turned into MS theses and be considered for three credits as part the master's degree requirement. In addition to being a research advisor, Dr. Krizek became our mentor, and he pushed us hard to complete our research program on schedule.

Northwestern University is on a quarter system with three quarters constituting an academic year. The master's degree required thirty-six credit hours. I had to complete thirty-three credits in graduate courses in the next three quarters (nine months) and then spend the summer finishing my thesis so I could graduate in August 1964. NU was a private university, and its tuition was on the high side or the academic year.

Fifteen grad students were enrolled in the master's and PhD programs, with soil mechanics as a specialty in the civil engineering graduate class of 1964. Four had master's degrees and were enrolled in the PhD program. They included Farrokh Screwala and Raj Khera, who had earlier come from India. Farrokh had graduated with a master's from Case Institute of Technology (later known as Case Western Reserve) while Raj had graduated with a master's from Ohio State. They had been in the US for a few years and were familiar with its educational system whereas Eiichi Yamamoto and Cheng, from Taiwan, were unfamiliar with the US academic system.

Prof. Jorj O. Osterberg (1915–2008) was a distinguished professor in the field of soil mechanics, which later became known as geotechnical engineering. The son of Swedish immigrants, Jorj was raised in the Bronx and had completed an undergraduate degree in civil engineering at Columbia University in 1935. His interest in soil mechanics led him to graduate school at Harvard University, where he studied under Casagrande *, and he earned a PhD from Cornell University in 1940. He was an authority on deep-caisson foundations for Chicago high-rise buildings.

- Arthur Casagrande (1902-1981) was a Austrian-born American civil engineer who made important contributions to geotechnical engineering.

With my limited exposure to soil engineering at the Mangla Dam, I was extremely excited to include the soil mechanics courses taught by Prof. Osterberg as the core courses for my master's. He had been on the NU faculty for over four decades and retired in 1985. No doubt he earned his place among the most noteworthy pioneers in the field of geotechnical engineering including his election to the National Academy of Engineering. Even a soil testing sampler is named after him (a tribute by Dr Krizek).

My research assistantship provided me $350 per month. I had to pay tuition quarterly at the rate of $750 per quarter. Deducting tuition would leave me approximately $2,000 for lodging, food, and entertainment for the twelve months. Being frugal by nature, I budgeted my expenses accordingly. Breakfast was simple—a glass of Tang in my room and a pint of chocolate or regular milk from the vending machines. The milk cost 10¢. Lunch at the university cafeteria consisted of sandwiches or burgers that would cost 50¢ or so. Dinner at the cafeteria was a treat. One could have soup, an entrée of chicken, fish, or beef with boiled vegetables, a piece of bread or a roll, and a dessert for $1.25, quite a bargain. However, the cafeteria was closed on weekends, so I would eat at a nearby Greek restaurant, Campus, at 832 Foster Street under the El that offered bargain dinners for students from 75¢ to $1.10. The dinner included a dessert—Jell-O or rice pudding. The other option was the Spot, known for its delicious pizza.

Dinner with Mike Mahoney, Yamamoto and Screwala(1964)

Alpha Epsilon Phi Sorority House (1963)

Dinner at the Alpha Epsilon Phi Sorority
Author at a Dinner with AEPhi Sorority

My Sorority Experience

I was the only student from Pakistan at NU. In the early sixties, Pakistan was eyed with much affection and interest; it was a newly independent country having won freedom from the British Empire after the partition of the Indian subcontinent barely sixteen years earlier. President Kennedy and Vice President Johnson were vowing to help Pakistan due to its strategic location and proximity to Russia. Evidence of that was the U-2 reconnaissance flights over Russia that originated from Peshawar.

One of the sorority houses, Alpha Epsilon Phi, found out that I hailed from Pakistan. It so happened that Carol Seinsheimer had visited Pakistan as an exchange student and had fond memories of the hospitality offered by her Pakistani host family. Through Carol, I was invited to their sorority for dinner every Wednesday at 6:00 p.m. I was the only male student at NU to share this dinner with the sorority girls. It was a formal affair. All the girls wore dresses and proper attire suitable for dinner. I had to be dressed in a tie and jacket. The dinner was a sit-down affair, with eight girls at each table and was presided over by the house mother, Aunt Edith, an elegant woman. It was a sumptuous four- or five-course meal including salad, a main course, side dishes of vegetables, and dessert and coffee served by student volunteers. It was a privilege I enjoyed for the entire academic year. The sorority girls ranged from freshmen to seniors, and they would treat me as a brother and sometimes openly talked about their daily activities, good and bad. The weekly dinners were a much-appreciated diversion at least for an hour from my otherwise busy schedule.

In addition to Carol, other sorority members I shared the weekly dinner with were Ruthie, Ronnie, Toni, Nancy, Reva, Karen, Linda S., Karol, Barbie, Debrah, Jane, Sheila, Diane, and Shelly Goldenberg, the class president. We exchanged greetings and gifts on Christmas and birthdays including mine. It was my first birthday celebration; until then, I had not celebrated my birthdays.

My Indian friends, Raj and Farrokh, lived on Foster Road two blocks away. We would get together on weekends, when Raj would prepare

Indian food including *dal* and *subzies* (vegetables), a welcome change from American food. Farrokh came from Mumbai, India. Raj originated from Punjab, India, but he had lived in West Germany and spoke German. Raj and Farrokh would often tease me about the unique favor bestowed on me of having dinner with forty-five to fifty girls in a relaxing atmosphere for an hour or so. It was an unforgettable and unique experience for me.

On weekends, I had time to relax somewhat. The Iraqi student was a devout Christian who attended Sunday Mass. Once, I accompanied him, and we sang the hymns together. He was married, somewhat homesick especially in a new environment, and under stress academically. After the first quarter, he quit studies and returned to Iraq. He must have failed to meet the minimum B average required for graduate students.

Among other Asian students I met on the campus was Hassam Tebayam, from Iran, who was majoring in the humanities. He later became a professor at the University of Colorado in Boulder. There was an undergraduate journalism student, Sabiha, from India, and there were several African students whom I befriended on social occasions.

Chicago's reputation for being the Windy City came true as winter set in. The trees became bare having been stripped of their leaves by late fall. One weekend, I ventured out to the movies. The Valencia Theater was over a mile away, and the walk was brutal. I had a cheap windbreaker jacket on, but I felt the wind freely penetrating through it. I saw a thermostat that read zero Fahrenheit, but that did not take into consideration the wind chill factor. It was more like minus 20 F. My walk took more than thirty minutes since I would interrupt it by taking shelter every five minutes in a store or alcove.

Some of the best movies I saw included *Lawrence of Arabia*, *Tom Jones*, *Dr. No*, *Move Over Darling*, *Hud*, and *Irma la Douce*.

Foster Families

NU and the Evanston Community supported foreign students through the American Foster Families program and shared traditional holidays including Thanksgiving and Christmas with foreign students.

The United Church Women of Evanston was active welcoming foreign students. Soon after my arrival, I received a letter from the chairman of the Overseas Student Committee of the United Church advising me that my name was given to foster relatives interested in welcoming me to their home. The committee obtained my name from the Foreign Student Advisor, Mr. Utley.

Before long, I received a letter from Mrs. Margaret Martin, who had volunteered to be my foster relative; she invited me to their home on Friday, October 25. I called her and accepted the dinner invitation. She would pick me up and take me to her home and back.

I was fortunate to be hosted by the Martin family, who were supportive of foreign students and in particular graduate students hailing from Pakistan. Prior to my arrival, the Martins had shared their holidays with another Pakistani student, Safdar Gill, who had returned to Pakistan. They spoke fondly of him. The family owned a home in Winnetka, a wealthy suburb of Chicago. Charles Martin was an attorney in a Chicago law firm, and Margaret was a housewife. They had three children— Mary, eighteen, Charles Jr., fifteen, and Larry, twelve. Mary was away at college.

On weekends and holidays, Margaret picked me up, and I shared dinner with the family; she then drove me to my residence. I became fond of them and kept in touch with the family for several years.

For Thanksgiving, I was invited by a host family in Lincolnwood. The informal dinner was hosted by the Eric and Helen Helmer family on Thursday, November 28, 1963. The guests included their children, Bill and David, and the parents of the family, Mr. and Mrs. Swanson.

Then there were others. Through the International Hospitality Center of Chicago, I was invited to visit a farm family in Minooka, Illinois, over a weekend. The farm was run by the Mann family, who owned livestock and grain silos. James and Jackie had two children fifteen and seventeen years old. I was given detailed directions as follows: "Take the Rock Island Railroad train leaving Chicago, LaSalle Station at 1:13 p.m., Corner of LaSalle and Van Buren, arriving in Joliet at 2:26 p.m. Upon arrival, you will be received by the hosts."

It was my first visit to a farm in Illinois. The farm grew corn and other staples and had animals including cows and pigs. The entire family worked hard and shared responsibilities. Susan, the daughter, a sophomore in high school, took me to a football game, where she was a cheerleader with pom-poms.

NU had a reputable drama school and had produced several actors and stage and theater personalities including Charlton Heston, Paul Newman, and Patricia Neal. Neal won Best Actress at the Oscars for her role in *Hud* that year.

My visits to Chicago were few, but I did visit the tallest building in Chicago then, the Prudential Building, which is sixty stories. From the top, one could see all the way to the steel mills in Gary, Indiana, while on the north and west were suburbs.

JFK Assassination

On November 22, 1963, I was working in the institute lab collating some research reports when I heard on the radio that President John F. Kennedy had been shot. I was stunned. I could not concentrate on my work.

President Kennedy was extremely well liked in Pakistan for his good looks, youthful appearance, and inspirational speeches. He was the youngest president of the United States. He had been in office for less than three years to implement his reformative agenda. His family and children were popular subjects in newspapers and magazines.

The youthful, thirty-fifth president accompanied by his attractive wife, Jacqueline, and Governor Connolly were in a motorcade in Dallas when he was fatally shot by Lee Harvey Oswald.

I rushed home. The apartment on the ground floor had a TV, and the tenants there let me watch. Everybody was shocked. We had lost a very admired president who left behind a young widow and two children, Caroline, age nine, and John, age three. The entire country mourned for him. Later, I watched in horror as Oswald (1939–1963) was fatally shot and killed by Jack Ruby two days later.

The funeral in Washington was an elaborate affair. I watched the entire funeral, which was televised live. The procession included the family and a riderless black stallion, a gift from Pakistan. He was buried in Arlington National Cemetery. Since the assassination took place near Thanksgiving, many students were away, and the campus was deserted except for foreign students.

In 1984, the Warren Commission released its findings concluding that Oswald had acted alone in the murder of President Kennedy. To date, the assassination has spurred numerous conspiracy theories surrounding his death.

1964 Spring Break—Visit to Washington, DC

I decided to spend spring break in Washington, DC. Mike Mahoney, a fellow graduate student, was planning on visiting his parents in Silver Spring, Maryland, and offered me a ride to and from Washington. I mentioned this to Jean Marie, who happily decided to accompany me to DC.

We departed Evanston for Washington on a crisp spring day in Mike's Red VW Beetle. Jean Marie and I were excited; it was my first road trip in the US. Our plan was to reach Maryland by late night, but when we were in Pennsylvania, a fan belt broke. The auto store would not open until 6:00 the next morning. We decided to sleep in the car. Luckily, the night was not so cold. We managed to get a few hours of sleep in the cramped space. We reached Silver Springs in the morning the next day and were warmly welcomed by Mike's parents.

Mike dropped us at the YMCA in downtown DC. The weather in Washington was pleasant. The cherry trees along the tidal basin around the Jefferson Memorial were in full bloom. The mall grass was green compared with the brown grass in Chicago. We soaked in the sun to get rid of the Chicago chill in our bones. Jean Marie and I walked around downtown visiting the Smithsonian museums, the art galleries, the mint, and FBI headquarters. We also toured Mount Vernon, George Washington's home, a fourteen-mile drive from downtown. We became American history students greatly appreciating the Declaration of Independence and the US Constitution formulated nearly two centuries earlier.

We visited the Booth Theatre where Lincoln was shot almost a hundred years earlier. President Johnson's photograph greeted us in every federal building. Only a few months earlier, JFK was the president, and his photo must have adorned all the federal buildings then. I was amazed at the smooth transition of power compared to rather undemocratic transfers of power in Pakistan. In 1958, I had witnessed a successful army coup d'état in Pakistan when General Ayub Khan took over and replaced the civilian government.

The only disturbing experience at the Y was that the toilet and shower stalls had no doors. It was an awkward situation for someone used to the privacy of shuttered doors in a bathroom. To avoid sharing with the other guests, I used the toilet and showers outside normal morning hours.

Ten years later, I visited Washington, DC again. My eldest brother, Parvez, was working as the chief economist at the World Bank. I visited DC at other times, but my first trip there was one of the happiest vacations I had and a much-needed breather from my hectic schedule at NU.

The Summer of 1964

In the 1960s, the university created an additional eighty-four acres (34 hectares) by means of a landfill in Lake Michigan. Among some of the buildings on these broad new acres are the university library, Norris University Center (the student union), and Pick-Staiger Concert Hall.

Jean Marie Nolf graduated with a master's degree in May 1964 and left for Belgium. The academic year ended in May 1964. I completed my thirty-three credits with a B+ average and was happy with the results. The sad part was the weekly sorority dining at the Alpha Epsilon Phi also ended. The campus became almost empty except for the foreign students.

Farrokh, George Shuraym, from Lebanon, and I decided to share a two-bedroom apartment with a living/dining area and a kitchen. The apartment was on Foster Avenue, a twenty-five-minute walk to the Tech. However, we could cook and entertain our friends with some Indian/ Pakistani dishes.

Raj was thrilled to bring Kamni Kaushal to the tech; she was visiting Chicago. A leading actress and heroine of India's Bollywood in the fifties, she often starred opposite Dilip Kumar. She was my idol during my teen years. Seeing her in person without much makeup and being older, I found her rather plain looking. In my fantasy, she was a larger-than-life figure on screen. Seeing her in person left me feeling let down. Years later, Raj named his daughter Kamni.

Dede Hansen, an undergrad student, and I were friends. She belonged to Delta Delta Delta sorority. She invited me to her parents' home in the Chicago suburbs.

As dinner was served, her father asked me, "Do you have any dietary restrictions?"

"I do not eat pork," I replied.

My response created a little change in the dinner menu. The family had prepared a roasted ham as the entrée. I was quickly served a kosher entrée. I felt as embarrassed as the host did. I thought the family knew that I was Muslim and would be familiar with our religious dietary laws, but after dinner, we laughed about it.

During the summer, the lake was a welcome relief from the unair-conditioned buildings though the tech rooms had ceiling fans. I was working on my thesis, which had to be completed by August. The thesis had to be typed. The CE Departmental secretary agreed to do the typing for $80. I agreed reluctantly.

My oral defense of my thesis went fairly well, but Professors Kondner, Krizek, and Basant made it clear that the degree did not make me a master of geotechnical engineering and that I had a great deal more to learn. I was awarded the MSCE degree in August as scheduled.

I was not present to receive my BSCE and MSCE degrees at convocations; I received both via mail. At NU, the annual convocation was in June; those graduating in August were awarded in that way the following year. I attended convocations at Swarthmore in 1983, RPI in

2000, and Boston University in 2014 and experienced the pure joy of marking significant milestones in my life. It more than made up for the missed opportunities.

The 1964 Civil Engineering Students

Some of the graduate students in the MSCE program were Kenneth Efferton, Farrokh Screwala, Raj Khera, Jim Horner, Eiichi Yamamoto, Bob Cheng, and Mike Mahoney.

Friends

Among the friends I made during this time were George Shuraym, Dede Hansen (Histand), Debbie Sigel, Hassam Tabayam, Kathi Coldway, Karen Grove Wald, Meredith Moss, Sue Fisk, and the Mann and Martin host families.

After graduation, Mike Mahoney settled in Sacramento, California. In 1968, he started the Kleinfeld office with twenty employees and was responsible for its tremendous growth as he rose to become the chair of the board. He retired in 1998. He and his wife, Judy, have been happily married for fifty-three years and are blessed with three daughters and eight grandkids.

Screwala and Raj Khera completed PhDs in 1966. Farrokh married Ellen and settled in Cleveland, where he practiced as a consulting engineer for nearly forty years before retiring. They have two sons. Raj Married Astrid and settled in New Jersey. He became a professor at NJIT.

With Dede Hansen at Chicago Zoo (1964)

George Shuraym

Class of 1964 with Prof. Osterberg visiting Chicago Building Foundations

Screwala and Nolf

With Farrokh Screwala at NU(1963)

With Susan at a Minooka Farm, IL.

At the NU Lake Front

Charles And Margaret Martins Family with an Iraqi student (1964).

The 1964 Presidential Election

The 1964 presidential election occurred less than a year after the assassination of President Kennedy. Lyndon B. Johnson, Kennedy's vice president, had been sworn in and tried to calm the national hysteria following the assassination. He urged the passage of Kennedy's legislative agenda including those involving civil rights.

During the summer, Chicago was bustling with Democrat politicians. I saw Hubert Humphrey, Johnson's running mate, when he visited Evanston.

A bitterly contested Republican primary took place between the conservatives and the moderates. At the Republican convention in San Francisco, the moderate candidate, Nelson Rockefeller, was unable to stop the nomination of the conservative Barry Goldwater, a senator from Arizona, who won on the first ballot. Goldwater selected William Miller of New York as his running mate.

During the 1964 election, Goldwater made moral leadership a major theme of his campaign and made little effort to woo the African-American vote. Johnson portrayed himself as pragmatic and level headed and portrayed Goldwater as a reckless person who might lead the country into a nuclear war. Democrats produced the famous Daisy ad, which showed a little girl picking flower petals as a countdown began for a nuclear explosion and a mushroom cloud. The ad was followed by Johnson's voice about the high stakes involved in the election. The ad was run only once, but it synthesized the view that Goldwater was too conservative.

Johnson won by a landslide securing more than 61 percent of the popular vote and 486 electoral votes. Goldwater won only six southern states accounting for 52 out of a total of 534 electoral votes.

Due to his legislative skills, Johnson was able to push a reform agenda including civil rights and clean air and water acts, forerunners of the initiatives on global warming fifty years later.

New York, 1964–1966

I needed a job. My foreign student advisor, Mr. Utley, had told me that as a J-1 Exchange visitor, I was entitled to obtain practical experience for a maximum of eighteen months in the US. Somebody up there had a plan for me; I got a break.

At an NU party, I ran into a marketing representative of Ebasco, who suggested I go to New York for an interview at the company's head office. The company would reimburse me for my expenses. It was a God-sent opportunity. My savings had dwindled to less than $1,000.

I took a Greyhound bus to New York, a twelve-hour trip. Ebasco Service's head office was in downtown Manhattan at 2 Rector Street, a block from Wall Street. After staying overnight at a hotel, I went to interview with John Scarola, the chief concrete-hydraulic engineer for the firm. His office was on the twelfth floor. After the interview, Bill Wells and Bill Zoino invited me to lunch at the Page restaurant on Greenwich Street. Wells headed the foundation group.

The interview went well. I was reimbursed over $200 for my travel and lodging expenses. With that cash in hand, I decided to stay in New York for several days and explore the city. During that short stay, I became familiar with the subway system and the city's landmarks.

New York is well known for its landmarks including the Empire State Building, a prewar, 102-story tower, Times Square with its neon lights, theaters and cinemas on 42nd Street, Wall Street and the New York Stock Exchange, and the UN building. I visited shops on Fifth Avenue including Saks, Tiffany's, and Macy's, and I visited Central Park. The Statue of Liberty was in the New York Harbor along with Ellis Island and Governor's Island accessible by ferry.

The 1964–65 World's Fair in Flushing Meadows was another attraction those days. To access the fairgrounds, a new train, the number 7, was added; the new Flushing line was built above ground (on an elevated steel structure) between Roosevelt Avenue and Main Street in Flushing. New York's subway system, which served Manhattan, Brooklyn, Bronx, and Queens, was a more elaborate underground system than Chicago's. The fifth borough, Staten Island, was connected in 1963 with the newly constructed Verrazano-Narrows Bridge, an engineering marvel with a main span of 4,260 feet (1,298 meters), 200 feet longer than the Golden Gate Bridge; it was the longest in the world until 1981. The double-decked, six-lane roadway rises 228 feet (69.8 meters) above sea level.

During my stay in the city, I called John Scarola at Ebasco and was told that a job offer with a starting salary of $700 per month was in the mail. It was indeed an attractive offer for a fresh graduate with no experience in the US. My experience at Mangla Dam must have come in handy.

I started looking for accommodations right away. I liked the Flushing Area. A new subway express line (number 7) to Midtown was added. Main Street, being the last stop for the train, would also assure me a seat. From Times Square, a local train would take me to Rector Street; it was a one-hour commute each way.

I found an apartment in a private home at 42–57 Phlox Place, a short walk from Main Street. The one-bedroom apartment was furnished, quite an upgrade from my NU rooming house. The bed was queen size, and the living room was big enough with a sofa and chairs for guests. It had a kitchen with stove and a small refrigerator. It was a ten-minute walk to the train station. The only item I had to purchase was a TV. Color TVs were quite expensive then; the price of a twenty-three-inch Magnavox color TV was $325, and I purchased one on an installment plan.

I signed up with a $20 check deposit. I had to get back to Evanston, pack my bags, and return to New York in a week. I bought some new clothes including a two-piece suit from Sears.

Back at NU, I bid farewell to Farrokh and George and wished them luck in their pursuit of PhDs in civil and electrical engineering respectively and returned to New York.

Ebasco was one of the largest design-construct firm in New York and perhaps in the US. It had been founded by General Electric in 1905 as the Electric Bond and Share Company (Ebasco). It provided engineering, consulting, and construction services for fossil-fuel or coal-based and hydroelectric power plants in the US and the five continents since 1935.

I joined Ebasco the third week of October, 1964, in the Concrete Hydraulics (CH) Department, which had some thirty engineers and three supervising engineers, Andrew A. Ferlito, James Mullarkey, and Bill Wells, supported by a team of between seventy and ninety designers. Another group, the Architectural Structural, had a similar number of engineers and designers.

Daniel Turner had joined Ebasco six months earlier also as a cadet engineer having graduated from Worcester Polytechnic Institute. He and wife, Lois, lived in Brooklyn. He and I hit it off right away. We often ate lunch at the cafeteria across Rector Street. One day, I was eating pea soup and noticed some pieces of meat in it. I asked Dan, "What is this meat?"

"It's ham," Dan answered.

That was the end of pea soup for me.

Our friendship lasted five decades. Lois was a schoolteacher and wrote poetry. She was also a great cook and an excellent hostess. We spent the July 4 weekend in Concord, Massachusetts, where Lois's parents lived. I got a lesson in history about the American War of Independence that began in Lexington and Concord. **Concord** is steeped in the history of the sword and pen. The site of the historic Battle of Lexington and **Concord**, the city provided the setting for the initiation of the American War of Independence honored at Minute Man National Historical Park.

I worked on several projects preparing construction specifications for concrete and grouting tunnels, hydraulic calculations for circulating water systems for power plants, and foundations for transmission towers.

Field Assignment in Blairstown, New Jersey

Ebasco had designed the first-of-its-kind hydroelectric power station called the pump-storage project. A pump storage is a hydroelectric project where the water is pumped from the lower reservoir to an upper reservoir during the night, when electricity rates are low. The stored energy at the elevated reservoir is released during the day to generate electricity. Known as the Yards Creek Pumped Storage Hydroelectric Station with an installed capacity of 420 MW, it was near Blairstown, New Jersey, near the Delaware Water Gap in Pennsylvania. It was constructed in 1964–65.

Due to an irregular rock foundation, there was water seepage from the upper reservoir during construction. For several months, there was around-the-clock investigation requiring borings and test pits to address the seepage issues. Bill Conway headed the investigation team and was supported by Joe Ehasz and me.

Blairstown, New Jersey

Blairstown is a small town near the New Jersey–Pennsylvania border. It did not have any motels or dining facilities. Elma's Diner on Main Street was a convenient place for lunch. Mimi Blevins worked there as a part-time waitress as she finished high school.

For lodging, I stayed at the Holiday Inn in East Stroudsburg, across the Delaware River Gap. The initial visit to the site turned into a six-month stay as summer turned into fall. The foliage in the Delaware Gap Mountains was very colorful.

We monitored the leakage around the clock. Bill and Joe worked the morning shifts, and I worked the night shift as I was a bachelor. Joe was married to Terri and lived in Bound Brook, New Jersey; he commuted daily to the jobsite. They were expecting their second child, Michael.

At night, fog would set in leading to poor visibility on the hill. A set of piezometers were installed around the reservoir to measure the seepage. A piezometer is a vertical standpipe with a perforated bottom to allow inflow of water thus measuring the water level at that location. The piezometer readings were taken at regular intervals including at night.

Due to the forest around the reservoir, I was warned of snakes including copperheads, which liked to coil around the cold piping. A first aid kit was on site in case one was bitten.

The Stroudsburg Holiday Inn was quite comfortable. It had a good restaurant, where I ate breakfast and dinner. The daily room rate was less than $10, and a good steak dinner would cost $7 including taxes and tip. My daily expenses totaled $22 including lunch and miscellaneous expenses.

I rented a 1965 Mustang and loved it. It was ninety miles from the jobsite to Queens. The Mustang, a two-seat sports car, was officially unveiled by Henry Ford II at the World's Fair in Flushing Meadows, New York, on April 17, 1964. It became very popular in the 1960s and beyond.

It would take me less than two hours via the Whitestone Bridge, Cross-Bronx Expressway, and the George Washington to reach the site via Route 46. Later, it turned into Interstate 80. I would go home to Flushing on the weekends. In the 1960s, there were no credit cards or even IDs. In order for me to rent the car, my company gave me a letter of introduction, which I gave the car rental company. I had a Pakistani driver's license that was apparently acceptable. There were tolls at the both George Washington (75¢) and Whitestone (25¢) Bridges.

One late evening while returning from the site, I was stopped in Blairstown. I was probably speeding. The cop asked me to produce a driver's license. I produced my Pakistani driver's license. It consisted of several sheets of reinforced cloth folded into a 4" by 4" booklet. The cop had never seen such a license before and was taken off guard. After some hesitation, he advised me to be careful and let me go.

1965 NYC Blackout

The Northeast blackout of 1965 was a significant disruption in the supply of electricity on Tuesday, November 9, 1965, at 5:16 p.m.; it affected parts of Ontario in Canada and Connecticut, Massachusetts, New Hampshire, New Jersey, New York, Rhode Island, Pennsylvania, and Vermont. Over 30 million people and 80,000 square miles (207,000 square kilometers) were left without electricity for up to thirteen hours. The cause of the failure was the tripping of protective relays on the transmission lines from the Sir Adam Beck Hydroelectric Power Station No. 2 in Queenstown, Ontario, near Niagara Falls.

The protective relays, which were designed to protect the line from overload, tripped and isolated Beck Station from all of southern Ontario. With no place else to go, the excess power from Beck Station flowed east over the interconnected lines into New York State overloading them as well and isolating the power generated in the Niagara region from the rest of the interconnected grid. The Beck generators, with no outlet for their power, were automatically shut down to prevent damage. The affected power areas were the Ontario Hydro System, St. Lawrence–Oswego, Upstate New York, and New England. With only limited electrical connection southward, power to the southern states was not affected.

New York City was dark by 5:27 p.m. The blackout was not universal in the city; some neighborhoods including the Maywood section of Brooklyn never lost power. Also, some suburban areas including Bergen County, New Jersey, served by PSE&G, did not lose power. Most TV stations in the New York metro area were forced off the air as well as about half of the FM radio stations as their common transmitter tower atop the Empire State Building lost power.

Fortunately, a bright full moon lit up the cloudless sky over the entire blackout area providing some aid for the millions who were suddenly plunged into darkness.

Power restoration was uneven. Most generators had no auxiliary power to use for startup. Parts of Brooklyn were repowered by 11:00 p.m. and the rest of the borough by midnight. However, the entire city was not returned to normal power supply until nearly 7:00 a.m. the next day, November 10.

The *New York Times* was able to produce a ten-page edition for November 10 using the printing presses of a nearby paper that was not affected, the *Newark Evening News*. The front page showed a photograph of the city skyline with its lights out.

Following the blackout, measures were undertaken to try to prevent a repetition. Reliability standards and improved coordination among electricity providers were established.

In contrast to the wave of looting and other incidents that took place during the 1977 New York City blackout, only five reports of looting were made in New York City after the 1965 blackout. It was said to be the lowest amount of crime on any night in the city's history since records were first kept.

By the late fall, it was getting cold at the upper reservoir of Yards Creek in the evenings. Bill suggested that we buy woolen shirts, long johns, and woolen pants, and I heartily agreed. The warm gear helped me through the end of my assignment. We purchased the warm clothing by mail. It was a harbinger of on-line shopping that became popular some fifty years later.

An Opportunity to See USA Unlimited—A $99 Package

On December 12, I telephoned John Scarola from the Blairstown site that my assignment was ending. John's message was clear: "Nash, I don't want to see you in office until the new year." That meant more than two weeks of paid vacation. I was surprised, but it was perhaps a reward for the hard work our team had handled.

I had to decide quickly. I did not want to stay in the city for the next two weeks. Greyhound offered a $99 See USA ticket with unlimited coast-to-coast travel with the caveat that such travel had to be completed within thirty days. It sounded very attractive. As a minimum, I could visit my friends at NU in Evanston and then travel west stopping at Denver, Salt Lake City, San Francisco, and Los Angeles. Returning from California, I could see the Grand Canyon. I would spend the Christmas holidays on the road. The cost of this unlimited pass would now be $577. I decided to travel at night to maximize my sightseeing during the day.

The first leg took me to Evanston, where the fall quarter was ending. I met some of my old friends and acquaintances on the quiet campus. From Chicago, I went nonstop to Denver arriving there in the early morning. Getting out of the bus, however, I felt tired and desperately needed a comfortable bed. I checked into the Brown Hotel for the few hours' sleep. It was expensive, $30 or so, but it was well worth the cost.

Denver

Denver, the state capital of Colorado, is known as the Mile-High City as marked on the Capitol Building. From the top of the building, the vistas were beautiful. Looking east, I saw flat hinterlands, but to the west, the Rocky Mountains presented a magnificent landscape with snowclad peaks. The air was clean and fresh. One of the attractions was the Denver mint, which I also visited.

Salt Lake City

The next stop was Salt Lake City, Utah. The attractions included the Mormon Temple and the Great Salt Lake, which is known to have the saltiest water on earth. Many years later, I found that claim to be challenged by the river leading to the Dead Sea in Jordan.

The visit to the Mormon Tabernacle Choir was a thrill. The tabernacle seated nearly 8,000 in a huge auditorium with a roof rising eighty feet. The acoustics were among the best. According to the tabernacle brochure, "The auditorium acoustics are so sensitive that you can hear a pin drop at the other end some 250 feet away." The 375 voices of the choir and the 10,000-pipe organ rendered "spine-tingling sounds from the Christendom's sacred music."

The Mormon Church

The Mormon Church is a branch of Christianity founded by Joseph Smith in the 1830s; he was martyred in 1844. The Mormon Church, also known as the Church of the Latter-day Saints, moved west under the leadership of Brigham Young into the valley of the Great Salt Lake in 1847. I ran into a young Mormon outside the church who was preaching. He gave me a copy of the Bible, which I still possess.

San Francisco

We crossed the Rockies at night into California and arrived in San Francisco in the morning. I took tours of the University of California Berkley Campus, the Golden Gate Bridge, and Fisherman's Wharf.

Eiichi Yamamoto was there working with a consulting firm. He was on a J-1 visa like mine. He took me to the Muir Woods National Monument north of the Golden Gate Bridge, the only redwood forest with trees over 2,000 years old. Redwoods grow only in the coastal region from San Francisco to Oregon. The trees have diameter as large as twenty feet allowing a car to go through the trunks of some that have been hollowed out. It was named in the honor of John Muir, a noted traveler, naturalist, and writer.

San Francisco is a unique city with hilly landscape, a famous cable car service, and crooked streets. The seafood at Fisherman's Wharf was extremely fresh and tasty.

Los Angeles

In Los Angeles, the city of angels, I took a guided tour. The tour guide talked of city smog and the jokes about it. I remember a joke in particular. "One day, the smog was so dense that a car was following the taillights of another car. Finally, the front car stopped and the driver came out. He walked over and asked the other driver, "Why are you following me?" The other driver asked, "Why did you stop?" The first driver said, "I've reached home and am parked in my garage."

In addition to smog, LA is known for its Disney Land, Universal Studios, Hollywood, and wealthy suburbs.

By then, I had traveled over 3,200 miles by road in less than fifteen days.

Grand Canyon

The last stop was at Flagstaff, where I took a tour of the Grand Canyon with very colorful stratified sandstone and deep caverns carved out by the Colorado River. The Grand Canyon is one of the seven natural wonders of the world. The guide narrated its history of formation through the millennia. I was impressed by the effects of wind and water on the rocky landscape consisting of sandstone, shale, and limestone with varying colors.

The return trip to New York was fast with transit stops only, and I was home before the New Year.

Greyhound had a well-advertised slogan, "Leave the driving to us." The slogan was true. The bus drivers were professional, experienced, and courteous, and they assured my complete safety as I slept well in the night in comfortable seats. It was perhaps the spirit of adventure that kept me going without much sleep on a bed.

1966 NYC Transit Strike

I was back in Queens at the turn of the new year, 1966. New York was being challenged by a looming transit strike that would paralyze the city for nearly twelve days. I was apprehensive. I had to show up in our downtown Manhattan office after my extended vacation at any cost. I took a cab to work on the first day of the strike with three other passengers; it cost me $8 for the trip from Flushing, Queens, to downtown Manhattan.

The transit strike also affected the commuters on the Long Island Railroad and Metro North, who used the subway system to reach downtown. The New Jersey residents had no commuting issues; they could ride the New Jersey transit trains including Path trains to reach downtown. Also, Jersey City was connected via ferry to Manhattan.

Joe Ehasz lived with his family in Bound Brook, New Jersey, and was unaffected by the transit strike. He offered me lodging, which I readily accepted. I accompanied him home via train that evening. I had to buy new set of clothes, underwear, and toiletries while I stayed with him for several days during the strike. Joe and his wife were extremely hospitable. Their son, Joey, was a less than a year old, and the family was expecting another child. I got to know the family well as a result of the transit strike. I ate a lot of Italian dinners those days as well as Hungarian goulash. Joe's family came from Hungary. Our friendship lasted several decades.

Dan and Lois had moved to Staten Island from Brooklyn in late 1965. Lois was expecting a baby. During the night of January 6, Dan drove her to Brooklyn Lutheran hospital. Their first child, Smyth, was born on January 7, 1966.

John Lindsey, a youthful, good-looking man in his forties, was the mayor of New York then. It was the era of the hippies, and Greenwich Village was a tourist attraction.

Refer to https://wikipedia.org/wiki/1966_New_York_City_transit_strike

The 1966 New York City transit strike was a strike in New York City called by the Transport Workers Union (TWU).

The twelve-day strike began on New Year's Day in 1966; the last trains rolled at 8:02 am. An injunction to end the strike was issued later that day, under the 1947 Condon-Waddling Act.

On January 2, the union reduced its economic demands, but the TA responded only by getting a judge's order for the arrest of the union leaders. Negotiations moved forward through mediators. On January 13, settlement was reached. The package, worth over $60 million, included wages increases from $3.18 to $4.14 an hour, an additional paid holiday, increased pension benefits, and other gains. Gains averaged nine percent for the next eight years.

Nancy Sinatra recorded a song during the strike, "These Boots Are Made for Walking"; it reached number 1 in the US Billboard Hot 100 and in the UK Singles Chart.

NYC Social Network

While living in Flushing, I ran into a young man who was working in the pharmaceutical industry and studying. Najam ul Ain hailed from Karachi. We soon became friends and shared weekends together. There was a small Pakistani community in New York at that time. N. M. Rashid worked at the UN information service. He was a well-known Urdu writer and lived on the East Side with his children, Yasmin and Shehryar. Yasmin, it turned out, knew my sister Shaheen. Then there was Anis Kabir, who also resided in Manhattan. This small Pakistani community met on weekends and shared meals and laughter.

Yasmin was a good singer, and so was Najam. Others joined in. Shehryar played the *tabla* (a pair of small drums for Indian subcontinent music played by hands) using stainless steel pots. It was a welcome change for the weekends.

Najam later returned to Pakistan and became the managing director of Sandoz. He married Anjum, the daughter of Salahuddin Hanif, a retired session judge. It so happened that I was related to Najam through Anjum. Uncle Hanif was the firstborn son of Dr. Sharif, who later married my aunt Iqbal after his first wife died.

Shehryar returned to Pakistan and joined the Foreign Service. Yasmin Rashed married and settled in Canada. Anis Kabir returned to Pakistan and married a civil servant in East Pakistan.

Another Pakistani family, stationed in New York, was Sarfraz Khan and Atiya. Sarfraz was working with the UN. Atiya Apa was the daughter of Azim Khan, who was my father's business partner Her younger brother, Nasim, visited New York; he was settled in the UK and was managing his father's (Azim Khan) textile business. It was summer of 1966, I invited him for a weekend escape visit to the Poconos. We had a great time there, reliving my earlier stay and happy memories.

Dan and Lois were like family too. For many years, Dan and Lois were my US contacts for family and friends visiting New York from Pakistan. When they acquired a pet dog, he was named Shaheen, based on my sister's name.

J-1 Visa Expires

Having worked for over eighteen months after my graduation, it was time to return home as part of the US J-1 Visa entry and exit requirements. John Scarola tried to convince me to work with an Ebasco subsidiary in Canada for the two years to fulfill the J-1 Visa requirements, but I was homesick not having seen my family for nearly three years. I decided to go home. I had come to the US on a plane, and I decided to return via ship.

> The Wavering Heart
> Since I was set to depart from your city
> Why then cast a dejected glance at its walls?
> The heart wanted to stay, but, how could I?
> When I first stepped into the unknown valleys
> The way memories from homeland implored me to return,
> The very same feeling overcomes me today:
> As if I would go through the same agonies and pains,
> As if someone would call me again, "Come back."
> (translated from a poem by Ahmed Faraz)

John and Grace Scarola Xmas Party (1964)

Author at Yards Creek Pump storage Investigation (1965)

With Lois Turner (1965)

With Dan Turner at Concord (1965)

With Najam and Friends in NYC (1965)

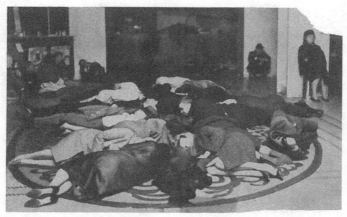

1965 Blackout -Stranded Guests **A Hotel Lobby in NYC (1965)**

Chapter 5

EUROPE ON
$5 A DAY

Returning from the US

I said goodbye to my colleagues and friends in New York and especially to Dan and Lois Turner.

My father told me that importing a US car to Pakistan would not be a good idea due to the high freight and customs duties. He preferred that I import a Mercedes from Europe instead with lower freight and import duties. I took his advice, but that meant selling my 1965 Chevy Impala, which was barely a year old. My brother, Dr. Parvez Hasan, had booked a Mercedes 200 sedan on my behalf that I was to pick up at the Mercedes-Benz Plant in Stuttgart, West Germany.

I sold the Impala for $2,000 at a loss of only $500. The cash transaction transpired in a diner on Queens Boulevard. I wired the proceeds from the sale to Stuttgart. I arranged to ship my books, clothing, and personal effects by sea to Pakistan. Ebasco's shipping department helped me with the packing and shipping.

I decided on a two-week sightseeing tour in Europe; I thought I might not get such an opportunity for a long time. I planned to visit my

Mangla friend, Nasir, in London, and my NU friend, Jean Marie Nolf, in Belgium before going to Stuttgart for the car. My itinerary was simple. After picking up the car, I intended to drive from Stuttgart to Naples.

My uncle Ghulam Hasan had driven from the UK to Pakistan in his Vauxhall a decade earlier. It was a much longer and more hazardous journey through Europe and Turkey, Iran, and Afghanistan. His trip was without a mishap except for a minor accident when a deer hit his car.

Those days, summer tours of Europe by US youths and college students were popular. They had a fancy to explore Europe with minimum expense. It was popular to stay at youth hostels, which provided economical lodging and interaction with other travelers. I purchased a copy of *Europe on $5 a day* by Arthur Frommer. He had enjoyed traveling around Europe on $5 a day paying $3 a day for a youth hostel and as little as 90¢ for a three-course meal. This book included all pertinent information including addresses of youth hostels in Western Europe.

I was excited about the educational, enriching experience as well as lessons in history. Since I would have a means of transportation, I could stay at the youth hostels cheaply and enjoy an experience of a lifetime in a rather untraditional way of seeing Europe.

Transatlantic Voyage

I sailed from New York on August 13, 1966, on board the SS *United States*. Is was a 50,000 DWT passenger ship regularly sailing between New York and Southampton, England. It would take five days to cross the Atlantic; that was considered the fastest transatlantic crossing by ship. Dan and Lois, Najam, Shaheen, and Shehryar were among my friends present on West 52nd Street for a very emotional and warm farewell.

Dan And Lois Turner at West Side Pier boarding SS United States 1966

SS *United States*

It was a luxury passenger liner built in 1952 for United States Lines built at a cost of $79.4 million. The ship was the largest ocean liner constructed entirely in the US, and it was the fastest ocean liner to cross the Atlantic in either direction. In its 1950s prime, this Titanic-sized ship offered one of the most stylish ways to travel between New York and Europe, but it was superseded by the jet travel era that followed.

On board the ship were nearly 1,800 passengers from all walks of life—students, family members of the US armed forces serving in NATO, and celebrities as well. The food was extraordinary with sit-down service and multiple courses, and passengers enjoyed high tea in the afternoon and entertainment after dinner. There were no phones or computers on board; we were on our own between the blue skies and the blue sea.

I was in the cabin class, but other young people and I would wander off to first class toward the bow. I ran into Shirley Maclain and her husband. The chance meeting was a thrill since I was a fan having seen most of her films including *Irma la Douce*.

London

After a restful five days, we reached the shores of England and berthed at Southampton in the early morning of August 18. There were nobody to welcome the arriving passengers, quite the contrary to the warm send-off I had received in New York. I boarded a train for London's Victoria Station in the late morning. Nasir Mohiyuddin, my friend from my Mangla Dam days, was working in London and had offered me lodging. He was a very gracious host and showed me around London. We visited Madame Tussauds, where we saw Ayub Khan's life-size figure as one of the new world leaders. We walked from Buckingham Palace to Trafalgar Square to visit the art galleries.

I also met Ahsan Ul Bari, who was also staying with Nasir and was on his way to the US for a master's in civil engineering. I must have mentioned to him my work experience with Ebasco, because after completing his studies, he joined the Concrete Hydraulics Department of Ebasco.

Nasir's apartment in Sheepshead bay was small, and the bathroom were dated. It required inserting coins for use of hot water for showers. It was quite a change from the modern bathrooms in the US that were fitted with an uninterrupted supply of hot water without requiring any coins.

Belgium

After nearly three exciting days in London, I flew to Brussels. I had written to John Nolf earlier about my flight and date of arrival and expected to see him at the airport. He welcomed me with a warm hug and drove me to his family home in Bruges, Ghent, a Flemish region in Belgium. John came from an established family in Ghent. His father was a ham radio operator. While in the US, John would talk to his family every Sunday via ham radio. His family, including his parents and a sister, made me feel at their home.

I was surprised to learn that John had planned a great four-day sightseeing tour of Belgium. His cousin joined us as we rode in a sports car. I will not forget the hospitality; I was not allowed to spend a penny on lodging, food, or entertainment during the four days I was with him.

Author with Jean Marie Nolf in Belgium (1966)

1966 Travel Route from Stuttgart (W Germany) to Naples (Italy)

Stuttgart, West Germany

I flew to Frankfurt, took a train to Stuttgart on August 22, and went straight to the Mercedes-Benz factory. The manager was expecting me. I was given a forty-five-minute tour of the factory, where a car was produced every fifteen to twenty minutes on an assembly line; there were no robots in the factory then.

I received the sales documents for the car, insurance, and maps for driving through West Germany, Switzerland, and Italy. My itinerary was to go through the Black Forest region in West Germany and then through the Swiss Alps into Italy. The 900-mile (1,500 kilometer) trip would require eight to ten days including nightly stops in Freiburg, Zürich, Lugano, Milan, Florence, Rome, and Naples. I intended to ship the car to Karachi from Naples and fly to Karachi from Rome. Being a scout, I was ready for the adventure.

A road map of my 900-mile journey, from Stuttgart to Naples traveling through the three countries is shown below.

As I left Stuttgart, I accidently met a German girl, Inge, at a cafeteria. She was in her early twenties and was a physical training instructor; she was headed north to Hamburg for a job in a secondary school. Upon my insistence, she agreed to travel south instead and share a part of my journey to Freiburg. She knew English well, and I liked her company and hoped she would accompany me for my entire trip south.

We exchanged our stories. Inge told me that she was in love with a young man from Israel, who was doing his mandatory army reserve training in Israel. They were planning to get married after he finished his training. I thought given the history of hatred between the Germans and the Jews, a marriage between a Christian and a Jew was rather odd. I might have told her so. I told her I was a Muslim returning from the US to Pakistan.

By late afternoon, we checked into a youth hostel in Freiburg. All youth hostels had separate rooms for males and females. In the evening, we went out to dinner at a restaurant. Inge ordered the meal for me since the menu was in German. I told her that my dietary restrictions prohibited me from eating pork.

The restaurant was lively and full of elderly couples. One diner exchanged greetings with Inge and talked to her. I thought of nothing of her small talk. We ate well and walked backed to the youth hostel and into our respective buildings.

I bid her goodnight, and she said, "Auf Wiedersehen. I'm heading north to Hamburg tomorrow." There was firmness in her voice. She had decided to part company. I had wished she would come with me at least as far as Basel, which was barely forty-six miles away and on the border between West Germany and Switzerland.

As we exchanged our parting words, Inge told me about the small talk she had had with the elderly gentleman at the cafeteria. He had asked her, "Are you married?"

Inge had replied, "Yes we are."

She was well aware of the delicate nature of the elder's question and had replied appropriately. In the midsixties, small towns in Europe were still quite conservative, and married couples were more respected than were unmarried couples.

Switzerland

The next morning, I traveled alone to Basel and then to Zürich. By late afternoon, I was in Zürich having traveled over a hundred miles from Freiburg.

Zürich was full of watch shops that offered world-renowned brands including Omega, Rolex, Cartier, Longines, etc. I bought some gifts there for my sisters, Yasmin and Mona. There were tourist everywhere.

Traveling through the Swiss Alps—snowclad but relatively bare mountains—was a unique experience. The air was warm, and heat was reflected off the mountains. The car had no air conditioning, so I kept the window open.

I reached Lugano, on the border between Switzerland and Italy, a distance of over 130 miles, in the late afternoon. I was struck by the vast lake and the buildings and cafés lining the streets. It was a very clean, soothing environment.

Most youths traveled on motorbikes or used public transport, so my pulling up to a hostel in my Mercedes raised eyebrows; people thought I was a chauffeur transporting the car.

Italy

A family in Milan whose daughter I had met in Lugano thought so too. However, they offered me a wholesome Italian meal with spaghetti and meatballs. Italians routinely drink wine with lunch and dinner, but I declined the generous wine offer.

At Florence, the Uffizi gallery, in the Piazza della Signoria, was a treat. As I entered, I was welcomed by the sculpture of "David" by Michelangelo.

An Unexpected Disruption

It was hot as I drove from Florence. It was the end of August, which is hot in Italy. At that time, two British hitchhikers had joined me for the Florence-Rome journey, 170 miles. Both girls were college students traveling to Naples. We intended to reach Rome by late afternoon, but we passed a small lake and suddenly had the urge to cool off. It seemed a nice, quiet, rural area with little traffic, and it seemed safe.

When we returned to the car fifteen or so minutes later, we saw that the car had been broken into. My wallet and briefcase containing my passport, traveler's checks, plane ticket, and more were gone. The only relief was that my companions had some cash in their baggage in the trunk.

We drove to the nearest town to report the theft. One girl knew Italian and tried to explain our losses to a police official, but he did not believe us. We had to drive back to the crime scene for further explanation. Finally, he typed up the theft report. As it turned out, the theft report was helpful in convincing various agencies of our misfortune that day.

We reached Rome late in the evening. I dropped the girls off at the youth hostel. We were hungry. I had no cash. Luckily, the girls had some cash and paid for my dinner.

I was able to find my way to Nazir Ahmed's home in EUR, a new suburb of Rome. My boy scout training was indeed helpful in locating their home because there was no GPS then.

Nazir Ahmed was married to Khalida, the older sister of my Bhabi (sister-in-law) Parveen. He worked for the Food and Agricultural Organization of the UN and was out of town, but Khalida and her kids were home. I was welcomed and given food and lodging for the next several days, and I received the emotional support I needed the most. It was my lucky day after all. It had ended well. I was grateful. Imagine the scenario if the Nazirs were away on vacation or out of the country! That possibility had never entered my mind.

Over the next several days, my two companions and I toured Rome. I had the transport, and the girls had enough cash to get by until I received replacement traveler's checks, but we were very stingy with our meals for the next few days.

I contacted the Pakistan Embassy in Rome for a temporary passport. The first secretary told me that the embassy would verify my particulars before reissuing a new passport, which would take time. Khalida Apa paid the passport reissuing fee and facilitated the whole process as she knew the first secretary. I was issued a temporary, one-way passport to Pakistan, PIA reissued my Rome-Karachi plane ticket, and American Express reissued the stolen traveler's checks.

I had sent a wire to Dan Turner in Staten Island requesting $300 from my savings account held by him, and he sent the money to American Express. Before long, all the travel-related issues were resolved. And Mercedes-Benz replaced the car window at no charge as it was covered by the insurance. The most important document was the car's import papers that were issued to me while entering Italy from Switzerland. I had casually stored these documents in the side pocket, and they had not been stolen. I was told by the Mercedes staff that had these papers been stolen, the car could not have been exported from Italy. I felt grateful. Somebody above was watching over me. All's well that ends well. I left Italy with good rather than bad memories. And I learned some important lessons about traveling.

The episode, however, delayed my departure to Karachi by at least a week. Pakistan Air Lines flights between Rome and Karachi were perhaps twice a week, so we drove to Naples, our last stop on our exciting journey. We found rooms at a youth hostel that was near the coast.

The honeysuckle flowers were in full bloom and filled the Naples summer air with their aroma along with the sea breeze. The youth hostel was a festive place; a good dream had come to an end. I bid farewell to my British friends, who had faithfully stuck with me throughout our ordeal. I had managed to travel on a slim budget of $5 a day in Germany, Switzerland, and Italy per Frommer's travel guide.

The next morning, I drove to the Naples dockyard to ship the car to Karachi. The shipping agent was a nice fellow, but I had to part with $300 as the fee for shipping the car to Karachi. The wire transfer from Dan Turner in Staten Island provided that.

I returned to Rome by train and had a memorable stay with the Nazirs. Guddu (Anwaar) was only seven or eight then. He spoke fluent Italian and had a curious mind and intellect. Her older sisters always helped their mother while Nazir bhaijan was away on business.

I ate a lot of Italian food during the week of my stay. In the evenings, I would take the kids to the playground. I was involuntarily marooned in Rome for a week waiting for the issuance of the passport so I could travel home.

I wrote about the delay in my departure plans to Abba ji via air mail informing him about the change in itinerary for the Rome-Karachi flight without giving any reason for the delay. The family must have been waiting for my arrival. Before my letter reached, a letter from Inge, whom I had met a week earlier, had reached Karachi.

Abba ji, being anxious to know of my whereabouts, had opened the letter from Inge addressed to me. In it, Inge thanked me for an unforgettable experience for a day of her life including the dinner in Freiburg and much more ... Upon my return to Karachi, Abba ji handed me the letter from Inge expressing regret that he had opened it. He was too discreet to ask about or discuss its contents. He was an understanding father indeed.

The summer of 1966 was truly memorable. First, the transatlantic journey followed by the land journey through the UK, Belgium, West

Germany, Switzerland, and last, the holiday in Italy, which was full of unexpected delight and adventure. Frommer's book was fully vindicated. I do not remember all the names of my fellow travelers who made it an unforgettable experience, but the two weeks enriched my life and gave me a better understanding of the world.

Lesson Learned

My 1966 memories of Europe will always haunt me; I learned valuable lessons about patience and reliance. I had met adversity with hope and resolve. God was perhaps testing me; help did come wherever I turned. The adversity was an opportunity. I never doubted the outcome and lived one day at a time.

The ability to deal with unexpected disruptions prepares you to deal with future disruptions. I urge every young individual to travel and explore the world to gain familiarity with different customs, traditions, and cultures and make this world a better place.

Chapter 6

ARRANGED MARRIAGES

I was back home.

I was finally in my parents' arms. I had been longing for that after a nearly three years' absence from home. Hugging my parents gave me real joy and happiness. The imam zaman that my mother had put on my arm was still with me; it had brought me safely home to Karachi notwithstanding my adventures in Europe.

My father greeted me at the Karachi Airport customs area and reminded me to fill the customs form for declaring unaccompanied baggage including the Mercedes shipped from Italy. His presence facilitated my custom formalities.

By then, our family had moved to 17 F, PECHS Block 6, a home that had been custom built in 1952. My father had the foresight and the stamina to construct our first home. The 1,500-square-yard plot was obtained from the government at a cost of Rs. 7 per square yard or a total cost of Rs. 10,500 ($2,000). On the plot, two identical, semi-attached homes (17 F1 and 17 F2) were built; my father and his youngest brother, Ghulam Hasan, owned them. Each unit consisted of reinforced block masonry load-bearing walls and a reinforced concrete flat roof. They had three spacious bedrooms with attached baths, large living and dining areas, kitchens with pantries, garages, and servants' quarters. The floors were finished in mosaic ceramic tile in the bathrooms and teak doors and windows. The plot sat on irregular ground consisting of limestone that had required excavation. It took an additional Rs. 60,000 ($12,000) for the construction of the two units. Initially, both units had been rented to well-heeled expatriate families from the UK and later Pakistan. The rent was Rs. 600 per month in the early 1950s.

Chacha G. H. never occupied his portion of the home; it was rented until 1977 and then sold to his nephew, Javed Hasan, for about Rs. 300,000 or so. The other half, our father's portion, was sold in 1999 for Rs 5.2 million, seventeen times the 1970 price and over seventy times the 1952 price. What a great investment! In 2018, the market value of this property was over Rs. 10 million. Pakistan's currency had been devalued by almost thirty times over those sixty years.

My father had retired. He was not in good health. He looked frail. He had suffered a hemorrhage in the right eye and had lost weight. His legs had poor circulation. One thing he enjoyed wearing were the cotton leggings I had used at the Yards Creek Project in the fall of 1965.

After completing an MA degree in international relations from Karachi University, my brother Jamshed was working for a private firm owned by K. Rehman in East Pakistan. Another brother, Behram, had earned an MBA from the Institute of Business Administration in Karachi and was employed at the Industrial Development Bank of Pakistan. Shaheen had received a master's degree in sociology and was working with the Census Bureau of Pakistan in Karachi. Yasmin was enrolled in a master's program in economics at Karachi University, and Mahjabin and Owais were studying at local colleges. My parents were proud of their endeavors notwithstanding the personal sacrifices they continually made to educate their eight children.

Bhaijan had returned from Saudi Arabia after five years. He had joined the West Pakistan government as chief economist and additional secretary with Planning and Development in Lahore.

Family Photo (1966) Karachi

Zafar and Associates

I got a job with a private firm, Zafar and Associates, Consulting Engineers, with offices on Drigh Road (later known as Shahrah-e-Faisal) two miles from home. That was convenient as I could come home for a hot lunch every day. I was hired at a monthly salary of Rs. 1,500, more than adequate to meet household expenses and entertainment.

Iftikhar Ahmed Zafar (known as I. A. Zafar) had worked for the Planning Commission but had left government service to set up a private consulting practice, and he was hiring young qualified professionals. He was a shrewd man with a phenomenal memory and an eye for talent. Over the next few years, he employed some of the brightest civil and structural engineers returning with MSCE degrees from the US and the UK. However, foreign-qualified engineers would come and go after a few years since his was a one-man show with little growth potential for young professionals. Among the engineering staff, I stayed the longest there.

Zafar and Associates had a professional collaboration arrangement with a German firm headed by o. Prof Lackner of Bremen, West Germany, for the design of additional berths and shed at the Karachi Port known as the Second Karachi Port Project Expansion as well as conducting engineering feasibility studies for a second port in Pakistan.

The latter study was to evaluate several ports along the Mekran Coast including Gwadar, Ormara, Pasni, and Sonmiani. Based on a cost-benefit analysis, Sonmiani was selected as the best location for a second port in West Pakistan.[15] As a result, additional hydraulic and geological investigations followed at Sonmiani, and I was intimately involved with those two projects.

The other major project was KESC Thermal Plant Expansion Unit 3 in partnership with a US firm, Laramore, Douglas and Popham of New York.

Azhar Ali had returned after completing his MSCE at the University of Illinois, Urbana-Champaign. Hashmat Ali had returned from the UK. They were responsible for the KESC Korangi Unit 3 Power Station Project. Akhtar Bokhari, who had returned with a MSCE from the University of Minnesota and I were involved with the ports, highway, and bridges.

The Structural Department was initially headed by a Hungarian, Karl Zwipp. The foreign qualified engineers were Abdul Razzaq Loya, Majeed Qureshi, Fida Sayani, Zain Anjarwala, and later Javed Uppal (with a PhD from the University of London) working on several buildings and other projects around Karachi, Dubai, and Abu Dhabi. The local engineers were Mahmood Alam and Maroof Kharkhi. There were several draftsmen and junior architects. Mian Fazakl Karim, who retired as the chief electrical engineer of Pakistan Railway (PWR), was a notable staff addition. Fazluddin Syed was the office manager.

During 1971–73, Pakistan's economy slowed down due to political unrest, elections, and subsequent events leading to the secession of East Pakistan, which was renamed Bangladesh. As a result, most of my colleagues left the firm to advance their professional careers in the US, and Zafar was forced to explore opportunities in the overseas market including UAE and Libya.

---

[15] In 1971, Bhutto's government selected Qasim Port, thirty miles west of Karachi, in the Province of Sind, for the second port.

Arranged Marriages

All the marriages in our family were arranged by our parents or elders in the family. The eldest brother, Parvez, married Parveen, daughter of (the late) Nazir Ahmed in 1962 while he was in Jeddah, Saudi Arabia.

Shaheen's Marriage (1967)

In 1967, Shaheen married Major Ahsan Yousaf Khan in Karachi. The wedding reception was held on an unbuilt plot adjacent to our 17/F home. My uncle, Group Captain Ghulam Hasan, was again made responsible for the main wedding reception and dinner. I became his deputy for managing the event. The *shamianas* (tents), furniture, and crockery were rented from Ruldoo and Sons and erected on the open ground a day before the reception. Food for over four hundred guests was prepared on the premises by professional chefs. The event was attended by family and friends.

Abba ji at Shaheen Wedding (1967)

Apaji and Bhabi at Shaheen Wedding

Shaheen and Maj. Ahsan Wedding (1967)

Jamshed's Marriage (1968)

The year started with a happy event in our family—the wedding of my second eldest brother, Jamshed, to Tehmina. It was an arranged marriage made possible through my eldest brother, Dr. Parvez Hasan. Jamshed flew to Lahore to meet his future wife just days before the wedding. It was a great source of happiness for my mother, who had not attended the wedding of her eldest son in Saudi Arabia some five years earlier.

Tehmina's parents, Prof. Abdul Hameed and Sakina, belonged to a well-known Kakezai family of Lahore. Sakina was the daughter of Miran Baksh and Amna. Abdul Hameed was a professor of botany at the Government College, Lahore.

Tehmina was the younger sister of Kaukab Shahbaz, who was married to Aitzaz Shabaz of Burma Shell and lived in Karachi. Tehmina came from a large family like ours; it included three brothers—Javed, Parvez, and Asad—as well as maternal and paternal uncles and aunts.

My parents flew to Lahore. The remaining family members including Behram, Yasmin, Mahjabin, and I traveled by train (Tezgam) for seven hundred miles. We were accompanied by the daughters of Aunt Nasim, Farhana, and Safina. The twenty-hour rail journey followed the left bank of the Indus River through Sind and Punjab Provinces making stops in Hyderabad, Nawab Shah, Sukkur/Rohri, Multan, and other places. At every stop, the vendors would storm the train windows offering snacks and beverages that we could buy without leaving our seats. We traveled economy coach class with overhead sleeping berths. Safina, an artist, drew caricatures during the trip.

The wedding lasted several days; it was a big family event. My father, being the eldest brother in his family, enjoyed great respect and love. It was the first wedding that was attended by most of our extended families including paternal and maternal relatives in Lahore.

The wedding was held at 7 A Waris Road under enclosed tents. The gas-heat lamps kept us warm during the cold winter night. The valima function was held in the grounds of my brother's residence at 21 Shah Jamal. I learned several years later that Jamshed had left Chittagong without an approved leave for his marriage. As a result, K. Rehman had sent a telegram to Lahore stating that his employment was terminated. Jamshed took it so casually; he threw the telegram into the waste basket and never mentioned this to any of his siblings, but he mentioned this to my father, whose instincts he trusted. It turned out for the better. Jamshed got a job in West Pakistan and escaped the riots and upheavals that followed in East Pakistan in 1971.

Chacha Ahmed Hasan and Chachijan Akhtar, Behram, Farhana, Rehana (1968)

Chacha Ahmed and Ghulam Hasan with Asad and Bilal (1966)

Abba ji and friends at Jamshed Wedding (1968)

Behram's and Yasmin's Wedding (1969)

Bhaijan was instrumental in making the next two weddings possible. Yasmin married Perwaiz Sheikh, a younger brother of Parveen, who was working in the Tea Gardens of Sylhet, East Pakistan. Behram married Ghazli, the daughter of Rauf and Naseem Malik. Both events were held in Lahore. Ghazli's father, Rauf Malik, was a successful businessman and owned flour and textile mills.

Many years later, Ghazli told me about her marriage proposal. It had been accepted by her parents without consulting her, but she had accepted their decision without hesitation because she trusted them. She, however, did arrange a sneak meeting with Behram made possible by her friends at a movie theater before the wedding. Her parents did not know about this sneak meeting.

Those arranged marriages were successful and vindicated our parents' and elders' decisions in matrimonial matters.

Behram and Ghazli with Apa ji and Auntie Shamim, Bilal and Mahjabin

Perwaiz and Yasmin with family (1969)

Mahjabin's Wedding (1970)

Mahjabin married Allaudin (Ali) Baqai in 1970, which was solemnized at the Beach Luxury Hotel, Karachi. It was an arranged wedding also.

Ali was the younger brother of Dr. Moinuddin Baqai, a close friend and a former colleague of Bhaijan at State Bank. He had graduated from NED College as a civil engineer and later obtained an MS from the University of South Carolina in Columbia. Our families had become quite close over the years being neighbors at the Pakistan Chowk and at the State Bank Flats in Karachi.

Mahjabin and Allauddin Wedding: Bhaijan, Uncle GH, Jamshed, Bilal, Shamim Hasan, Sonia, Air Commodore Ghulam Hasan and Musarrat(1970)

A Business Opportunity Turned Sour

In 1970, a business opportunity arose that might have changed my professional career. Philco-Ford of USA was setting up satellite stations in Karachi and Chittagong. Hussain Nasir, an engineer working for Devcon, approached me with a possibility of securing the contract for constructing the pile foundations for the Chittagong satellite station. We agreed to establish a firm by the name of Nasir Foundation with Allaudin Baqai as managing partner. The five partners contributed Rs.

10,000 as individual equity. We had drilling, boring, and piling equipment fabricated and shipped to Chittagong. We considered this a great business opportunity. Ali flew from Karachi to Chittagong to supervise the work. My sister, Mahjabin, joined him later.

In 1970, the Mujib-ur-Rehman Political Party won the elections as the majority political party of Pakistan with PPP, led by Zulfiqar Ali Bhutto in second place. However, Bhutto failed to yield and wanted to form the central government as prime minister. The elections held under the martial law administrator, Yahya Khan, were considered fair by all parties.

By March 15, 1971, the people of East Pakistan were in a defiant mood. The government–Awami League negotiations held between March 16–24 in 1971 failed to resolve the political issues. General Yahya banned the Awami League and accused Mujib of being an enemy of Pakistan. The Mukti Bahini in East Pakistan decided to agitate against the West Pakistanis in the Eastern Province. Punjabis in particular were the main targets.

Mahjabin and Ali were in Chittagong and were vulnerable targets for Mukti Bahini. They were staying at the Agrabad Hotel. Avery, representing Philco-Ford and overseeing the satellite station construction, was there as well. As the Mukti Bahini agitation grew, the safety of the West Pakistanis became a serious issue in Chittagong. The Mukti Bahini came to the Agrabad Hotel looking for the Baqais. Avery was able to hide the Baqais in a hotel walk-in closet for several days. Avery provided them food and drink from his meals. Mahjabin was expecting a baby in June that year. She recited the Qur'an (*Sura Yasin*) often, and God listened to her prayers.

On March 24, 1971, the Pakistan army launched a military action, Operation Search, to arrest the prominent Awami League leaders, disarm all Bengali troops, control all the naval bases and airfields, ensure the safety of towns, and reestablish the writ of the government. The Baqais were rescued from the hotel. The army major who raided the hotel wanted to be certain that they were indeed from West Pakistan. They did not speak Punjabi, but my sister, due to her physical features, complexion, and light-brown hair, was readily recognizable as hailing from West Pakistan.

Ali and Mahjabin had a miraculous escape from torture or possible death at the hands of Mukti Bahini had they been caught. They safely returned to Karachi via a merchant ship.

No Deal

We were young entrepreneurs with no idea of the road ahead. We had completed our first project under the new firm involving the piling work for the satellite station and were in negotiations for other contracts in Chittagong. During the summer of 1971, an East Pakistani businessman offered to buy our drilling equipment for Rs. 200,000 ($20,000), which was way above our cost. But without consideration or consultation with his partners, Ali rejected the lucrative offer. The Bengali businessman told him rather sarcastically, "You'll have no future in East Pakistan. I'll possess your drilling equipment at no cost."

It turned out that the businessman had been right. Six months later, war broke out with India, and East Pakistan seceded and became an independent nation. Ali and I had been too naïve to foresee the political climate developing that led to the disruption and further instability in East Pakistan. An opportunity had turned sour. It was time to change directions. Ali decided to move. At that time, the US was offering immigrant visas to qualified engineers and doctors. He left for the US in the summer of 1972.

Third War with India

The third war with India took place in November 1971 and resulted in the fall of Dacca to Indian forces on December 16 and the eventual surrender of over 80,000 Pakistan army troops to India. It was a great humiliation.

Captain Ahsan Siddique, my maternal cousin, was deployed in East

Pakistan and fought against the Indian army. His bravery against the enemy was cited even by the Indian chief of staff, Field Marshal Manek Shaw. He was awarded the Sitara-e-Jurat, the third highest military award in Pakistan, for his valor He was also a POW and held by India for a year.

The defense of Kamalpur refers to the battle at Kamalpur near the border in the war of 1971 and the Bangladesh liberation war. The defense of Kamalpur by Captain **Ahsan** Malik and his 140 men would be an epic event in any army's history. He had seventy soldiers of 31 Baloch and the same number of paramilitary troops; all fought magnificently against great odds.

Other POWs in our extended family included General Arif and Masood Mufti. The latter is a prolific writer and has written about the fall of Dacca and POW internment in India. Masood Mufti was married to Bushra Khan, daughter of Shamsa and B. A. Khan. Shamsa (1920–2015) was Sonia's paternal aunt.

A new country Bangladesh was born out of the ashes of East Pakistan in 1971.

A Marriage Made in Heaven

The fall of East Pakistan was otherwise a blessing for me. The parents of my future wife, Sonia, were settled in Chittagong and were very prosperous. Sonia's father, Misbahuddin (M. D.) Ariff, was a prominent businessman and the director of the Ispahani Company's Tea Division. Being an expert tea taster, he was also responsible for blending tea. The East Pakistan riots disrupted their affluent lifestyle, and the family was forced to flee to Lahore in the spring of 1971.

Apa ji had met Sonia at a wedding party in Lahore. She must have been quite impressed with her since she formally asked for her hand on my behalf without even consulting me. I had not seen Sonia or met the family before, and I had no knowledge of this development. Apa ji had proposed through N. D. Yousaf, who was a half-brother of M. D. Ariff.

In the summer of 1972, Sonia and her family moved to Karachi, and we were officially engaged. Sonia and I had one date chaperoned by my younger brother, Owais, a lieutenant in the Pakistan army having graduated from the Kakul Military Academy in the spring of 1971. We drove to the Quaid-e-Azam Mausoleum a few miles away. On the way, our Toyota broke down. I left Owais with the car to see to its towing and returned to Sonia's home in a rickshaw. It was a short date lasting less than an hour.

Prior to the wedding, our families got to know each other. Sonia's father used to affectionately call my mother Mami ji (equivalent to a maternal aunt) because his older half-brother was a real nephew of my father's only sister, Iqbal. My brother Parvez and his family visited from the US. He had joined the World Bank in 1970 and left Pakistan. Also, my uncle Ghulam Hasan and auntie Shamim visited the Ariff family during the summer and fall of 1972.

The wedding took place in January 1973 in Karachi. I became the wedding planner for my wedding making all the wedding arrangements including arranging for wedding dresses for Sonia, jewelry, ordering new furniture, arrangements for the photographer, and the wedding reception at Beach Luxury Hotel. By then, I was used to this after several marriages in the family. This would be last wedding of our family in Karachi.

The wedding was a lavish affair. My near relatives in and outside Pakistan including the family of Bhaijan, Chachas J. H. and G. H., and my sister Shaheen and her husband, Ahsan. Jamshed and Tehmina came from Lahore. Asad Hasan came also. Among my office friends, I. A. Zafar came as well as Fazal Syed, Mian Sahib, Uppal, Abbas Shahid, Shahid, and Najma Sherwani. On Sonia's side, her uncles N. D. Yousaf, S. D. Asif, her aunt Shamsa and B. A. Khan with their children came. Ali missed the wedding since he was in the US. It was a weeklong affair with *mehndi*, *nikah*, wedding, and valima receptions.

On our honeymoon, we traveled through Lahore, Rawalpindi, and Swat. On our way to Saidu Sharif, Swat, we stayed in a rest house. It was January. The snow was several inches deep. Our car, not equipped with snow tires, was stuck on the road. There were no snowplows for removal of snow; however, villagers were more than willing to push our car out of the deep snow.

Owais and Lubna Wedding(1976)

Owais and Lubna Wedding (1976)

Sonia signing the Nikah paper, witnessed by her uncle Dr. Asif (1973)

My Nikah Ceremony- Imam, Perwaiz and Uncle Ariff (1973)

With the Groom Family (1973)

Groom and Bride with family (1973)

With Azim Khan family(1973)

With Naima and Naz(1973)

Valima Reception AT Beach Luxury Hotel (1973)

BA Khan, SD Hanif and ND Yousaf families (1973)

With Hasan Family (1973

With Apa ji, Mami Sakina and Samia (1973)

Chachas Jamil and Ghulam Hasan with nephews (1973)

Sonia with Dad and Aamir at wedding Reception (1973)

Sonia playing with snow in Swat (1973)

Sonmiani Port Project

I was working on the Sonmiani Port Project, a proposed port on the Arabian Sea approximately sixty miles from the Port of Karachi in Baluchistan. Our firm had earlier performed a feasibility study for a well needed second port along the three-hundred-mile coast of Pakistan. While Gwadar and Ormara were natural harbors, they were away from road and rail facilities connecting the hinterland to the port facilities. Additional hydraulic and model studies were being performed to establish the detailed design in consulting with Lackner and Associates, a West German firm specializing in the design of ports.

A visit to the site would consume a full day. We had to cross the Hub River and wade through knee-deep water since there was no bridge. The road was a single-lane highway with unpaved shoulders. The final eight miles to the site was a track only. A four-wheel vehicle was a necessity. The German hydraulic specialist, Ing. Kohl, was in Karachi. We would make the trip together often.

The Pakistan government headed by Zulfiqar Ali Bhutto decided to build a port in Sind instead, barely twenty miles from the existing port. It was a political decision. Some thirty years later, a port at Gwadar would be built with the help of the Chinese with new infrastructure links to the hinterland.

Marriage Realities

Marriage brings forth new realities and thinking. While I was happy in my job with Zafar and Associates, I was unsure of the political climate and my long-term professional development working for a private engineering firm with a sole owner, which was typical for the entire country. The work was awarded more based on contacts and less on merit. The political climate put a damper on economic growth. There were a few large engineering firms outside the government agencies WAPDA or CONSULTPAK. I had been working in Pakistan for six years. It was time to explore other opportunities.

During the summer of 1973, as Sonia vacationed with her parents in Ceylon and Singapore, I decided to explore a return to the US. I wrote to Ebasco for employment with the firm. I had been in touch with the staff at Ebasco CH Department. Andrew A. Ferlito (AAF) had replaced John Scarola as chief. He offered me a job in the CH Department as senior engineer starting at $1,500 per month. It was indeed great news. It seemed as if AAF was waiting to hear from me.

When Sonia returned from her Far East trip, I shared the news with her. Initially, she was reluctant to go, but her father apparently convinced her, and she agreed to go for a year. We did not know what lay ahead. Sometimes, our actions unbeknown to us are dictated by a higher authority.

Becoming an Immigrant

I was eligible to return to the US as an immigrant along with my family any time.

Earlier in 1965, Ebasco's HR Department had submitted a petition on my behalf to the US Immigration and Naturalization Service during my employment there. This petition was approved, and I had been notified of that by the US Embassy in 1967.

I applied for the immigration visa at the US Consulate in Karachi. The application required character verification and police, educational, and health records for Sonia and me, but before too long, our travel plans were finalized. Our recently purchased bedroom furniture, the car, and other items had to be sold to generate the travel funds including a vacation in Europe.

The 1968 Toyota Corona was sold for Rs. 40,000 ($4,000). The car was over five years old and had cost Rupees22,000. I got the price I wanted, which surprised my mother-in-law, Duroo. The proceeds were adequate for our travel including a two-week vacation in Europe.

In October, after emotional goodbyes with family, we embarked on our memorable trip that would take us through Rome, Paris, Madrid, and London for nearly three weeks. I was really excited that I could share my memories of Europe with Sonia.

In those days, communication was mainly through mail, and there were no cell phones. I had written to Khalid and Imrana, Sonia's first cousin, who was stationed in London, about our flight information and arrival date. If there were change in plans, I had to notify them via telephone, an expensive proposition.

When we got to Rome, we called Khalida Apa, but there was no response; Nazir Bhaijan and his family were away for the weekend, so we checked into a hotel. A day later, Nazir showed up and took us to their EUR apartment. He and Khalida Apa were gracious hosts. At the end of our stay lasting three days, he dropped us off at the airport.

Paris

Our next stop was Paris, where we stayed at the Champs-Élysées Hotel. Over the next three days, we visited Notre Dame Cathedral, Pigalle, and of course the nightclubs. Paris is a haunting city; it grows on us with every visit. Climbing to the top of Notre Dame reminded us of Anthony Quinn in *The Hunchback of Notre Dame* hanging onto the rope of its huge bell.

Madrid

Madrid is as historic as Rome or Paris. It's famous museum, the Prado, large boulevards, and statues of kings and queens display its past grandeur. Its known for its margaritas, olives, flamenco dancing, and bullfights. The bullfight season was over. Sonia did not enjoy the olive-based food; it made her nauseous. We left for London on Iberia Airlines.

London

We stayed in Wimbledon, the famous suburb of London, where the annual tennis tournament is held. Khalid and Imrana with their new-born, Abid, lived in a detached, three-bedroom house and were quite settled. Khalid was working for BCCI. They were extremely hospitable and generous to us and showed us around London including a visit to the Buckingham Palace, Trafalgar Square, and Madame Tussauds. Sonia went shopping on Oxford Street.

London is like a second home for Indians and Pakistanis with its English language. The British ruled the subcontinent for over a hundred years and left a legacy of love and hate.

Our memorable vacation ended sooner that we had thought. We were also out of money as well when we arrived in New York. I had to get back to work.

Chapter 7

THE EBASCO STORY

The Power of a Dream

The story of Ebasco is rooted in the powerful dream of Thomas Alva Edison (1847–1931), a great American inventor who was the first to harness electrical energy and demonstrate lighting systems in streets and buildings in Menlo Park, New Jersey.

A dream of Thomas Edison Dream (1879 Plaque)

Ebasco Headquarter at Two Rector Street NYC

Wikipedia offers a detailed history of Ebasco.

The Electric Bond and Share Company (Ebasco) was organized by General Electric and prior to its breakup was the largest electric power Holding company in the United States. In 1905 it was a wholly owned subsidiary of General Electric Company (GE).

In 1924, GE divested itself of Ebasco and it became a public-owned company.

In 1927, Ebasco moved to Two Rector Street adjacent to the Trinity Church in the Financial District in downtown Manhattan. It's a 24-story prewar building which came to be known as the Ebasco Building. Ebasco' s headquarters in New York City had over 1,000 employees, and it controlled companies in 33 states worth $1.25 billion.

Ebasco was forced to divest its holding companies and reorganize due to the passage of the Public Utility Holding Company Act of 1935. Ebasco filed suit against the Act, claiming it was unconstitutional but lost. The Securities and Exchange Commission ordered the break-up of Ebasco' s holding companies known as American Power & Light Corp. that included 35 subsidiaries and the Electric Power & Light Corporation with its 24 subsidiaries, until they conformed with the 1935 act. Ebasco could retain control of its foreign electric power holding company known as the American & Foreign Power Company (A&FP).

After its reorganization, the company evolved into a major design and engineering company of both fossil fuel and hydroelectric power generation facilities. It was the leading engineering and construction company, in the early part of the 20th Century completing the first hydroelectric station at Buckhorn for Carolina Power and Light Company in 1908, the first steam station in Texas in 1914, and later, the first nuclear power plant in Italy in 1963.

Ebasco had become one of the major US architect-engineers, coordinating the design of many nuclear power plants both in the US and abroad. On May 22nd, 1956 Ebasco' s subsidiary, American & Foreign Power Co. announced plans to build two nuclear power facilities in Latin America, very likely in Cuba since they held 100% of the country's electric production. Other major nuclear construction plans included the Tsuruga and Fukushima Nuclear Power Plants in Japan and Chin Shan Units 1 &2 in Taiwan as well as consulting work for a nuclear plant in Spain.

As the firm grew in 1960's during the advent of Nuclear Era, it added space in other offices at 19 Rector and 21 West Street. It became the gold standard in the Power Industry. It was extremely successful as the premier US based architect-engineering company, performing all aspects of Licensing, design engineering, purchasing and construction management of many nuclear power plants both in the USA and abroad.

In 1980, Ebasco consolidated its three downtown locations and moved to the Two World Trade Center (WTC), leasing 14 floors totaling 591,000 square feet, between 77 and 93 floors.

By the 1980s, EBASCO had three divisions: EBASCO Engineering, which provided engineering design and A/E services, EBASCO Environmental, which provided environmental engineering and science services, and EBASCO Constructors, which provided construction and construction management.

Prior to the 1993 bombing at the WTC, Ebasco had moved some of the offices to Lyndhurst and to Princeton, NJ and downsized its presence at the WTC.

From an initial focus on the Power Business, designing steam, hydro, and nuclear power plants, the firm was later diversified in the 1980's and was engaged in the design and construction of Infrastructure Projects, including Bridges, Tunnels, Dams and Water Resources.

In 1994, Ebasco was acquired by Raytheon Corporation for approximately $210 million in cash and was merged with the Raytheon Engineers and Constructors. EBASCO Environmental was sold to Foster Wheeler, Inc., becoming Foster Wheeler Environmental.[16]

At the time of the 9/11 terrorist attack in 2001, Ebasco had downsized its Manhattan office to 190 employees after expanding its offices in Princeton, New Jersey. The limited loss of lives (thirteen) on 9/11 as described in chapter 1 was a result of the transfer of staff to other offices and staff attrition.

In 2000, Raytheon sold the engineering and construction business to Washington Group International (WGI) for $730 million. WGI had approximately 25,000 employees in over forty states and more than thirty countries. Its primary areas of expertise were infrastructure, mining, industrial/process, energy and environment, and power. It was acquired by URS of San Francisco for $3.1 billion in November 2007. As of June 2013, URS had more than 50,000 employees worldwide in nearly fifty countries. In 2014, URS was acquired by AECOM.

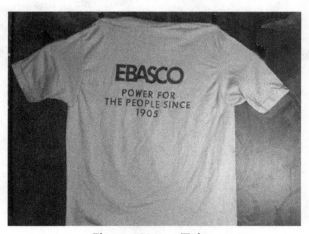

Ebasco 100-year T-shirt

---

[16] http://en.wikipedia.org/wiki/Ebasco_Services.

*Commemorating The 100th Anniversary
of The Founding of Electric Bond & Share Company
1905-2005
The Ebasco 25-Year Club June 4, 2005*

100-year History of Ebasco Project Photos

1983 Ebasco Services 25-year Award Dinner

1986 Ebasco 25-year Club Luncheon

Nuclear Power Era—A Personal Remembrance

The 1970s was a significant period for accelerated construction of nuclear power plants in the US. Ebasco was responsible for engineering design for nuclear plants in Louisiana, Florida, North Carolina, Texas, Tennessee, and Washington. Ebasco's nuclear projects extended to the mid-1990s with retrofits mandated by the Nuclear Regulatory Commission (NRC).

AAF was the chief engineer in the Concrete Hydraulics Department of Ebasco when I rejoined the firm in 1973. As a result of organizational changes during the nuclear era, the CH and Structural Departments were merged in 1979, and Joe Ehasz became the chief civil engineer. Joe headed a large group of civil engineers and designers assisted by George Kanakaris, Allan Wern, and Enver Odar as deputies from 1979 to 1991. Kanakaris was the chief civil engineer from 1991 to 2001. Odar also headed the Special Analysis Group and later became a project director for the retrofit nuclear projects.

I was involved with the civil engineering design of the nuclear projects from 1974 to 1986. I was the staff engineer and a specialist in concrete technology in the Civil Department, which enabled me to work on several of the firm's nuclear projects including Waterford Unit 3 in New Orleans, St. Lucie Unit 2 in Fort Pierce, Florida, WPPSS Units 3 and 5 in Olympia, Washington, and Shearon Harris Units 1–4 (later downsized to one unit) in Raleigh, North Carolina.

Nuclear plants are very complex and conservatively designed to be structurally strong with redundant mechanical, electrical, and instrumental components. The primary and secondary shields of nuclear plants are made of heavily reinforced concrete to capture the gamma rays emitted by the splitting of atoms in a reactor. The primary shield wall houses the nuclear reactor and auxiliary equipment including cooling pumps. The secondary shield building is circular in design, 180–200 feet in diameter and extending over ten stories in height with a hemispherical dome to accommodate the steam generators and other equipment. The building is topped with a dome roof and is designed to absorb impacts from tornados, missiles, and aircraft. The secondary shield building concrete structure is constructed by a slip-forming process, which allows for speedier construction. The concrete in a nuclear plant may require as much as 200,000 cubic yards and 6 million pounds of steel reinforcement. It is built like a fortress.

The several phases of a nuclear project from the initial prefeasibility to the final construction require detailed environmental and licensing issues governed by the NRC. This entire process usually takes six to ten years, which in turn subjects the project personnel to various emotions ranging from enthusiasm to exhaustion.

Project Phase	Result
Prefeasibility	Enthusiasm
Feasibility	Exuberance
Design/ Regulatory Delays	Disillusionment
Construction Issues/Delays	Panic and Hysteria/Change in Personnel
Completion	Exhaustion

I found the above to be generally true during my professional life.

Waterford Nuclear Plant, New Orleans

New Orleans is unique. The French Quarter boasts of excellent cuisine and jazz music; it is a place for fun. People cruse on the Mississippi River on traditional paddleboats.

Waterford Unit 3 was the third power plant on the site following two fossil-fuel units on the river. The site was adjacent to the river levee, which protected the low-lying landscape.

New Orleans is below river level and is protected by an elaborate levee system on both riverbanks as well as Lake Pontchartrain to prevent inundation. The city was flooded severely by the disastrous Hurricane Katrina in 2005 that caused a severe breach of the levees and inundated the city for months with heavy loss of property. The city was virtually uninhabitable for several years.

My first visit to New Orleans was in 1974; I was accompanied by Ping Chiu Liu (PCL, but generally known as PC), who was the civil lead. We witnessed the installation of the common mat foundation for the nuclear plant island structure. PC and I became good friends as we worked together and traveled often to the jobsite.

We usually stayed north of the city at a Holiday Inn. The site was accessible via the Huey P. Long road and rail bridge over the Mississippi. The bridge, the only link between New Orleans and the west bank, Gretna, provided an overview of the historic French Quarter. The bridge was long with narrow lanes, and the usually heavy traffic during the rush hours challenged motorists, who shared the road with trucks. There was a local ferry crossing for vehicles also, which was very slow during rush hour owing to its limited capacity.

Our favorite restaurant those days was a steak house, Ichabod, in the French Quarter. PC and I would relish twelve- to sixteen-ounce sirloin steaks. Following dinner, we would walk the streets, generally limited to pedestrian traffic, stop in at small clubs, and listen to the jazz music of Al Hirt, the well-known musician.

During the day, we would watch the concrete placement in the large common foundation for the reactor building and other category I, safety-related structures. Due to poor alluvial soil conditions and a high groundwater table, the common mat was ten feet thick and was provided with a waterproofing liner on the exterior.

Sonia would often join me on such trips for up to two weeks at a time. I could not afford to pay her roundtrip airfare between New York and New Orleans, which cost several hundred dollars, but our company allowed engineers to travel first class since we often traveled in the evening, and I learned from my colleagues that I could exchange my first-class ticket for two economy-class tickets at no additional cost, and that allowed Sonia to join me on extended trips.

We usually stayed at the Gretna Holiday Inn on the west bank. During check-in, the hotel clerk would routinely list two guests in the register for billing. I was unaware that the number of guests would appear on the invoice as well. I submitted my expense account (including receipts for lodging, car rental, etc.) to AAF for approval after returning from a trip. He called me into his office. He was looking at my lodging receipt attached to the expense account. "Nash, I assume the other guest on your hotel bill was your wife?" I was stunned and dumbfounded, but I answered in the affirmative. AAF told me that he would process it for payment but that the client might refuse to pay for the additional guest. He was politely advising me to refrain from including the second guest on the hotel bill.

I found out that the difference in cost between a single guest and two guests was $1.88 per night in the 1970s. After this incident, I made sure that the clerk would exclude the second guest and create a separate bill for my wife, which I paid. AAF never questioned my travel expenses afterward. I cannot forget how discreetly my superior reprimanded me and gave me a lesson in ethics.

I was also in New Orleans during Mardi Gras, Fat Tuesday, in February. The French Quarter comes alive with visitors from all over the US and even abroad. The festivity extends for several days with exuberant parades and spectators, excessive drinking, and lewd behavior. A large contingent of police, though tolerant, prevent any extreme behavior.

The girls and women standing in the balconies above the streets in the French Quarter would shower the crowd below with plastic beads as souvenirs and offer inviting gestures to the passers-by. It is a unique experience of entertainment expressed during this festival, which marks the beginning of Lent in the Christian calendar.

A milestone during construction was the completion of the secondary shield building, two hundred feet in diameter and rising some ten stories above the foundation. The four-foot-thick reinforced concrete structure was slip-formed continuously at the rate of six to eighteen inches per hour. It was perhaps one of the first shield buildings constructed in this manner. The slip-forming operation was facilitated with continuously moving formwork equipped with jacks embedded in the concrete.

St. Lucie Nuclear Plant, Unit 2, Fort Pierce, Florida

AAF directed Leopold Gertler and me to oversee the slip-forming of the shield building for Unit 2. Leopold Gertler (Leo) was a senior colleague in the Civil Group. James P. Burket was the civil lead engineer and was already on site for the slip-forming operation.

I flew from JFK to West Palm Beach via a direct flight. Renting a car, I drove through West Palm Beach lined with palm trees, manicured lawns, and gated estates on Route A1-A to Fort Pierce, where the nuclear plants were.

It was fall, but at night, the mosquitos were vicious in areas inaccessible to the sea breeze. Leo and I took turns witnessing the around-the-clock slip-forming operation. The area was well lit. The high vantage point of the building allowed a view of the Atlantic Ocean to the east and the Indian River to the west. We were there to expeditiously resolve any field change requests or other deviation requests from the design specification to facilitate construction.

Satsop Nuclear Plants (WPPSS) Unit 3 and 5, Olympia, Washington

Ebasco was involved in the design and construction of the Washington Public Power Supply System (WPPSS) Units 3 and 5. I was involved in overseeing concrete mixtures design, selection, and testing, and I made many trips to the site. The New York–Seattle transcontinental flights were long and tiring particularly the return flights at night known as redeye flights. The units were 70 percent complete in 1983 when the financial collapse of the Washington Public Power Supply System's bonds occurred and they became worthless. It was a shocking experience.

Corrective Action Plans for the Nuclear Plants

From the early 1980s through the 1990s, Ebasco was engrossed in providing services to implement the monumental and unprecedented activities of the Corrective Action Plan (CAP) in assisting utilities in obtaining fuel-loading permits and operating licenses, which were initially denied due to whistleblower allegations of unsafe design conditions and formal objections by intervening groups. Ebasco involvement in the CAP at Comanche Peak and Watts Bar Nuclear Stations, owned by Texas Utilities (TU) and Tennessee Valley Authority (TVA) respectively, is provided below.

Comanche Peak Nuclear Power Station, Glen Rose, Texas

Comanche Peak Nuclear Power Station (CPNPS) Units 1 and 2 are southwest of Dallas and Fort Worth near Glen Rose, Texas. Each unit is a pressurized water reactor and rated at 1150 MW. The construction of Unit 1 began in 1974, but the operating license was denied due to allegations by a few whistleblowers that the design and the construction of the plant structures, systems, and components were not safe. The whistleblowers worked through an intervenor, Citizens' Association for Sound Energy (CASE). The Atomic Safety and Licensing Board was formed to monitor the situation, and CASE was a part of that board. The edict was that the utility was to perform a complete reevaluation of and as necessary correct all aspects of design and engineering, generate backup calculations and other paperwork to support and document the reevaluation and redesigns, and perform a complete, independent validation of the installation. This called for an unprecedented, enormous, and very expensive effort that was implemented in two-prongs: design validation and postconstruction hardware validation.

Ebasco was one of the three companies working on these projects. At the height of the effort, Ebasco had close to 1,400 engineers, designers, CAD operators, and other support personnel working at Glen Rose and its home offices. As part of their efforts, Ebasco also provided subject-matter experts to a number of hearings to defend the work performed and to keep CASE informed of progress made.

Unit 1 was finally granted an operating license, and fuel was loaded in April 1990 followed by Unit 2. CPNPS was the next to the last nuclear plant to operate in the United States.

Watts Bar Nuclear Power Station, Knoxville, Tennessee

Watts Bar Nuclear Power Station, Units 1 and 2, was thirty-five miles southwest of Knoxville in Spring City. Its pressurized water reactors utilize containment ice condenser technology. The reactor and the nuclear steam supply system were provided by Westinghouse. Unit 1 started construction in July 1973. Cost overruns, reduced power demand, and other factors resulted in TVA's stopping construction in 1985.

In 1992, with the concurrence of NRC, a corrective action plan to validate the existing design and an upgrade to the latest requirements and to demonstrate the adequacy of the existing structures, systems, and components of Unit 1 was initiated. Ebasco, with TVA engineers, performed the various components of the CAP to demonstrate the adequacy of the completed program. The 1167 MW Unit 1 went online in May 1996. Unit 2 was given an operating license later.

Watts Bar units have a distinction of being the last nuclear power plants in the US.

Three Mile Island Nuclear Plant

Refer to https://quizlet.com/206495772/science-flash-cards/

The Three Mile Island (TMI) accident was a partial meltdown of reactor unit 2 (TMI-2) of Three Mile Island Nuclear Generating Station in Dauphin County, Pennsylvania, near Harrisburg, and subsequent radiation leak that occurred in 1979. It was the most significant accident in U.S. commercial nuclear power plant history.

Refer to https://www.world-nuclear.org/information-library/safety-and-security/safety-of-plants/three-mile-island-accident.aspx

The accident at unit 2 happened at 4 am on 28 March 1979 when the unit 2 reactor was operating at 97%. The cooling malfunction led to partial meltdown of the core. The reactor did shutdown automatically, but the relief valve failed to close, leading to release of some radioactive material.

The 1979 accident at the TMI nuclear plant became a doomsday scenario for the nuclear power industry, which never recovered from the negative public opinion generated by this accident. The release of a small amount of radioactive material into the atmosphere caused panic about the safety of such plants, which was never overcome by the facts supporting the plant's safety.[17]

As a result of the TMI accident, the NRC ordered the utility companies to develop means to neutralize hydrogen buildups inside nuclear reactors.

Ironically, the TMI accident was preceded by the 1979 movie *The China Syndrome* starring Jane Fonda and Jack Lemmon, which aroused negative publicity by those opposed to nuclear plants. In this movie, the safety operations of a nuclear plant were shown to be distorted and compromised by crooked individuals.

Chernobyl Power Plant

Refer to https://rayharris57.wordpress.com/2016/04/27/chernobyl-birds-dropping-out-of-the-sky/

On 26 April 1986, reactor four suffered a catastrophic power increase, leading to explosions in its core. As the reactor had not been encased by any kind of hard containment vessel, this dispersed large quantities of radioactive isotopes into the atmosphere and caused an open-air fire that increased the emission of radioactive particles carried by the smoke. The accident occurred during an experiment scheduled to test the viability of a potential safety emergency core cooling feature, which required a normal reactor shutdown procedure.

The Chernobyl Power Complex, about 130 kilometers (81 miles) north of Kiev, Ukraine, and about 20 kilometers south of the border with Belarus, consisted of four nuclear reactors of the 1000 MW design. Units 1 and 2 were constructed between 1970 and 1977, while units 3 and 4 of the same design were completed in 1983.

---

[17] Three Mile Island, Wikipedia.

- The Chernobyl accident in 1986 was the result of a flawed reactor design that was operated with inadequately trained personnel.
- The resulting steam explosion and fires released at least 5% of the radioactive reactor core into the environment, with the deposition of radioactive materials in many parts of Europe.
- Two Chernobyl plant workers died due to the explosion on the night of the accident, and a further 28 people died within a few weeks as a result of acute radiation syndrome.
- Some 350,000 people were evacuated as a result of the accident, but resettlement of areas from which people were relocated is ongoing.[18]

The 1986 Chernobyl accident was a catastrophic nuclear accident that perhaps was a huge setback and a major factor in the demise of the nuclear industry. The plumes of the radioactive material, which covered the town of Pripyat and out 150 miles, remained active for more than thirty years.

Nuclear Plant Maintenance, Upgrades, and Spent-Fuel Storage

In early 2000, the Nuclear Group of the company was involved with the maintenance of the operating plants with the implementation of mandatory upgrades and with design, licensing, and construction of the sites' independent spent-fuel storage installations (ISFSI). With the absence of expected and federally provided spent-fuel storage and repository facilities and with the cancelation of the work at the Yucca Mountain repository facilities in Nevada, the utilities with operating nuclear plants were faced with a huge dilemma. The in-plant spent-fuel storage capacities were rapidly diminishing and urgently required a near-term storage solution that involved transferring the spent fuel in specially designed storage casks and storing them in the protected area of the plants on heavy, safety-related, reinforced, concrete storage slabs.

The company provided the design, licensing, and construction

---

[18] https://www.world-nuclear.org/ … /safety-of-plants/chernobyl-accident.aspx. Updated April 2020.

support services to various utilities including ISFSI pads at the Peach Bottom, Limerick, and Fermi 2 nuclear plants as well as related modifications for the spent-fuel transfer and transport to the cask storage areas.

Demise of the Nuclear Plant Industry

Some factors responsible for the early demise of the nuclear industry were cost overruns caused by evolving design enhancements as a follow-up of the TMI accident mandated by NRC regulations. In addition, the public opposition to the plants by the whistleblower allegations and intervenors was the fatal blow.

In fairness, it should be noted that the actual performance of a nuclear plant designed for a life expectancy of forty years and its safety and reliability have been better than expected. However, the issue of the safe disposal of spent fuel has yet to be resolved.

After the 9/11 attack on the WTC, the safety of the nuclear plants being subjected to a Boeing 757 plane hit and the debate of a catastrophic nuclear accident was revived. The thirty-six-year-old Indian Point Nuclear Plant on the Hudson River in Westchester, thirty miles north of New York, owned by Con Edison, had its share of safety concerns, and one of its reactors was given the lowest safety rating by the NRC. After 9/11, plant critics, activists, assorted dissident scientists, and not-in-my-backyard public officials joined hands in raising fear of a nuclear catastrophe. While the nuclear plant has a lot of safeguards to protect it, the attack from air by a large plane was never postulated for the Indian Point nuclear units.

Infrastructure and Water Resources Projects

With the reduction and slowdown of nuclear projects in the US, Ebasco refocused on infrastructure and water resources projects. During the post- nuclear period, some of the notable infrastructure projects handled by the AECOM legacy firms included the following.

Sidney A. Murray Jr. Hydroelectric Station

Sidney A Murray Hydroelectric Project, Vidalia, LA (1991)

Sidney A Murray Preassembled Plant Structure Floating to its site

Ebasco completed a five-year, lump-sum, turnkey contract to engineer, design, and construct the S. A. Murray Jr. Hydroelectric Station. This 192 MW facility was the nation's largest low-head power plant. The plant consisted of eight bulb turbine generators with twenty-seven-foot-diameter runners, the world's largest at that time, with operating heads ranging from eight to twenty feet between the Mississippi River and the Old River control outflow channel.

The steel structure for the power plant was built in a shipyard and towed to the site on the Mississippi River thereby allowing simultaneous construction of the powerhouse and foundation and reducing the time and money required by conventional construction methods. The hydroelectric complex was to be integrated into the existing Army Corps of Engineers' Old River control system. As a result, all design was completed in accordance with the pertinent Army Corps of Engineers' standards.

The project involved in part a 5,000-foot intake channel from the Mississippi and a 9,000-foot outlet channel to the Old River overflow channel, relocation of 5,000 feet of levee, and construction of 4,000 feet of new levees requiring over 2.5 million cubic yards of dry excavation and 15 million cubic yards of dredged excavation.

Bi-County Tunnel Water Tunnel Project, Maryland

Ebasco provided design and construction management services for the Washington Suburban Sanitary Commission (WSSC) Bi-County Tunnel Rehabilitation carrying drinking water from the Potomac River to Prince George County in Maryland. As part of the design, annulus grouting between the steel and concrete lining was performed successfully. The project won an award from the local ACI chapter.

WSSC Bi-County Tunnel Rehabilitation Design
Team (1993) Author receiving ACI award

San Roque Multipurpose Project, Philippines

San Roque Multipurpose Project in Philippines (2002)

The 200-meter-(650-foot) high San Roque Dam on the lower Agno River on Luzon Island, Philippines, was completed in 2002. The earth and rockfill dam, the twelfth highest in the world, is one of several major features of the San Roque Multipurpose Water Resource and Hydroelectric Project. The project's three diversion tunnels were plugged, and the impounding of the San Roque Reservoir began on August 8, 2002. On November 19, 2002, the 345 MW power plant synchronized with the National Power Corporation (NPC) grid with electric generation was transmitted for the first time, just four years and eight months after the initiation of the design.

Through its legacy firm, AECOM provided engineering, procurement, and construction for this massive project under a complete turnkey, lump-sum, fixed price, design and build contract.

Rainbow Hydroelectric Redevelopment

AECOM, through its legacy firm, provided all civil, structural, mechanical, and electrical engineering design, preparation of plans, specifications, and studies in support of the redevelopment of the Rainbow Dam hydroelectric facilities. The design package for the general construction contract was completed early in 2010. AECOM, through its legacy firm, provided construction management and engineering during construction for the project and managed the replacement of substations at other nearby PPL-owned hydroelectric plants and the replacement of associated transmission lines in the Great Falls area. The project was completed in 2013.

AECOM Hydro Team for Rainbow Hydro Project (1912)

Ebasco Colleagues Remembered

Ihsan Ul Bari. Ihsan was my colleague at Ebasco. Our paths crossed in 1966 in London, when he was coming to the US and I was returning to Pakistan. When I immigrated to the US, he was working in the Concrete Hydraulics Department of Ebasco. He married an Iranian, Mahwash, and had two beautiful girls. Subsequently, he was posted in Mexico and worked as the civil lead on the Lugana Verde Nuclear plant on the Gulf of Mexico in the 1990s.

One afternoon, the entire family was at the beach in knee-deep water. The undertow was strong, and Mahwash found herself being dragged away by the strong currents. She shouted for help. Ihsan went to save her and brought her back to safety. Meanwhile, he suffered a heart attack and lost his balance. He was swept away by waves. There was no lifeguard on duty there. I had lost an old friend who was working hard and looking forward to a brighter future for his family.

Frank Bakes. Frank was a civil engineer who migrated from Slovakia. He left Ebasco and worked in New Jersey with Burns and Roe. He specialized in power plants' circulating water systems.

In 1995, on a visit to Seoul, South Korea, he became a victim of one of the deadliest accidental building collapses. The Sampoon Department Store, opened in 1990, was a popular mall that attracted over 40,000 people per day. Another floor was added in the early 1990s.

He was in the store to purchase gifts for his family before returning home to the US when the roof of the store gave way. The entire five floors collapsed within a minute or so. Over 502 people died. Many survivors were pulled to safety, even some fifty hours after the collapse.

Frank Bakes was not one of them. He was only fifty-eight. His wife, Maria, became a widow. His dreams remained unfulfilled.

John R. Fotheringham. Another colleague with whom I shared good memories was Dick Fotheringham. It was a coincidence that when I first joined Ebasco, I sat at his desk; he was away on US Navy Reserve duty. I knew him by his nameplate. When I returned to the US in 1973, I sat across from him at 21 West Street. He was handsome, humorous, and humane. He commuted from Asbury Park, New Jersey, every day, a train journey that took him two hours each way. Even then, he was always in the office before others.

He was the lead civil on the St. Lucie Nuclear Plant in Florida. He owned a boat and would spend time on it during weekends sailing and maintaining it. When an opportunity arose in 1978, he transferred to the Ebasco West Coast Office with his sailboat; that was agreed to by Andrew Ferlito, our chief concrete-hydraulic engineer.

After 9/11 destroyed our offices and my entire technical library, he thoughtfully sent me some design documents I had lost with a note, "I hope this replenishes some of your losses." I had not even asked him for the missing documents. It was a purely voluntary and considerate action. I will not forget his humanity.

In 2005, he was managing the firm's Seattle office and was involved with the Swift hydro project. I met him briefly there. He had lost weight and appetite. He had been diagnosed with pancreatic cancer and died shortly after. Even in his last days, he smiled. He was a brave soldier. I lost an old friend. His wife, Patricia, lost a devoted husband. Their children, Ross and Susan, lost a loving father.

Satindar Sethi. Satindar hailed from the Indian subcontinent. We both came from middle-class families and sought better lives in the US.

Satindar graduated with a BS in electrical engineering from Pilani, India. It was always his intention to seek a better life in the US as one of his older brothers had done. However, he put off prospects of his own marriage and career to support his parents and sisters until they were married with dowries. He married Gargi and came to New York in 1970.

He was a hardworking, ambitious, and aspiring individual. He joined Ebasco and settled in Staten Island. When I moved to Staten Island in 1976, we became neighbors as well as friends.

Their children, Shikha and Puneet, were encouraged to excellence by Satinder and Gargi. They graduated from Tottenville High School and Staten Island Tech at the top of their respective classes; both attended Harvard University. Shikha became a doctor and married in 2000.

Gargi's father, K. L. Sabhrawal, lived with the family. Though he was in poor health, he was an optimistic individual. He loved his grandchildren. He and I enjoyed talking in our native Punjabi language.

When the 1993 WTC bombing occurred, Satinder was also stranded in the South Tower. He immediately called home that there was an electrical problem and that he would be home early. However, he did not reach home until much later. He was covered in soot from walking down eighty-four flights of emergency staircases and assisting others. Gargi was astonished and remarked, "Kya Hua? Bhoot bun key Aaiy Ho," "What happened? You look like a black ghost."

Prior to the 9/11 attack, Satindar had left Ebasco after the company was acquired by Raytheon and pursued investments in local businesses and real estate; therefore, he did not suffer the agony that those colleagues who continued working in the WTC did; he was vacationing on an Alaskan cruise at the time. As a result of 9/11, domestic flights were canceled, and he stayed in Vancouver for several days before returning home.

Throughout their time together in the US, Satindar and Gargi invested a great deal of time, effort, and savings to assist family members emigrating from India. Satinder encouraged and supported his family, friends, and even assiduous strangers and invested in their education and their careers. Satinder was a major donor to the reconstruction of the local YMCA as well as a donor to Arsha Vidya Gurukulam and to the establishment of the Staten Island Hindu Temple, where he was a board member. After 2010, Satinder was afflicted with an undiagnosed neurological disorder that gradually worsened. His community, friends, and family gave him loving support until he passed away far too early in 2014.

Leopold Gertler (1927–2017). Another colleague I came to know personally was Leo. I first met him in 1973. His desk was across an aisle in the Ebasco 21 West Street office. He had just completed the Ludington Pumped Storage Project in Michigan, which was ranked the best engineering project in 1972.

I always enjoyed his company though he was several years older than me. He was a straight person and disliked backstabbers and malicious schemers. His family was a survivor of the Holocaust during Hitler's regime.

He was born in Romania and had immigrated to the US with his wife, Coca, in the 1960s.

He was an engineer's engineer; he covered all design aspects with thoroughness and an eye to perfection. During the late 1980s, Leo was the project engineer on the Sidney A. Murray (Vidalia) Hydro Project in Louisiana assisted by Edward O'Connor and John Kwan as leads. I was responsible for the concrete design specification for filling the cavities of the PPS with over 100,00 cubic yards of flowing concrete.

We often took trips to construction sites together. On October 19, 1987, Leo, George Kanakaris, and I were in New Orleans, where the preassembled power plant was being fabricated at the Avondale Shipyard.

One night, George Kanakaris joined Leo and me for dinner at a Cajun restaurant. George asked,. "Have you heard the news? The stock market has tanked."

The stock market had indeed crashed. It was the worst drop in its history. The Dow Jones Index had fallen 508 points, 22.6 percent—big news. The economic recovery from an earlier recession had been going on for several years. At that time, my investments were limited to Ebasco's investment plan. My heart sank a bit. But then I realized, *I have an important job at hand. The market will come back.* This rationale calmed me, and we continued with the dinner consisting of fried crawfish, a New Orleans delicacy, and Cajun food. I remember that Leo was particular about the sauces and ingredients in the food and always checked before ordering an entrée. I have relished spicy Cajun food in New Orleans since the 1970s, when I often ate in the French Quarter during the construction of Waterford Unit 3.

Leo was the backbone of our design team responsible for the hydro development at the San Roque Project. His experience in tunneling, penstock design, and powerhouse design was invaluable for a fast-track completion.

Coca, his wife, was his love and passion. When she called the office, he always answered it immediately giving no regard to the matter at hand; he never made her wait to talk to him.

When 9/11 occurred, he was vacationing on Long Island. Coca had asked him a few days before, "Why don't we go away for a few days?" That surprised Leo; Coca had never asked him something like that. Normally, he never took off from work except for a scheduled vacation.

Leo thought for a moment and agreed to take a few days off. Coca thinks that God had directed her.

During the 1993 WTC bombing, Leo and Coca had been away from the city as well. It is rather unusual that Leo was an absentee survivor of both attacks.

He retired in 2015. His empty desk at 1 Penn Plaza remained unoccupied until we moved to another floor. He had a heart attack in July 2017. He was in rehabilitation for few days. God gave him enough time to sort out his financial affairs. He was recovering well. Then on August 1, 2017, he called Coca to come. By the time she reached the rehab unit, Leo had passed away.

Murray Weber (1921–2018). Murray Weber was born on September 10, 1921, in New York. He graduated from City College in 1942 with a BS in civil engineering. He served the US Army as an engineer during World War II. He married Doris in 1946; their marriage lasted seventy-two years.

They had two daughters and a son, who had five children. Most members of the family are working as teachers or professors at US universities.

Murray joined Ebasco in 1970 as supervising engineer for the St. Lucie Nuclear Plants in Florida. Upon their commissioning, he headed the structural design team responsible for the Shearon Harris Nuclear Project 1973–1987. He was a responsible professional engineer who would thoroughly review all the design details that could affect construction. I accompanied him during the construction of the Shield Building at Shearon Harris. He was an experienced engineer who could resolve construction issues in a timely fashion. Anis Baig, an engineer at Ebasco, remembers some good advice he received from Murray: "Don't sign a drawing unless you've verified all the details."

He was also an adjunct professor at a local college for many years.

I was a part of the project team for the Shearon Harris Project occupying the entire eighty-first floor in the WTC. Over two hundred engineers, designers, and managers worked on the nuclear project in North Carolina.

In 2018, Rashil Levent and I went to see him and his wife at their apartment in Queens. He was ninety-six and in frail health with visible injuries on his body from falling quite often, but his mind was sharp; he vividly recalled names and events going back thirty years. He considered his condition as a fait accompli with a smile that was real. He was proud of his grandchildren, especially Joel Blecher, a history professor at George Washington University.

Blecher had recently written a book, *Said the Prophet of God—A Hadith Commentary across a Millennium*. It is a classic textual analysis of the sayings of Prophet Muhammed (peace be upon him) interpreted over the last millennium through early and classical Arabic sources and offering new avenues for the study of religion, history, and law. He even showed me a paper clipping of the book review.

During the Christmas holidays in 2018, I learned the sad news of his death through a letter. For many years, Murray and I had exchanged season's greetings. This ritual was now transferred to his wife, who broke the news of his passing away.

George A. Kanakaris (1929–2017). George immigrated to the US from Greece when he was barely six. He was raised in New York City and attended Stuyvesant High School, a symbol of excellence in education for over a century. He earned a BSCE from City College followed by a MSCE from Columbia University. In 1957, he joined Ebasco's Concrete Hydraulics Department and worked on several hydro, pumped-storage, and nuclear projects in the US, Greece, and Japan including Fukushima 1 and 2.

George took over the reins of the Civil Engineering Department from Joseph Ehasz in 1991 and remained in that position for ten years. He was in the South Tower when the bomb went off in 1993 but was absent during the 9/11 attack.

He was a thorough engineer with administrative and management skills for overseeing a team of over four hundred design professionals at its peak.

George passed away in 2017 at age eighty-eight. He left behind a loving wife, Anna, two children, and three grandchildren.

A very comprehensive history of the Ebasco Holding Company is provided in the following URL reference.

https://eur01.safelinks.protection.outlook.com/?url=https%3A %2F%2Fwww.wikiwand.com%2Fen%2FElectric_Bond_and_Share_ Company&data=02%7C01%7C%7C7a606bbdc99a4338a 29408d7d2437304%7C84df9e7fe9f640afb435aaaaaaaaaa aa%7C1%7C0%7C637209059439024480&sdata=F4XZSy- eYn2CZ8AMhzqME039e3z%2FuSsnBgsfJpOAsRg4%3D&amp ;reserved=0.

Receiving Service Awards –Resch (45), Hasan (40),
O' Connor (40) and Levent (40) -2014.

Russ Christensen and Fred Gatti at Ebasco Reunion Lunch

Joe Falbo with Gesztes

O' Connor, Ehasz, Hunter and Gertler (2008)

With Hunters and Gertlers (2008)

Fred Gatti and Brenda Towe (2008)

With Amy and Joe

With Gesztes and Levent

With Leo Gertler and Bob De'Angelis

Bill Jacques and Dan turner

With Jerry Zerboulis. Mac Ismail

Falbo, Healy and Ehasz

Fiala, Keilbach, Ruggeiro, Levent

With Anis Baig, Dave Hunter and Lekh Batheja

Mike Pavone, Bob Resch, and Joe Ehasz at Resch's Retirement (2015)

Kula, Shiam Goyal and Dave Hunter

Van Nam, Leo, Shiam, Hau, Dave and

With Kirit Dave and Ish Patel

With Hildebrand and Lynda

Andy Ferlito with the Vines

Joe and Joanne Ehasz

AECOM Team HydroVision Conference, Portland(L to R): Wayne Pietz, Mike
Pavone, Rick Dulin, Cameron Isaman, Doug Harzog, and Joe Ehasz (2015)

Chapter 8

HOME SWEET HOME

Staten Island

In 1976, the bicentennial birthday of the US, we moved to Staten Island, the smallest of New York's five boroughs and a residential community with a population of less than 500,000 that offered affordable housing. At that time, Staten Island was not connected to the New York City Subway system, but ferries took commuters to Manhattan.

A few years later, we moved to Huguenot, on the south shore of the island and within a short walk of the train station. The township was named after the early Dutch settlers who came from Amsterdam. Our home there was a two-family place on a dead-end street. It had been custom built and belonged to an Italian family who was forced to sell it as is without a certificate of occupation. Sonia and I loved the unusual layout and French doors and windows. All the bedrooms and the kitchen were on the second floor, so it could not be described as a real colonial house. We liked the extra space including a full basement; we anticipated visits from family and friends.

Financing as well as the as-is status of the house were big questions marks. The Pasqualis' mother agreed to give us a second mortgage. My lawyer, Sy Leinseider, told me of the risk of buying the home as is. Being an engineer, I felt the risk was acceptable. With a 25 percent down payment, the monthly mortgage would be $1,500 since mortgage interest rates were around 15 percent then. Jimmy Carter was president; inflation was being fought at the monetary and fiscal levels with the slogan Whip Inflation Now (WIN). Paul Volker, the Federal Reserve Bank chairman, was a proponent for raising interest rates to fight inflation.

The good news was that our Springville home sold at a premium, which allowed me to make the large down payment, and the rental income from the apartment helped us. It was a decision I did not regret, but I took out additional life insurance to cover the risk.

At closing, the sellers surprised us; they would not vacate the home immediately. We had sold our other home and had to vacate that day. Upon considering our situation, we were allowed to move into the ground-floor apartment while the furniture was stored in the basement.

The contract had not addressed these issues. In addition, the sellers had told us that they would take the lighting fixtures and some other fittings, which was probably unreasonable, but I felt sorry for the sellers. Here was a family who had a dream house but that dream was being shattered by economic circumstances. They were in a desperate situation; I agreed to the demands.

The move had taken a toll; we decided to take a week's vacation in Canada.

Our neighborhood was predominantly white; we were the only Asians on the block. The neighbors welcomed our nuclear family; Saad, barely three, was the youngest kid in the neighborhood. Mike Materia, a retired fire chief, lived across the street on nearly an acre of property with a manicured lawn. He had fig trees and brought his harvest as gifts for us. Vincent and Kathy Harzewski and their daughters, Stephanie, eight, and Caroline, five, lived next door. Other neighbors were Mike and Peggy Anastos and Mary and Gary Etlinger with their children, Dino and Royce.

Radha and Najam with their son, Syraj, became our first tenants renting the two-bedroom apartment. Najam and Radha had emigrated from India. Syraj was older than Saad and kept an eye on him while playing in the street. They were among the best tenants over the next several decades.

Being a dead-end street, we had advantages of extra parking and quiet—no through traffic. However, during the winter, snow on our street would not be removed as the plough could not turn around. The neighbors had to pitch in to shovel it. Vincent and I shared the honor of ploughing the entire 250-foot street during heavy snow in 1986.

The Huguenot home was our home for several decades. It was a welcome abode for our families and friends in Pakistan, the UK, and India. Usually, it was full of visitors during the summer with relatives coming and going. I introduced our visitors to Vinnie and Kathy whenever I could.

Aamir, Sonia's brother, immigrated to the US in 1983, and Yasmin, my sister, immigrated to the US in 1986 with her two sons. Our home became an open house for our Pakistani and Indian families.

One day, Vincent could not control his curiosity. "Nash, are you running a hotel?"

I laughed and told him it was our Eastern custom to host and entertain relatives; it was deep rooted in our family. We had seen the way our parents had welcomed guests in our homes even when we lived in small apartments with limited space and conveniences. Such values, however, are on a severe decline in the East and West.

Our move to the South Shore meant better public schools for Saad. IS-75 opened in 1988, and Tottenville High School was within walking distance—less than a mile away.

The Staten Island Ferry

The Staten Island Ferry is a New York landmark. The service, operated by the Department of Transportation, provides around-the-clock service between Staten Island and Manhattan. The twenty-five-minute trip in the harbor passes Ellis Island and the Statue of Liberty, national landmarks, the former being the entry point for the early immigrants and the latter being the freedom and independence symbol, a gift from France. The ferry provides breathtaking views of the harbor, the Hudson River, Manhattan's skyline, and the East River Bridges and the Verrazzano-Narrows Bridge between Brooklyn as well as the New Jersey skyline. For over four decades, I took the ferry from Staten Island to Manhattan. The Ebasco offices were a short walk from the ferry terminal.

In the 1970s, the ferry ride cost 5¢ each way, but that later went up to 25¢ for the round trip. Eventually, the ride became free since the costs of collecting the money were deemed to be more than what the fares brought in. This was equitable for the Staten Island residents and put them on par with the residents of the other boroughs, who had access to the city's subway system.

The ferry was a respite from the noise of the city; the commute was very relaxing with cool sea breezes particularly during the summer, a welcome relief from the heat of the concrete jungle of Manhattan. In the mornings, the boats, which run at fifteen- to thirty-minute intervals, allow the commuters to enjoy breakfast on board, read the paper, or put on makeup. In the afternoon and evenings, the tired commuters enjoy a quick nap and wake up refreshed upon hearing the announcement that the boat is approaching the shore.

In the fall and winter, the sunset with its orange glow over New Jersey is a beautiful sight. While the morning atmosphere is subdued and on the quiet side, the afternoon boats are full of tourists who take photos and selfies with the Statue of Liberty in the background. The ferry is a huge attraction for more than a million tourists visiting New York.

The Staten Island Rapid Transit is a train service on Staten Island between the north and south shores. The system with over twenty stations is over eighty years old. It provides twenty-four-hour service with express trains during rush hours. The service is reliable even in inclement weather. I do not remember a service disruption except during unusual blizzard conditions in 1986.

Apa ji's Last Memory—Wedding of Her Grandchild

Apa ji came from Pakistan in May 1989. She was in poor health. She was diabetic and had had sciatica for as long as I could remember, but she flew over 10,000 miles to attend her first granddaughter's wedding. We met her at JFK. She was in a wheelchair and escorted by an old family friend who had attended to her during the flight from Karachi to New York. She was in frail health but in good spirits.

She occupied the guest bedroom in our home. She had stayed there a few years earlier. She noticed something missing on the wall and asked, "Where did the picture of Abba ji disappear to?" She was referring to an old photo of my father and his younger brother, Ahmed Hasan, during a visit to Karachi. I had to explain that the frame had fallen and the glass had broken.

Sonia called my mother Mami ji, the same salutation by which her Uncle Ariff addressed my mother. My mother was nearly seventy-six. She needed help with hair coloring and getting ready for the big wedding. Sonia helped her.

Samia, daughter of Bhaijan, was the first grandchild born in the Hasan family. The wedding was to be held in June 1989.

My brother Parvez was then the chief economist and director of planning at the World Bank in Washington, DC. He was involved with the economies of the developing countries in Asia, including Philippines, Korea, and China.

Invitations were sent to relatives in the states and as far away as Pakistan, Saudi Arabia, and Italy. It was truly a world event as relatives came for the festivities, which would last several days.

We had bought a new Volvo 740 earlier that year. Saad was eleven and learning to play the piano. He could play some tunes on a keyboard.

We left for Bethesda on a Thursday in June. We were warmly received.

Some of the guests from Pakistan included Bhabi's brother Col. Tanvir, sister Sajida and her husband Brigadier Afzal, brother Waheed, and brother Jamsheed and his wife, Ismat. Baji Saeeda arrived from

Jeddah with her daughter, Ayesha, and son, Pasha. Anwaar(Guddu) and his wife with kids, came from London. Saeed and Majeed (children of Javed and Naima) came from Arizona, where they were undergraduate students.

On Bhaijan's side, Yasmin and our family came from Staten Island and Ali and Muna from New Jersey. Bilal's family from Connecticut, and Mussarat, Nauman, with their children and Uncle G.H. and Shamim aunty came from Alabama. All the above families were provided comfortable lodgings at home, with friends, or at nearby hotels.

Apa ji was in high spirits meeting the relatives, sharing stories, and enjoying the great hospitality of the hosts. She and Baji Saeeda stayed at 7907 Springer Road. The rest of the guests were offered lodging a few miles away with the Khurshid family. It turned out to be very comfortable accommodations for the three of us. Baqais stayed at Kirmanis, and Paeji and Yasmin at Rana's home.

The formal functions included a *dholak*, *mehndi*, *nikah*, and the wedding. The first three events were hosted at 7907 Springer Road while the wedding took place at a mansion some forty miles away in Virginia.

The nikah ceremony was unique in that Samia and Bruce read a statement following the official marriage. Bruce had met Samia at Swarthmore College. Bruce was in love with Samia and wanted her hand in marriage. He had no hesitation about converting to Islam, which was considered a prerequisite in our moderate Islamic family.

The mehndi (*henna*) was a colorful event held on June 9. A large tent was put up in the backyard to accommodate over a hundred guests. The ladies sang and danced, men followed, some in Punjabi *bhangra* (a popular dance of Punjab region associated with beating of drum for fast rhythm) style and others in Western style. The night was clear—no threat of rain. It had rained the previous day, and the ground was slightly wet. The fun lasted into the early hours.

The wedding was held at a wooded and secluded lodge in Maryland on June 11. On the wedding day, I went to supervise the arrangements for the reception at the lodge. It had plenty of parking and open space for a banquet. The exterior was well illuminated with small colored bulbs decorated like a *dulhan* (bride).

The dignitaries arrived after sunset. I was part of the self-appointed reception committee. One of the guests I remember escorting was M. M. Ahmed, a former finance minister of Pakistan.

While the wedding party was traveling to the lodge, Sonia was driving the Volvo. She came across a large piece of obstruction in the road, which appeared to be unavoidable. The Volvo rim and tire won the skirmish with the large obstruction without malfunction or delay. An accident would have disrupted the wedding reception. It had been a close call.

The food was catered by Bombay Palace, and the sweets (*mithai*) came from Shaheen Sweets. My brother-in-law, Paeji, is not known to be a dessert person unlike the rest of Hasan family. That night, however, he was indulging the hot *gulab jamuns*; I saw four on his plate. I could not resist photographing the event.

After brunch the next day at a restaurant, Apa ji stayed in Bethesda while the rest of the family returned to Staten Island.

Saad with Nana (1978)

Safdar and Zeba with Saad (1979)

Aamir Wedding

Salim And Rehana Ahmed

Jamsheed, Majid, Col. Tanvir and Saeed (1989)

Samia and Bruce with Sonia, Apa ji and Saad

Bruce and Samia Wedding (1989)

Samia and Bruce Lamb with Apa ji and Baji Saeeda (1989)

Family with Bobogul (1992)

Saad At Mount Rushmore (1991)

With Azhar and Kausar Ali, Sami and Hajira at Boat Club, Karachi (1991)

Bruce and Samia visiting Karachi- with Behram's family (1991)

Chacha Ghulam Hasan and auntie Shamim

MB K Malik with Daughter Rehana (1993)

Sonia with Saeed Hai family

With friends Safdar and Samiullah

Akram And Nasreen Mughal

Aamir and Kamran Hameed

Yasmin and Ajmal Khan with Uncle Ariff

Shazia and Fidya Agha

The Hasan Family in Islamabad (1991)

Saad with parents and Nana in Las Vegas (1987)

Ambareen and Mian Naveed Jawaid Wedding (1994)

Javed Hammed family -Aneela Wedding (1993)

Naveed, Khurrum, Behram, Asad and Najam (1993)

Asad Hasan and Khurrum Hameed (2009)

Khurrum and Abida Malik with sons (1993)

Aneela and Omar Wedding ((1993)

Kaukab with family (1993)

Kaukub and Tehmina (1993)

Aitezaz Shahbaz and Parvez Hasan

Mama Yousaf with Mami Sakina and Lubna (1993)

Reza first birthday with parents, Nana and Nani (1996)

Reza Lamb with Nana (1996)

Yasmin with family on her Graduation with MBA degree

Bilal, Ali, Perwaiz, with Shams and Adnan (1996)

The family gathering with Auntie Shamsa and Sajida Baqai (1993)

Sonia, Salman and Parveen with Dr Tahir, Ali and Perwaiz (1996)

Mario and Seeme with Ahsan family in Boston(1997)

The three in-Laws in Staten Island: Ahsan, Perwaiz and Ali (1997)

The Three Sisters (1997)

Bilal with Zulekha and Jehan Hasan

Duroo, with husband Ariff and Brother

Auntie Sudha, with Daughter and Saad

Dr. Naila with Mother

Dr. Tahir and Naila family

Usman and Saima Wedding (1999)

With Brig, (retd) Ahsan, Maj (retd) Owais, Behram and Dr. Farid Baqai

The Hasan Siblings (1999)

With Yawar, Taiq (Rikki) and Owais (1999)

Chaudri Sardar and Sher Mohammad (1999)

Our Former Family Home: 17/F/PECHS, Karachi (2011)

The Hasan Family (1999)

Sonia, Safina and Lubna

Imran, Maria, Saadia and Saad

Saima and Usman Hasan with Ghazli, Irfan and Taimur (1999)

Abid Majid Wedding (1999)

Auntie Najma, Sonia, Fariah Hasan and Saadia (1999)

Naveed and Farah Hasan with Asad

Shezad, Fawwad, Farhan and Saad

Saad, Saam and Yasser

Rehana and Friend

Shezad and Salima Yousaf with Mother and Ambareen

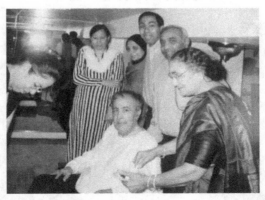

MD Ariff's 80th Birthday- with sister Shamsha and family (1999)

MD Ariff Birthday Participants (1999)

A Family Graduation

Saad graduated from Tottenville High School in 1996. With good grades and SAT score, he was admitted to Rensselaer Polytechnic Institute (RPI) in Troy, New York.

RPI is the oldest engineering college in the US; it opened its doors in 1825. It was an all-male college for 120 years, when it admitted female students.

In 2000, Saad graduated with a BS in electrical engineering. It was a huge milestone in our lives. He was keeping the family tradition of focusing on education. He had followed his cousins, Samia, Sameera, Usman, Irfan, Sarah, Hamid, and Ali, who had graduated from various universities in the US between 1980 and 2000. To celebrate the occasion, we invited the immediate family including my brothers and sisters for the graduation ceremony and made lodging arrangements in Albany for a weekend in June. My brother Behram and his wife, Ghazli, who were visiting from Pakistan, joined the group. Other family members included Bhaijan and Bhabi, Parwaiz (Paeji) and Yasmin, Ali, Mona and Eddie, and Irfan. We gathered in Linden, New Jersey, late Friday afternoon and drove to Albany. Sonia's cousins, Pushkar and Gauraf, joined us the next day.

During our stay at a Holiday Inn in Albany, several incidents apart from the graduation made the weekend memorable. First, a dinner plan went awry. Due to some misunderstandings and the absence of cell phones, only two carloads made it to the intended restaurant; the third car ended up at another restaurant.

The next morning, we got together for breakfast at a restaurant. Ali's old Mercedes's radiator was overheating, so I escorted him to a Mercedes-Benz dealer in Albany. The radiator's hose required replacement. It took us several hours while others in our party waited anxiously to get to the convocation at the Albany Coliseum.

Finally, around 1:00 p.m., we left in three cars and pulled into a garage that was within walking distance of the coliseum. In our excitement, we ignored a small sign that stated, "This garage closes by 10:00 p.m. on weekdays."

The graduation ceremony was the fulfillment of our dreams and indeed rewarding. Sonia and I were proud parents and very grateful for Saad's achievement. He had secured employment with Accenture (then known as Andersen Consulting) as an analyst. He had gotten the job without any help. It reminded me of my first job, which I secured without any help.

Following the graduation ceremony, we had a sit-down dinner that lasted beyond 10:00 p.m. When we got back to the garage, the gate was locked, and no attendant was in sight. We were stunned and felt helpless not knowing the solution to our misery.

Saad's Rensselaer Polytechnic Institute (RPI) Graduation Convocation(2000)

Saad Graduation Dinner at Albany (2000)

Saad greeted by Hon. Shirley Ann Jackson, President, RPI

A Garage Door Opens to Prayers

Other families had failed to see the sign concerning the 10:00 p.m. closure as well. Of all of us, Bhaijan was the most disturbed; he was scheduled to catch a flight to Pakistan from Dulles Airport on the following Monday. Having been appointed by President Musharraf as the chairman of the Debt Committee, he was to provide recommendations on the Pakistan economy and its debt burden issues, and he was to speak at an economics conference at the Institute of Development in Pakistan honoring him.[19]

Ghazli was at the Holiday Inn with Irfan as she had been unwell and did not attend the graduation ceremony. She was probably anxious as well about our whereabouts and unaware of the events at the coliseum. Yasmin was praying for a miracle for the garage to open somehow. As we waited, the local press got word about our being stranded. A reporter showed up and began interviewing our family. It was a hot story for the late-night news in Albany that carried the headline "Out of Town People Stranded in Albany.

A TV reporter asked Behram, "Where did you come from?"

"I came all the way from Pakistan," he replied in an excited voice. He was aware that he was live on TV. Behram had come from Karachi to visit his son, Usman, in Indianapolis when he heard about Saad's graduation and decided to attend. The eldest brother, Parvez Hasan, and his wife, Parveen, had come from Maryland. Ali had driven from Linden, New Jersey. Yasmin and our family had come from Staten Island. Two other families had come from Vermont and Connecticut.

The hullabaloo continued. The police showed up and left. They explained to us that they had no authority to open the garage. Being Friday, the garage would be closed for the weekend and open on Monday morning. We had planned for a luncheon for the visiting families in Staten Island, the following day, Sunday. Our plan was in jeopardy!

During our difficult situation, Saad joined us with his friends. He had heard about the lockout. After discussing the situation at hand, he left with his friends.

An obvious option was to stay in Albany until Monday, when we

---

[19] The high-level debt committee was established to suggest a strategy for reduction of debt burden and a system for better management of public and external debt. The other committee members were the government officials, with Dr. Ashfaq being the secretary of the commission. The report was released in March 2001.

could collect our cars. But that was not a viable option for Bhaijan, who had to be in Maryland by Monday for his flight.

I was almost certain there was a better solution. I started to walk around the area for some sign of help. Being the weekend, restaurants were busy even though it was late. As I walked, a ray of hope came; it was the fire department attending a call from a restaurant. I approached the crew leader and explained our distress. He was sympathetic and willing to help. I was told that the fire department had the authority to break the locks of the garage, but the presence of the police was necessary. He called the police. The garage door lock was broken. Within fifteen minutes, our dire and hopeless situation had a happy ending. We repossessed our cars and left Albany. Our plans for the luncheon on Staten Island remained unaffected. This episode made the 2000 graduation ceremony a memorable one. It was obvious that a higher authority was listening to our distress call and responded in a timely manner. Miracles do happen.

Y2K

The **Y2K** bug, also called Year 2000 bug or Millennium Bug, was a problem in the coding of computerized systems that was projected to create havoc in computers and computer networks around the world at the beginning of the year 2000, but the beginning of the twenty-first century year was rather uneventful. The Y2K uncertainty had led to great anxiety resulting in a rush to software adjustments including four digits for a calendar year instead of the two digits used previously. It had been timely resolved before the beginning of the new millennium.

Sabin's and Adnan's Wedding

In the spring of 2001, the wedding of Sabin, the daughter of Musarrat and Dr. Nauman Qureshi, took place in Athens, Alabama, where my cousin, Musarrat, daughter of Chacha G. H., who married Dr. Nauman Qureshi in 1978, lived. Nauman was a graduate of King

Edward Medical College, Lahore, and specialized in internal medicine followed by a fellowship at Northwestern University. He was practicing as a nephrology specialist at the Athens-Limestone Hospital.

Chacha G. H. had retired from the Pakistan air force with the rank of air commodore, and he had immigrated with his wife, Shamim, to the US in the 1980s. They also lived with the Qureshis in Athens.

The entire Hasan clan in the US in addition to the Qureshi clan from Pakistan would attend the wedding. Asad and Talat, with their son, Farhan, came from Pakistan. They stopped in New York on their way to Alabama. At my insistence, they agreed to drive with me from Staten Island to Athens, over a thousand miles.

Asad had recently retired from the government civil service having served in important federal positions. His last position was as the secretary of the senate, the functional head of the secretariat. All communications, orders, and reports authorized by the chairman are issued under the signature of the secretary. Similarly, all communication by the members including notices of bills, questions, motions, and resolutions are addressed to the secretary and received by him after a long service.

We stayed in Roanoke, Virginia, overnight with the Sherwanis. Shahid was an executive with Yokohama Tire. Being an old friend, he and his wife, Najma, were happy to host us. Najma made a delicious dinner and made us comfortable for the overnight stay. It was a happy reunion with an old friend even though for just one night.

Bhaijan flew from Reagan Airport to Huntsville. Bhabi could not come since Samia was expecting a baby. She was with Samia and Bruce in Cleveland. Saad and Sonia flew from Newark.

The out-of-town guests were accommodated in a motel in Athens. Upon reaching the motel, Bhaijan realized that he had grabbed the wrong bag at the airport baggage claim. He called the airlines, who delivered his bag before the Mehndi function. He was greatly relieved.

Behram was in Indianapolis visiting his son; they drove from Indianapolis. Farhat and Rukhsana with their daughter, Naureen, drove from Cleveland. Nauman's parents, Shaukat and Nasim Qureshi, and their children came from Lahore.

The mehndi was an all-women event. Men, even close family members, were not allowed to attend. Bhaijan took us to the nearest restaurant for the dinner.

The wedding was held in the Huntsville Ballroom. It was a sit-down dinner for several hundred guests, and it included speeches from the bride's and groom's families.

After the wedding, we returned to New York. Farhan came to see me at the WTC office. He was the last family member to visit me there. I showed him around my office and gave him a short tour of the complex. He admired the vistas of New York not knowing the towers would be destroyed in a few months later; such memories haunted him.

Adnan and Sabin wedding (2001)

Sonia, Auntie Shamim, Fatima, Dr. Nauman and Asad Hasan(2001)

With Chacha Ghulam Hasan, Behram and Bhaijan

Adan, Bhaijan, Asad and Farhan (2001)

Sabeen Wedding Participants (2001)

Dr. Nauman and Musarrat Qureshi with daughter Fatima

Sarah's and Mustafa's Wedding

Sarah's and Mustafa's wedding was scheduled for October 13, 2001. It was difficult to postulate the impact of 9/11 on our lives and routines. Initially, there was great uncertainty about the upcoming wedding, barely a month away, as Bhaijan was delayed from returning to the US from overseas. All transatlantic flights had been canceled. However, the flights resumed a week after the attack, and Bhaijan was able to fly home. My having survived the WTC attack was a relief for the immediate family planning the wedding.

Sarah was my sister Mona's daughter. The family lived in Linden, New Jersey. We met often on weekends including occasions when other family members would visit us from overseas to celebrate Eid following Ramadan, birthdays, and anniversaries. Ali was also a good cook who was full of vitality and enjoyed companionship; that was an added attraction for such a get-together.

Mustafa was the son of Bakhtiar and Shahnaz Khan. He had enlisted in the army for active duty in 1994; upon discharge, he joined the national guard for six more years; that provided for his college education.

The family decided that postponing the wedding was not an option. It was a good decision and perhaps therapeutic for our family after 9/11.

The wedding was held in Philadelphia. Sonia helped with setting up the stage. The guests included Uncle Ghulam Hasan and his family, who drove from Alabama. The Bhaijan family came from Bethesda. Saad was the master of ceremonies. From the groom's side, Bhaijan made the speech. The high point of the speech that I remember was that the Hasan family had healthy genes and it was a gift for which the family should be grateful.

It was the first family gathering after 9/11. We were grateful that there was no disruption to the planned event. Life goes on even after a disaster. Picking up the pieces and moving on is always a better option.

Mustafa and Sarah Khan

Our Son's Marriage

One of our happiest memories was the wedding of Saad with Mariam, which took place in the spring of 2006 in Manchester, UK. It was not an arranged marriage; Saad had met Mariam in New York when she was visiting with her mother. I do not know the details, but it was apparent that they were meant for each other. Sonia had been after Saad for some time to look for his life partner in the Staten Island community with several potential matches, but marriages are made in heaven. Saad brought Mariam to our home, and Sonia and I liked her immediately.

Saad and Mariam became engaged in the fall of 2005, when Sonia and I met Mariam's parents, Islam and Salma, in Manchester.

We left for Manchester on March 15, 2006, and were received by the Chaudhris and taken to their home for a sumptuous breakfast. We stayed at a nearby inn as their guests.

Our wedding party besides Sonia and me included Yasmin and Perwaiz, Mahjabin and Ali, Eddie, Sarah, and Mustafa. Bhaijan and Bhabi came from Pakistan. Usman joined the party from Indianapolis, and Samia joined us from Cleveland. Dr. Abdul Rehman accompanied by his wife, Razia, and daughter, Naheed, came from Staten Island. Other extended family members included Abid, his wife, Mariam, Babar and his wife, and Salma, who came from London.

Following the nikah, a mehndi reception was held at the Nawab Restaurant, which was largely attended and included dances by the young and old in a festive setting. The Chaudhris and their friends entertained us with their performances. Even Islam B than seventeen milesexcelled in a solo performance.

The wedding was held at the exclusive Lowry Hotel, and it was a formal affair. The *sehra* was read by Dr. Rehman. I gave a short speech following the father of the bride, Islam Chaudhri. I spoke of my parents' wedding in Amritsar, India, over seventy years earlier. For that wedding, the bridegroom party had traveled from Batala to Amritsar seventeen miles on a train, but that took nearly a day whereas our Newark-Manchester flight, a distance nearly twenty times greater than seventeen miles, had taken less than seven hours. The world has really changed and become closer.

After the wedding, we arranged for a day tour of the Lake District. It was a fun outing with transportation costs borne by Ali, and lunch was hosted by Bhaijan. Being early spring, we were the only diners at the restaurant and were treated with much attention.

The wedding was followed by a valima reception held back in the US at the Hilton Double Tree, Somerset, New Jersey. It was a repeat of the celebrations held in Manchester on April 29. That time, the Chaudhris with their children and friends totaling twenty or so were our guests. It was also a memorable event attended by over four hundred guests including the immediate family and relatives and our Staten Island community.

Saad and Mariam Wedding, Manchester (2006)

Saad and Mariam Wedding, Manchester (2006)

Saad and Mariam with parents, Manchester (2006)

Saad and Mariam, with her parents and siblings

Saad and Mariam Valima New Jersey-Friends

The Office Friends at Saad wedding reception at Hillton

Islam Chaudri, Dr. Rahda and Najam Syed

More Blessings

In time, we became the proud grandparents of two lovely children, Hannah and Adam. Both are adorable kids filled with curiosity and a thirst for knowledge and travel. Hannah loves to sing while Adam has a passion for soccer.

The torch has been passed to the next generation and beyond. While Sonia and I do not have any memories of our grandparents, our grandchildren will no doubt remember sharing some great memories of travel in Europe and Africa with us. When we visited Cape Town, Adam was barely three. He spiritedly climbed the last fifty steps to the top of the 4,000-foot-high Table Mountain and said, "I did it! I did it!"

In addition we witnessed other weddings of the Hasan family including Usman, Aiysha, Umer, Kamil and Zainab during the 2000-2012 period

Aiysha Wedding Reception Ladies Line-up (2001)

Aiysha wedding participants

Aiysha and Atif with Owais and Lubna and Ghazli

Farhat Family wedding Cleveland

Umer and Saba wedding (2009)

Kamil and Aiysha Wedding (2009)

Kamil and Aiysha Wedding (2009)

Zainab and Hassan

Brig (retd) Ahsan, Naveed, Najan, Ruby, Kehkashan,
Shaheen, Lubna, Ali and Maj (retd) Owais

Zainab and Hassan with family

Saleem Wedding (2011)

Vincent J. Harzewski (1940–2017)

Our neighbor Vincent J. Harzewski, a lifelong Staten Island resident of Huguenot, died in Portsmouth, New Hampshire, where he lived for his last three years near his daughter Stephanie's home, on March 25, 2017.

He worked for fifty years in the baking industry beginning as a baker for Buda Bakers and then at Interstate Brands. He loved to work with his hands. Vincent was friendly and helpful individual. He took pride in parenting his daughters.

Vincent was more than our neighbor. He was ready to help us settle in and made us welcome. His daughters became Saad's best companions;

he was the youngest kid on the block. His sharp mind and intellect always amazed me. He was an avid reader as well. He could fix and replace car components with ease and was a handyman.

One late evening in the middle of winter, I got a distress call from our tenant. The front door had become unhinged. I called Vincent for help. He came over and fixed the front door without even mentioning the lateness of the hour. He was an angel one could call always. I will not forget that episode.

After his retirement, his diabetes got worse. It affected his leg, which had to be amputated. But his smile was always there. I visited him after the amputation at a New Hampshire nursing home. The place was near his daughter, Steph, who was a professor of English at the University of New Hampshire

Before Caroline was married, he told me about one disappointment in his life: "Nash, I will never be a grandfather." I was struck by his words of despair. His did not know, but God was listening. Before long, his younger daughter was married. Awaiting the birth of his grandson kept him going as his crosses became heavier, but he was able to see his grandson after all.

The last two days before the death, he underwent brutal dialysis. He was a hundred percent ready when the call came; he finally welcomed it. He was joking with a nurse's aide and took his last breath in the middle of a sentence.

He was the loving husband of forty-nine years of Kathleen (Kathy), father of Stephanie and Caroline, grandfather to Athelstan, and father-in-law of Christopher Axthelm.

The in-laws- Ali Baqai and Bakhtiar Khan with spouses

Salman and Jilani with spouses, Parveen and Fizza (2011)

Hannah with Nani

Hannah with Nana

The NED Alumni- with Bashir, Siddique, Ali and Samiullah (2011)

Saad, Mariam with Hannah and Adam

Shamsa Auntie with daughters and Sonia (2011)

With Col. (retd.) Ahsan Siddique and Kehkashan (2011)

Farida with Shaheen and Ahsan, London (2012)

Mazhar Malik with grandson in London (2012)

View from Table Mountain, Cape Town, South Africa

Usman, Saima with Saram (2013)

Anil Pahwa and Ruby (2013)

Sonia in Morocco (2013)

With Bhaijan, Masood Mufti and Abid Hasan (2014)

Brig, (Retd) Ahsan with Brig. (Retd) Afzal and
Sajida Khan with Daughter (2014)

With Dr. Fariduddin Baqai (2014)

The Future Hasans: Saram, Iman, Hannah and Adam Hasan

Shezad Hasan Family (2014)

Sonia with Pasha and Julia in Napierville (2014)

Visiting Lake Louise, Canadian Rockies with Zaheer and Pat Chaudri (2015)

With Zia Khan (2015)

With Sonia and Pat Khan (2015)

Adam scoring a goal (2017)

Hannah and Adam (2017)

Thanksgiving with Mustafa and Sarah Khan Family (2017)

Sonia and Bushra Waheed (2018)

Api Nasreen (2018)

With Zain and Javeda Anjarwala (2018)

Hannah with Grandma In San Francisco Bay (2018)

With Vincent Grandson and family

Hannah Play in Alexandria

Majeed and Shahina Qureshi with Azhar, Kausar, Sonia and Sana (2019)

Javed Hasan with daughters, Saba and Sarah, and Sonia (2019)

Chapter 9

DREAMS, MORTALITY, AND AWAKENING

Dreams Do not Die
Dreams do not die. Dreams, unlike hearts, eyes or
breath,
Do not vanish or scatter Or wither away with death.
Dreams, they are light Melody and Breeze
They cannot be stopped by hideous mountains,
These flags of light, sound and breeze,
Will not bow, even in execution's square.
(excerpt from *Banished Dreams*, a collection of Poems
by Ahmed Faraz)

Our Mortality

Death is a certain and natural part of our mortal life. Modern scientific knowledge has proposed alternates, and people are living longer and healthier lives, but death is inescapable.

Death and Life—The Islamic View

Death, a fact of life, is repeatedly addressed in the Torah, the Bible, and the Qur'an. Death is part of the cycle of life, and subsequent resurrection is shared by the Abrahamic religions and is a clear example of God's absolute power and human beings' dependency on the divine. According to Islamic belief, the *ruh* (soul) departs from the body at the time of death, as the organs stop functioning.

Christianity, Judaism, and Islam share many similar notions about death with some notable differences. Judaism tends to emphasize the importance of living a good life here on earth and as such has a less-defined concept of an afterlife. Christianity strongly focuses on Christ's death and resurrection as opening the way to eternal life and is more concerned with understanding the afterlife than is Judaism. Islam shares with Christianity a belief in the ultimate importance of the next life as well as the resurrection of the physical body on the Day of Judgment.

Dreams

Dreams can happen at any time during sleep, but we have our most vivid dreams during a phase called REM (rapid eye movement) sleep, when our brains are the most active. **Dreams** may help people learn more about their feelings, beliefs, and values. Images and symbols that appear in **dreams** will have meanings and connections that are specific to each person. During sleep, we sometimes relate to the metaphysical world around us. The dreams take us into the past or the future and on a journey of our imagination and spiritual existence. Dreams are sometimes real. Dreams are reminders; they are connections with the past and even with the future. Dreams are also source of spiritual rejuvenation and even excitement.

Ahmed Faraz (1931–2008) was a well-known Urdu poet from Pakistan. His real name was Syed Ahmed Shah, but he was known by his pen name, Ahmed Faraz. He was awarded posthumously with the Hilal-e-Pakistan by the government of Pakistan. His poems were translated into English language as *The Banished Dreams*; they reflect the fight to deliver humanity from bondage, despair, heartbreak, and suffering, and they make us conscious of our humanity.

Some of his poems are included in various chapters of this book.

Dreams about Abba ji

My brother, Behram, was posted with the Industrial Development Bank of Pakistan in Dacca, East Pakistan.

In early 1968, my father was told of a dream or a vision by Iqbal Siddiqui, a respected religious figure in Karachi. He had visions of violence and riots in East Pakistan. He saw fires erupting out of control. He told my father to get Behram out of East Pakistan as soon as possible. The actual riots did not begin until March 1971, but they led to the secession and the independence of East Pakistan, Bangladesh.

In May 1968, Behram had a dream that Abba ji had died. It was very upsetting for him while awaiting release and transfer to Karachi, West Pakistan. I had a similar dream while I was visiting Bangkok in connection with a coastal engineering course sponsored by the SEATO school during May–June 1968. The dream was about my father's illness. I recall writing home about it; phone calls were still expensive in the sixties.

Behram and I had a similar dream while far from home. In less than ninety days, a family tragedy came our way. Behram and I were fortunate to be in Karachi at the time of our father's sudden illness and were at his bedside during his last hours.

Abba ji's Last Dream

It was Friday, September 13, 1968. I got ready for work and came downstairs at 7:30 a.m. As was my routine, I went to Abba ji's bedroom before breakfast. "Assalam O Alaikum," "Peace be upon you," I greeted him.

"Wa Alaikum As-Salam," he said returning my Islamic greeting.

Abba ji had had a dream that night. He was visibly elated. "I saw Deputy Sahib last night." He was referring to his deceased *mamoo*(maternal uncle) Abdul Hameed, who had died nearly a quarter of a century earlier. "He came to get me." He gestured with both hands as a sign of beckoning him from above. I did not pay much attention to it, and I left for my office at Zafar and Associates.

Later in the afternoon, I accompanied Abba ji for the Friday (*Jumah*) prayers at the PECHS Nursery mosque. As we returned, the phone rang. It was Bhaijan calling from Lahore: "Parveen had a baby girl this morning. It was a Caesarian section, but mother and baby are doing fine." That was truly great news on that Friday the thirteenth. My father had been anxiously awaiting the news. He was relieved and happy to become a dada (grandfather) for the third time.

The next morning, September 14, I heard that Abba ji had had chest pains during the entire night. He had a history of angina and took medication regularly. He was lying in bed and did not look well. He must have been patiently waiting all night for us to call the doctor. In those days, the doctors made house calls even at night, but Abba ji didn't want to disturb our sleep. I immediately called the cardiologist at Naveed Clinic, who came right away. He probably injected some blood thinner, which reduced his chest pains, and he also gave him a sedative. The cardiologist advised us to monitor Abba ji's condition and to admit him to Naveed Clinic if his pain or breathing became worse.

Abba ji's condition did not improve during the day. As evening approached, Javed Hasan and Naveed, our first cousins, came to see us. Naveed was visiting from Islamabad, where he was deputy secretary of Audits and Accounts. Javed worked with the Airport Development

Authority. It was good to see them as it distracted us from the serious situation.

At around 9:00 p.m., Abba ji's condition turned serious. He was in considerable pain. We called for the ambulance and rushed him to Naveed Clinic, a few miles away. I volunteered to go with the ambulance and to stay by his bed.

At the clinic, he was probably injected with more morphine after consultation with the cardiologist. He was semiconscious. His heart was apparently failing. Due to the late hour, no doctor saw him. The staff knew his condition was grave, but they did not tell me. He was still breathing on his own.

During the night, I was aware of his muffled voice reciting verses from the Qur'an. I thought he may have been seeing the angel of death hovering around him and waiting for the exact time to extract his soul. Perhaps he was surrounded by the souls of the deceased relatives including his uncle, Deputy Sahib, who had visited him two night earlier.

It was agonizing to see him suffer. I felt helpless in the dark hospital room, I could not sleep. I kept him in my prayers during the night vigil. I was hoping he would wake up and say something.

But he did not.

The next morning, Apa ji and Behram came to relieve me. I went home and briefly spoke to my siblings at home and said something like, "No improvement." I slept for several hours.

By midday, Abba ji had breathed his last. It was as if lightning had struck. The 17-F PECHS home was instantly turned into a funeral home.

The family including my brothers in Lahore and my uncle Ghulam Hasan in Rawalpindi were informed immediately. Azim Khan's family, particularly Saleem and Naeem, were extremely helpful in making the funeral arrangements. The dead body was brought home in a van provided by Azim Khan's family. In Pakistan, a dead body was kept at home since there are no funeral parlors. His body was washed in the Islamic tradition and covered with a *kafan*, an unstitched white muslin. Owais, the youngest sibling, helped the *maulvi* (a muslim priest) in the washing ritual. Ice blocks were brought in to keep the body cool overnight. Uncle

GH was instrumental in getting a burial plot in the PECHS cemetery from his spiritual guide, Iqbal Siddique, who owned several such plots in the cemetery for his family. My brother Parvez left his wife, Parveen, who was still in hospital after the delivery and flew to Karachi that evening.

The earlier two dreams of the sons had come true.

Several years later, I discovered that Abdul Hameed, my father's uncle, had died on September 13, 1943, some twenty-five years earlier, the date of the birth of Abdul Hameed's son, Tariq Hameed, as well.

Several months later, a conversation with a respected elder relative took place. He told me, "When I drive by the PECHS graveyard, I see that Sheikh Sahib is happy in his grave." He was referring to my father by his surname. At that time, I paid little attention to his words. He was perhaps referring to the virtuous deeds of Abba ji during his life that earned him a peaceful internment until the Day of Judgment.

Over the years, I have dreamed of deceased relatives and can appreciate somewhat what I also heard from others about such dreams and their relevance. One dream about Abba ji was related to me by Uncle Ghulam Hasan in the 1990s. He called me from Athens, Alabama, where he lived with his daughter, Mussarat, and her husband, Dr. Nauman Qureshi, a nephrologist. He said, "Last night, Bhai Sahib came to me. He seemed upset that I forgot to remember his death anniversary. I also saw you praying in one corner."

My uncle was really grateful to his eldest brother for educating him and arranging his marriage. He had failed to remember his brother's death anniversary date during his prayers that night while I had not. It was also a sign that our prayers and supplications are always being heard and even acknowledged indirectly in heaven.

Jamshed's Unfulfilled Dream

Sonia and I were naturalized in August 1979. We took the Pledge of Allegiance to the US at Prospect Park, Brooklyn. Becoming citizens was a special milestone in our lives. As Sonia and I hugged, tears of joy welled up in our eyes. We had a new identity and responsibility. We were now a part of the growing Muslim community in the US. "We will be able to vote now too," I said to Sonia.

We applied for US passports immediately, but our travel to Pakistan was somehow delayed for several months. At that time, I was frustrated with the delay.

By Thanksgiving, we were ready to leave. Saad was almost eighteen months old then, a toddler who was still in pampers; a suitcase full of them was among our luggage. We were really excited about this trip to Pakistan with the addition of a new family member and our US identity.

We landed in Karachi in early December. Saad was a toy to the Ariff household; Nana Ariff and Nani Duroo were thrilled with their first grandchild. Also, Apa ji was extremely happy to see her ninth grandchild. The Karachi weather was mild and really pleasant; the evenings were filled with relatives and friends. Hamida was still available as nanny and looked after Saad, which permitted Sonia to relax and socialize with family and friends.

Our next leg of the trip took us to Lahore, where we stayed with my brother, Jamshed, and his wife, Tehmina, at their 81 H Gulberg III home. Their children, Aneela, age nine then, and Kamil, age two, played with Saad. Jamshed was as executive of Pakistan National Oil (PNO). He also showed me a house under construction on which he had put a down payment, but he was interested in immigrating to the US. I agreed to file petition papers for that as soon as I returned. He wanted to pursue a career in hotel management in the US.

Our stay in Lahore was short, but thanks to Jamshed, I met the extended family and relatives including Uncle Nasir, Khurrum, and my friend Ijaz, who was principal of the Polytechnic Institute there.

On our last day, after the Fajr prayer, we visited the shrine of the great Sufi saint, Syed Ali Hajweri, more affectionately known as Data Sahib. That morning, Jamshed was showing symptoms of high blood pressure, and his eyes were red. When I asked him if he was taking any medication, his response was less than satisfactory. We relished a sumptuous breakfast of *puri* and *halwa*, our last meal together, before we left for Rawalpindi by air. It was truly a memorable family reunion.

The next morning, the phone rang in Rawalpindi. It was a nervous Behram calling from Karachi that Jamshed had suffered a stroke and was in a coma. It was unbelievable. His smiling face and farewell hug at the Lahore airport were still fresh in my memory.

The news was grim. The families from Karachi and Rawalpindi were bound for Lahore. Arranging the airplane tickets at the last minute was a big hassle, but connections helped. We were back in Lahore less than twenty-four hours after we had left. Apa ji, Behram, and Ghazli arrived from Karachi that evening, and 81 H became a temporary hotel for two dozen or so relatives; it was a logistic challenge to handle food and other issues for the crowd.

Details about Jamshed's condition and medical assessment poured in. It was clear that the stroke had been massive and his chances of recovery were slim. The doctors had stated that the first twenty-four hours following the stroke were critical. It was less than twenty-four hours then, and Jamshed was still in a coma and fighting for life with our prayers.

Before long, the struggle was over. Jamshed's body was brought home to Gulberg. Tehmina had become a young widow with two very young children. My mother had suffered another shock of losing a son eleven years after the death of her husband. The family had lost a loving brother.

All the relatives came to Jamshed's residence. Duroo Aunty flew from Karachi, Shaheen and Ahsan from Rawalpindi, Parvez Hasan from the US, and Uncle G. H. and family from Rawalpindi. The local relatives were Uncle Jamil and family, Mami Sakina, Mama Yousaf, and Uncle Ahmed Hasan's family.

Uncle Ariff sent a cable to Ebasco in New York about the death in the family and requested an extension of my leave. Upon my return to New York, I found that my absence was treated as funeral leave, and I was fully compensated for the absence.

It was only a few months earlier that my uncle Ahmed Hasan has passed away and the family had not recovered from the loss. Khurrum and family came. He really was sad having lost a brother, as he had memories from his Karachi days. Mian Fazal Karim, an old friend from

Zafar and Associates, came to pay his respects. Another notable friend of the family, Saeed Ahmed, son-in-law of Azim Khan, came from Karachi.

Jamshed had died on Monday, December 16, 1979. He was only forty-three and in the prime of life. He had not planned to exit that way and so suddenly. His ambitious plans for himself and his family remained a dream. It was also a reminder that our worldly lives are temporary and uncertain. The Qur'an reminds us,

Every soul will taste death, and you will only be given your compensation on the Day of Resurrection. So, he who is drawn away from the Fire and admitted to Paradise has attained. And what is the life of this world except the enjoyment of delusion. (Sura 3:185)

"Inna Lilahe Wa Inna Ilahe Rajeoon," "We belong to God and there we shall be returned."

The family stayed for the *quls* (*soyem*). Bhaijan joined the family from the US.

The house at 81 H Gulberg had three bedrooms. Most of the family slept in makeshift beds set up at night in the den and lounge areas. Fortunately, my sister-in-law Ghazli's parents' home was nearby in Gulberg, and her maternal uncle (*mamoon*) lived next door. We enjoyed their hospitality. Gazli's dad, Uncle Rauf, was fond of cricket. He entertained us with snacks and tea as we watched the Pakistan cricket team playing a test match on TV.

By default, I took charge of the kitchen supplies for the out-of-town family and other guests. There were dozens of eggs and fresh bread for breakfast. The eggs and chickens came from Al-Khair Poultry in Farhat Hasan's shop in the Gulberg market. Three meals were cooked every day.

Brother Jamshed was buried in the Miani Sahib graveyard, one of the oldest in Lahore, in the company of her mother-in-law, Sakina, who had passed away in 1977. It was a sudden blow to his young wife and kids and family and friends. His loss was best expressed by my cousin, Khurrum, who was also his close friend. He wrote me several months after Jamshed's death,

Jamshed was a true friend who shared both the happy days and the sad events with his friends. He was sincere and loving person. His loss at the crossroad of my life would not be forgotten easily and he would be remembered always.

He sent me two couplets of a poem: "Kitni Yadain Gum Afroze say Jaag Ut-thi Hain Girtay pattun say Bahar'un ka Khial ata hay," "My memories are jogged with the lighting of a candle. It's like remembering the spring with the fall of the leaves."

Khurrum became my friend, and the friendship torch was passed to the younger siblings for the next fifteen years. He died in 2004 from lung cancer leaving behind a lovely wife, Abida, and two sons; that closed another memorable chapter of my life.

Tehmina, a very young widow with two small children, Aneela and Kamil, was helped by the immediate family particularly Kakub and Aitezaz Shabaz (Jaji) during the difficult period. Tehmina got a job with PNO, which helped financially in raising the children. Aneela became an MD while Kamil became an electrical engineer and earned an MBA from Lahore University of Management Sciences(LUMS). The two are married and pursuing successful lives. I often wonder that if my brother were alive, would he have done better than that? Tehmina played a dual role in raising the kids and made sacrifices in doing so.

Some four decade later, Kakub, Tehmina's older sister, and Aitezaz mourned the death of their son, Duffy, who also died suddenly at age forty-two. For the surviving parents, such a loss of a child in his prime is difficult to endure without faith in God and submission to His will.

There were similarities in the departure of Jamshed and Duffy from this world.

Apa ji's Unfulfilled Dreams of Returning Home, 1989

It was Sunday, October 15, 1989. The phone rang. Bhaijan said that our mother was in a Bethesda hospital due to severe stomach pains. Being Sunday, no doctor was available. It came as a surprise to us; though she was a diabetic, she had maintained generally good health since her arrival in the US five months earlier. She was homesick and scheduled to return to Pakistan in September. Her reservations were modified at the suggestion of Behram. She was upset at the delay and wanted to return home badly. To appease her, Bhaijan took her to stay in Bethesda.

The following day after returning from office, I called the hospital around 6:30 p.m. My mother told me that her gall bladder enzyme levels were very high and that the doctors had decided on surgery the next day. My sister-in-law, Parveen, who was attending her, was to return shortly after dinner. Sonia and I tried to reassure her about the surgery and wished her a full recovery. As soon as the call ended, I started planning on seeing her right after the surgery.

The phone rang in the early morning of October 17. Bhaijan apologized for not having called during the night. It appeared that soon after our telephone conversation the previous evening, Apa ji's heart had stopped. A code blue was declared, but efforts to restore her heart had failed. The doctors wanted a postmortem to determine the cause of her death; we refused that based on our Islamic beliefs.

We left for Bethesda in the afternoon after I went to the office to inform my boss about the death in family and to request funeral leave. I was told that I did not have to come to the office to inform them. Ebasco was always been very sympathetic and supportive in our bereavement.

The funeral prayers were held at the Islamic Center, Washington, DC, on October 18. Prior to that, we visited the funeral home. Apa ji looked peaceful in her eternal sleep. Her face was young and full of bliss without any signs of age. Sonia observed that too. Apa ji had prepared well for her departure from this world; she had always prayed for a quick death while she was on her feet. She did not want to suffer any disability or a long illness. My parents were fortunate enough to not have suffered extended illnesses and to have departed from this world quickly.

While she was in the hospital, Apa ji had expressed her wishes to be buried in the US. After the funeral prayers, she was buried at the Lebanon Cemetery in Prince George's County, Section 203, Islamic section. Her final resting place is surrounded by trees, has shade most of the day, and is on relatively high ground. The cemetery is near the Beltway (I-495), and easily accessible from I-95 via New Hampshire Avenue Exit 29S.

It was more than a coincidence that soon after her death, I was assigned to work on the Bi-County Tunnel Rehabilitation Project that would supply water to the Washington metropolitan area. The water main tunnel runs at depths of 50 to 150 feet under the beltway. I was associated with the project for nearly three years through design and construction, and that afforded me an opportunity to visit my mother's grave often for *fatiha* (prayer)

Prior to leaving for the US, Apa ji had visited Quetta, where she stayed with eldest daughter, Shaheen, for several months in the spring of 1989. Her husband, Lt. Col. Ahsan, was taking a staff college course there. Upon her arrival in Karachi, she remembered a debt she owed to a goldsmith; she visited the goldsmith and paid off the small balance (Rs. 200–300) due for a jewelry item made earlier. The balance had remained unpaid for several years, yet the timing was perfect. She will never again see the goldsmith. She was debt free upon leaving this world.

Looking back, it appears that Apa ji had been giving her goodbyes to her children one by one first in Quetta and then in Karachi, New York, and finally Maryland. I had lost both my parents and had been deprived of their prayers and supplications for our well-being. I remained in Bethesda to offer prayers and reminisce about the good life our parents had given us. All the siblings felt a vacuum in our lives that would take a long time to heal.

She had been born in Amritsar, India, and married before finishing high school. She had raised eight children. She became a widow at age fifty-four. She saw all her children get married. She had seventeen grandchildren at the time of her death. She faced the loss of her son, Jamshed, bravely. Finally, she was able to participate in the wedding of her firstborn grandchild, Samia.

She was fond of good clothes and good food. During the early years in Karachi, she had a tight budget to run the household on; she managed a tiny kitchen from early morning to late evening preparing three full meals daily for a large family and managing the daily needs of her children. I never heard her complain.

In 1948, upon arrived in Karachi, she decided to remove her *burqah* (head-to-foot veil) for outdoor shopping visits. It was a daring act for a woman those days in a conservative Muslim society since she had always worn a burqah outdoors in Punjab.

She was very hospitable and had a warm heart. She would always welcome relatives for lunch or dinner without hesitation. She was an excellent cook who was always eager to learn new recipes.

She was a happy person and played a positive role in our lives. For over two decades, she was the matriarch of the family. She inspired us through her regular letters and kept us informed about news of the extended family.

Asad's Dream

Asad, a first cousin, was my close friend. We have shared good memories for most of our lives. He visited me in Mangla during my first engineering job. One time, he confided in me about his sweetheart and love, and I said, "I know," though I had no clue about it.

He asked, "If you know, then tell me her name!"

"Her name starts with a T." I was guessing but with confidence based on a voice within.

Asad was dumbfounded. It was true. Talat was his sweetheart.

They married and had three wonderful children, Fawwad, Farhan, and Nabil. Asad retired from civil service after long and meritorious service in 2000.

His last visit to the US was in 2001, before the WTC attack. His son, Farhan, came to my office at 2 WTC and was the last relative to visit me there.

He celebrated his seventieth birthday in a hospital in Islamabad. His heart was failing. I called him from Staten Island to wish him well. Over the phone, he shared his last dream: "I see some strange figures who are surrounding my bed, but they are kept at a distance. There appears to be a line on the floor that they are unable to cross." He died peacefully a few days later. The angel(s) of death were hovering around to take his soul at a specific time.

I have also dreamed of my death and seen people surrounding my body in a mosque mourning my loss. I want to say something but am unable to speak. I wake up next to my wife. I am still alive.

A Heart Attack Repeats after Thirty-Five Years

It was just past midnight on September 14, 2003. I was ready to hit the bed after a long day and a dinner party at Sham's and Tania's home on Staten Island. I had already changed into my night suit after performing the *Isha* prayers. I lay down for a moment and suddenly realized I did not feel good as I normally did at night. It was an instantaneous, sixth-sense message from deep within—I was having a heart attack. There were no usual signs of pain in the arms or chest or breathlessness accompanied by heavy sweating—typical symptoms of a heart attack. At that time, I did not know that a deposit of plaque had landed in an artery and had caused a clot that was depriving my heart and brain of oxygen, but I knew something was wrong with my heart.

A day earlier after dinner, I had felt some heaviness in my chest after a long day at the Hudson Bergen Project in Jersey City. I thought it was indigestion. For two months, I had an assignment in the Jersey City office preparing final documents to be handed over to the NJIT. Due to its remote location, I drove every day. It was different from my regular job in that it required public transportation to New York and involved several miles of walking each day.

I went for a short walk to the Woodrow Plaza, a shopping center a mile away. The fall evening air was pleasant and comfortable. After walking a few blocks, I felt short of breath; fatigue compelled me to stop. The symptoms disappeared after several minutes. After the walk, I felt a little better. When I got home, I didn't mention this to Sonia and had forgotten about this incident until that moment. Many heart patients have symptoms that come and go, which confuses them. That time, however, I responded to the distress signal. I told Sonia, "I'm having a heart attack!"

"Are you sure? Maybe you had a gas attack and heartburn." She tried to reassure me. "Just go to bed and you'll be fine." Her remarks had some validity; I had indulged that evening in spicy food topped by two helpings of dessert, *ras malai* and *kheer*. But I became convinced that my discomfort was not gas related or indigestion. "I'm going to the hospital," I said.

Luckily, Saad was home for the weekend. He had been working for Accenture based in North Virginia and drove home on weekends.

"Dad, I'll drive you to the hospital," he said sensing the firmness in my tone.

We raced to the Staten Island South Shore Hospital less than two miles away. As we approached Hylan Boulevard, there was a red light. There was no traffic on either side. After hesitating, he drove through it as if he had read my mind. He felt the emergency as well.

Within minutes, we were in front of the hospital's emergency entrance. "Help! I'm having a heart attack!" I shouted to an attendant outside.

Before long, I was in the emergency room being examined by a physician. Time is everything in a heart attack. All must recognize the danger signs even if they doubt them and get immediate help. I was given some injections instantly, probably blood thinners. I threw up twice in the examination room, but that helped relieve the heaviness.

The doctor completed his examination and said, "Yes, you're having a heart attack."

By that time, Sonia, my sister, Yasmin, and her son, Zahid, who was an MD, had arrived.

Southshore Hospital had no facilities for angioplasty or heart surgery, so I went by ambulance to North Shore Hospital in Staten Island without stopping for red lights.

I was rushed upstairs to the Heart Institute, where Dr. Snyder explained the angioplasty procedure. A two-part catheter tube was inserted through my groin area to the heart coronary artery. The secondary catheter had a deflated, cylindrical-shaped, empty balloon at its far end. The balloon was inflated to open the blockage in my artery. I was somewhat sedated, but I watched the screen as the catheter tube was routed to open the blockage. I was perhaps given more sedatives and went to sleep again. A pump was attached to my foot to keep the balloon inflated in the blocked artery. It was Sunday morning, September 14. I had survived a heart attack. I had been lucky.

Exactly thirty-five earlier on September 14, 1968, my father had a massive heart attack and did not survive after being admitted to a hospital in Karachi. He was sixty-eight. It was perhaps more than a coincidence that my father's maternal uncle, Abdul Hamid, had died of a heart attack on September 13, 1943, at age fifty-four. He and my father had been smokers while I was not. Also, I had no sign or dream as my father had thirty-five years earlier about his recall.

While I was at the hospital, a debate had begun at home about my heart surgery options. Dr. Ansari, a cardiologist and a respected elder of the Pakistani-American community on Staten Island, preferred that the heart surgery be performed at the Lenox Hill Hospital in Bronx. The well-respected and experienced surgeon at that hospital was on vacation. At North Shore, Dr. Meggin had established a new heart institute. Dr. Mazhar Malik, a close family friend and neighbor, recommended Dr. Meggin, who had moved from New York University Hospital in Manhattan to Staten Island. I agreed to stay at North Shore Hospital for the surgery.

While being prepared for the surgery and having my chest hair shaved, I felt calm. The heart pump attached to my leg was working. The nurse, a big and burly person with a smiling face, put me on the stretcher and took me to the operation theater. He told me he would visit me after the surgery. On hearing this, I felt reassured about the outcome. I was sure God would give me another chance.

I was operated on in the early morning of September 15, nearly thirty-two hours after the initial heart attack. The surgery was long and traumatic. The family was told that there were complications during the surgery that delayed the restoration of my heart from the heart-lung machine. I was in the recovery room for over eight hours while family and friends prayed outside.

A Dream during Surgery

My family in New York, Alabama, and Maryland and in Pakistan were earnestly praying for me, and their prayers were being heard.

During my surgery and recovery, I dreamed that I was flying solo over the deserts of Saudi Arabia trying to reach Mecca for pilgrimage, a sacred religious journey for Muslims. However, there appeared to be delays in the air traffic flow represented by red lights. As soon as I would recite a verse from the Qur'an, the red lights would turn green allowing me to proceed. The sequence of red and green lights continued throughout my surgery and recovery period. I also dreamed that I was climbing a cliff and was unable to reach the top, surrounding Mecca, to view the *kaaba (Haram Sharif in Mecca- built by Prophet Ibrahim)*. It was an extremely difficult climb, but I was persistent. Perhaps those dreams represented my spiritual state and resolve. I remained positive about the outcome of the heart surgery. God was testing me. I was being given a second chance. It was time to reawake and reflect on my life.

I woke up on Tuesday morning some twenty-four hours after surgery. I had been transferred from the recovery room to a semiprivate room I shared with another heart patient on whom Dr. Meggin had operated. I was grateful to be alive and well after the quadruple-bypass surgery. Except for some discomfort in my chest, emotionally, I had survived surgery well, but my roommate appeared to be in much discomfort.

The visits from many family and friends were comforting and reassuring. I remember that one morning, a friendly face, someone in a green jacket, was standing near my bed smiling at me.

Initially, I had difficulty breathing through my nose. My chest felt very tight as a result of the eight-inch incision into the rib cage for the open-heart surgery and subsequent closure with stitches. I was given a suction pump apparatus to perform breathing exercises to open my clogged lungs as a result of the surgery. It was quite difficult breathing for a day or two. Sometimes, when I would fall asleep, I would be awakened suddenly as if I were choking. Gradually, my breathing became automatic with the breathing exercises. A normal, healthy person does not appreciate the gift of life and effortless breathing. It was an awakening to realize this.

I was given painkillers on Tuesday night; as a result, I hallucinated most of the night. I felt I was drowning as the water rose in Times Square above the tall billboards. I was struggling for air and woke up. The following day, I told the nurse that I did not want any painkillers. After consulting with the doctors, she consented to my request. I had no more hallucinations.

I did not know that part of my heart muscle had been permanently damaged. The arteries for the transplant had come from my legs, which were bandaged. I was given a red pillow to squeeze against my chest to prevent opening the stiches. I felt more humility than ever before.

I am convinced that the prayers of my loving family were responsible for my successful surgery and quick healing. It was a miracle indeed. I was grateful for the overwhelming support from the Staten Island community. The Almighty had given me another life extension.

Perhaps I had some unfinished business left in this world.

The doctors and the nurses were very happy with my prognosis. I had no swelling in my legs. The stitches were healing well. I was walking daily around the ward under supervision. I was even allowed a home-cooked meal, which Saad brought me.

I was discharged five days later after I demonstrated that I could walk up some stairs without assistance. I was happy to be home in the loving arms of my wife and with other family members who had kept a close vigil and said prayers for the entire week. Saad had taken off from work and was home for the entire week.

I was prescribed painkillers and several medications including iron pills and laxatives. I never took the painkillers. Within twenty-four hours after taking the iron pills, I experienced severe constipation. Until then, I had occasionally experienced diarrhea, but I had never been constipated. I discontinued the iron pills after consulting with the doctor, and I felt immediate relief.

My recovery would require a minimum of six weeks with some initial physical therapy and daily nurse visits at home. Initially, I could walk only a quarter-mile uphill on Marcy Avenue before I felt tired. While recovering at home, I told Sonia about my dream and my intention to perform Hajj. The next Hajj would be in late January, barely four months away. Hajj is performed during prescribed dates in the Islamic month of Zul-Hijja. I asked her, "Would you accompany me for Hajj?"

She answered in the affirmative.

I felt relieved. It has been my desire to go to Hajj in the preceding years, but Sonia had been reluctant when this subject was raised. Hajj is one of the pillars of Islam and requires Muslims who can afford it financially to go to Mecca on a pilgrimage at least once in their lifetime. Her change of heart was due perhaps to her desire to look after me during the long and arduous journey. The trip would require the approval of my cardiologist.

The postsurgery don'ts list was long; I could not lift anything weighing more than eight pounds, and I could not bend down or drive. I ignored one of the don'ts; I would lift the milk bottle (a gallon of milk weighs over eight pounds) without being concerned. I also started driving to the doctor's and therapist's offices after two weeks of rest. I always felt comfortable driving.

Sonia and I would often drive to the Wolf Pond Park in the afternoons, eat lunch or snacks in the lovely, cool, autumn air, and watch the waves roll up to the sandy shores of Staten Island. Such trips were refreshing indeed.

In December, I resumed work on the Hudson Bergen Light Rail Project. I attended the Christmas party at the Hotel Algonquin in New York with Saad and Mariam, who drove me there. Several of my colleagues including Leo, Shiam, Ed, Dave, and Rash welcomed me with hugs. I felt happy to resume my normal activities after a nearly three-month absence.

Pilgrimage (Hajj) to Mecca

In December, Dr. Pulijal performed a stress echo test and gave me permission to travel. She was fully supportive of my intention to undertake the sacred journey.

I made reservations for the Hajj trip. Sonia was concerned about my health. She had agreed to come to Hajj though it was a long and arduous journey requiring travel to Saudi Arabia and performing prayers and essential supplications in Medina, Mecca, Mina, and Arafat. By accompanying me, she could watch over me.

We left New York on January 21, 2004, via a chartered Saudi Arabian flight. We had booked our travel through Dar-el-Salam. The first part of the journey would take us nonstop to Medina. As we waited in the departure lounge, we had a surprise meeting with a colleague, Ahmed Jalil, who with his family was making the spiritual journey as well.

We arrived in Medina about twelve hours later and went through customs. Our US passports were collected by the local custom authorities. The only IDs we had were photos bearing the Dar-el-Salam badge and a wristband identifying our group number. We hoped to retrieve our passports on the day of our departure from Saudi Arabia.

In our group, which consisted of US citizens only, were doctors, engineers, and other professionals and businessman from all over the US. The Hajj packages ranged in price from $4,000 to $7,000 depending upon the type of accommodations and the number of persons in a room, etc. In most of the packages, the men and women were separated and shared rooms with up to three others. It was a great spiritual experience we shared with strangers all focused on fulfilling the Hajj *manasik*, all the rites and ceremonies to be performed by pilgrims in and around Mecca.

Our stay at Medina Darul Iman Hotel lasted three days; it was across from Masjid-e-Nabvi (Haram). It would take few minutes to join the prayers after the *azan*. The masjid had been greatly expanded to accommodate up to a million people for the prayers. The interior was air conditioned and furnished with Persian rugs and cool marble floors, a very welcoming refuge from the desert heat.

The daily rituals were focused on the five compulsory prayers and optional Nafal prayers. The streets, bazaars, and shops were full, and the hotels were packed with pilgrims. Since the Haram mosque (Masjid-e Nabvi) was open twenty-four hours, many *Haji*s spent most of their time there meditating and reciting the Qur'an between the prayers; that limited time for eating and sleeping.

On January 26, we wore the *ihram* and offered the two Nafals at the Haram before flying to Jeddah. By the time we landed in Jeddah, I had developed a severe cold and kept on sneezing. I recited the *Talbiyah* during the forty-five-mile bus ride to Mecca. By the time we reached the Haram Sharif in Mecca, my cold had vanished as if it had never existed. Perhaps it was the *zikr* that did it. The Talbiyah (Arabic at-Talbīyah) is a Muslim prayer invoked by the pilgrims as a conviction that they intend to perform the Hajj only for the glory of Allah.

I was able to do the *tawaf* and *sai* rituals with my normal zeal and enthusiasm. We stayed at the Ash-Shuada Hotel, a five-minute walk to the Haram Sharif.

On the seventh of Zul-Hijja, we departed for Mina, where we stayed in air-conditioned tents. The over 100,000 tents made it a temporary tent city coming to life for a week or so during the Hajj period. The camp facilities included squatting-type toilets, running water, and shower stalls. Each tent housed twelve people. It reminded me of my scouting days. The meals were sumptuous. In addition, there were food shops for those with larger appetites.

A Turkish doctor shared the tent with me. He had had heart bypass surgery too. Under advice from his cardiologist, he was carrying a nitro-glycerin pill to mitigate chest pains. I told him of my recent bypass, and he was surprised that my doctor had not prescribed nitroglycerin for me.

On the ninth of Zul-Hijja, we left for Arafat by buses after sunrise and spent the day there until sunset. The large tent was air conditioned. It was a long and tiring day; some, being old and weary, even slept. The *imam* exhorted us to engage in prayers.

Outside our tents were some 2 million people, a sea of humanity exposed to the harsh sun and heat in the open in Arafat with Mound Arafat in the distance. As far as the as the eye could see were worshippers clad in white *ihrams*, people of different colors and races braving the heat with calm observance and solitude in the barren and shadeless landscape. At sunset, our imam made long *duas* and supplications for forgiveness and acceptance.

We proceeded to Muzdalifah reciting the Talbiyah. At Muzdalifah, we offered the combined *Maghrib* and *Isha* prayers in earnest. We spent the night at Muzdalifah sleeping under the open skies in two-piece unstitched ihrams. The starry night reminded me of my boy scout days; I slept on a blanket on the ground. I picked up twenty-one pebbles during our stay in Muzdalifah.

On the tenth of Zul-Hijja, we left Muzdalifah after the *Fajr* prayer and walked on foot to Mina for the ritual of throwing stones at Satan's pillar, one of the ritual acts that must be performed on the Hajj. It is a symbolic reenactment of Abraham's hajj, where he stoned three **pillars** representing Satan's tempting the prophet Ibrahim on his way to sacrifice his son.

The Hajj manasik also traces the footsteps of prophet Abraham, who was commanded to sacrifice his son, at Mina. While he was doing so, a ram had appeared as a sign of divine acceptance of his sacrifice. For his unwavering devotion and sacrifice, he is mentioned as Klalil-Alllah (friend of God) in the Qur'an.

As our group slowly approached the first pillar, a stampede occurred. I lost my balance and my slippers and ran to safety. Within minutes, nearly 250 people died and a similar number were injured. It was one of the worst stampedes during Hajj resulting in a significant loss of life.

This symbolic throwing of stones at Satan's pillar is performed at Mina for three consecutive days. I did perform the ritual later that afternoon followed by shaving my head; the restriction of Ihram is removed. I went to Mecca for Tawaf Al-Ifadah in the evening.

We stayed at Mina until the twelfth of Zul-Hijja and returned to Mecca for the Tawaf Alwadah. *(This the farewell visit of the Kaba before departing home)* I was able to perform all the manasik of Hajj to my utmost capacity without feeling any restraint or fatigue or showing ill effects from my recent heart surgery. Few people at the Hajj knew about my heart surgery and thought I was a normal older person.

Sonia was housed separately with the women and checked on me often; when I would not show up for several hours, she would be concerned. My legs showed no swelling or discomfort. In fact, I walked from Muzdalifah to Mina, four miles, without difficulty or fatigue. Also, I did indulge again in the rich desserts. It was indeed heartening that I accomplished Hajj with ease and satisfaction.

In the following years, several thousand people were killed during this event. Recently, a protective wall and other improvements have reduced the number of large death incidences.

We returned to New York; the spiritual journey lasting a fortnight had come to an end. We were back to our material world. During the two weeks, there had been no TV to watch or newspapers to read, and it seemed that time had stopped. The focus was on prayers, meditation, and supplications with earnest thoughts seeking forgiveness and salvation of our souls.

Masjid Nabvi, Medina

Masjid Nabvi, Medina

Haram Sharif, Mecca

Haram Sharif, Mecca

Awakening

I was truly grateful for God's grace and blessings in performing the pilgrimage with ease and devotion throughout the two-week sacred journey. My family had reservations about my taking the arduous journey so soon after surgery, but I was confident that my heart was sound again. I had fulfilled my dream. I was restored physically and spiritually.

In retrospect, the heart surgery was an essential detour in my life to enable the fulfillment of my pilgrimage dream. That became a blessed awakening.

Duroo's Last Words—2005

The phone rang. It was the morning of Saturday, April 12, 2005. A Brooklyn Hospital nurse was told me, "Duroo Ariff passed away this morning at four thirty."

Sonia and I drove from Staten Island to Brooklyn Hospital Center on Dekalb Avenue. Duroo was already in a body bag. The nurse opened it to reveal her face. She looked peaceful. She showed no effects of the needles and the suffering she had endured the last three years. We had been at her bedside only the night before.

Sonia had told her about our upcoming travel to Pakistan on April 15 for a family wedding. My cousin Asad's middle son, Farhan, was getting married in Lahore followed by a valima reception in Islamabad. It was an important family wedding.

"We will be gone for three weeks," Sonia had told her.

She nodded and moved her lips as if saying, "Go ahead. I'll be fine." She could not speak since she had undergone a tracheostomy. She gestured and communicated in a sign language. She had positive vibes around her. Her face was serene and peaceful without any anxiety. She was a religious woman.

Aamir, Sonia's brother, was there as well. He was concerned about her health. She had been moved to Brooklyn Hospital from a nursing home as her condition had deteriorated lately. Duroo was diabetic. She was on insulin and was fed by a tube in her stomach. She also had glaucoma, but her spirits were always up, and she always had a smile on her face. She had died in her sleep barely six hours after our visit.

Her body was brought to Casey Funeral Home in Staten Island for an Islamic funeral and burial. As she was washed by a group of woman, including Sonia, she showed no signs of needles or marks on her body that she had endured during her extended illness. Her body has been fully restored upon death with no sign of her protracted illness or needle marks. After the funeral prayers at Masjid An-Noor, she was buried with her loving husband, Misbahuddin Ariff, in the same grave.

She had joined her husband, whom she loved immensely, some eighteen months later. They were the happiest married couple; they always showed their immense love for each other regardless of their health issues. We felt grateful for God's mercy and grace in selecting the timing of her death. He allowed us adequate time for her burial without affecting our travel plans. I have often wondered about the scenario if her death had occurred after we had left for Pakistan. Who would have arranged for the befitting burial she deserved? And what about the regrets of not attending her funeral prayers? Duroo had made sure that even when she left this world, it would be easy for us. She was always looking out for us. Her prayers were answered. God took us without disrupting our plans or making us regret having left her behind in the hospital.

I learned a lesson that day—We should always be grateful. God has a plan for us.

We flew to Lahore on April 15 without a change in our itinerary. A Qur'an reading and Fatiha was held in Lahore at Aunty Shamsa's and her son, Sikander's home in Lahore.

Asad's son, Farhan, was married in Lahore; it was a memorable family get-together. Uncle Jamil, ninety-seven, was the most senior elder at the wedding, Auntie Shamsa being the other.

Uncle Jamil and Aunt Hanifa passed away the following year.

Safdar's and Zeba's Unfulfilled Dream—2005

During our stay in Islamabad, I met up with Safdar, my old friend and classmate from NED. Safdar had recently retired from the Pakistan Tobacco Company and was living at the Margalla Towers, luxury condominiums occupied mostly by elites and expat staff. It had 24/7 security, and visitors were screened before entry. Safdar's family occupied a spacious fifth floor condo with an unrestricted view of Margalla Hills, a soothing sight.

Safdar and his wife, Zeba, took us to lunch, and Safdar talked about his comfortable retired life: "I'm really having fun being retired. I'm relaxed as I play golf every morning. I come home and eat lunch and then rest in the afternoon. I'm then ready for an outing in the evening. Sheri, why don't you and Sonia come back and share this good life?"

I thanked him for his remarks. I told him I would think about it.

Safdar and Zeba had named their son after our son, Saad. He had really liked our Saad, who was a year old when he visited the US in 1979. Safdar's son had received admission to higher studies in Canada, and the family was planning to travel to Canada in the fall of 2005.

Barely four months later, a powerful earthquake struck Islamabad. The October 2005 earthquake hit the northwest Pakistan with a severe seismic blow in the morning. The earth in Islamabad shook violently for twenty seconds or so. The Margalla Towers, a twelve-story apartment building, was the only structure destroyed, but some seventy-eight people, including the entire Safdar family, died in their apartments. The secure building had an unannounced seismic intruder that bypassed the 24/7 security and gave little notice to its occupants to escape. Other buildings in the immediate vicinity suffered structural damage, but there were no casualties.

I had lost a dear friend. He and I had shared many happy memories over a half-century. Their dream remained unfulfilled. The saying "Man proposes and God disposes" was true in this case.

The loss of life and property from the 2005 earthquake was immense. My brother, Parvez Hasan, also owned a lavishly furnished three-bedroom apartment in the same building; he lost all the furnishings except for a steel trunk in the earthquake, a 7.6 on the Richter scale.

Ali Baqai's and Zaki Sher's Car Accident—2007

Our phone rang the night of Sunday, July 15, 2007. Mustafa said, "Dad is in the hospital. He had a car accident."

Sonia and I rushed to Newark University Hospital Level 1 Trauma Center, a good thirty-minute drive on the Garden State Parkway (GPS) from our home. We took the outer bridge and went north on GPS to Exit 145. We prayed along the way. We saw Ali partly conscious with a visible head wound and other body injuries. He appeared to be in bad shape.

Earlier that day, Zaki Sher, a close friend and business partner of Ali, had come to Linden, New Jersey. They decided to drive down to Edison, New Jersey to buy some meat to cook for dinner. It was a less than four miles to Edison via the Garden State Parkway between Exits 136 and 132. While returning around 2:30 p.m., their 230 Mercedes driven by Ali was hit on the driver's side. Zeki Sher was on the front passenger seat. The other driver pushed them with such force that the Mercedes turned over, hit a light pole, and landed in the low area near Exit 136. Ali and Zeki were severely hurt. Zeki Sher's injuries were so life threatening that he was transported via helicopter to the Newark University Hospital trauma center. Even the parkway traffic was temporarily suspended. Ali remained conscious during the accident and in the hospital.

The initial prognosis was not good. Both had head injuries. Ali had arm and leg fractures. Ali was conscious while Zeki Sher was not. Ali had been wearing seat belt that day while Zeki Sher had not. Normally, the reverse was true. Zeki Sher often reminded and teased Ali to fasten his seat belt.

It was late in the evening when he was able to provide the nurse his residence landline telephone. The hospital was then able to contact the family by late evening. When we heard the story later, it was a miracle he was alive. Zaki did not come out of coma. He died three months later.

Ali was transferred to RFK Medical Center in Woodbridge. The doctors found a tumor in his large intestine, which was surgically re-moved; it was cancerous. His heart was affected too. He went through a heart bypass at the Jersey City hospital. Doctors said that the accident was a blessing in disguise as without it, the cancer might never have been detected. After RFK, he went through rehabilitation and physical therapy at the Highlands for six months.

According to her daughter, Sarah, upon her father's return home after the rehabilitation, there were visible changes. She recalled, "The man who was dressed from head to toe and shoes shined and a tie tied by seven a.m. would stay in pajamas unshaven and walk around with a blanket around him. Personally, it was a very difficult time. Luckily, Alhamdulillah, Mustafa, and I were living with my parents; that was a blessing in that we were able to support one another during this time.

"We would take turns going to the hospital multiple times a day to visit him and speak with doctors. Ibrahim was three and Sulayman was only nine then. Interestingly, Sulayman had a speech delay around age two that we believe might have been due to the trauma that occurred when he was little as his daily life was disrupted. The boys' grandfather, who was such a large part of their daily lives and who was so involved with them, was suddenly no longer there."

It took years for the family to adjust to taking daily care of their patriarch. His comeback from a life-threatening accident and related health issues was perhaps a miracle and a result of the prayers, devotion, and tremendous support from his immediate family, who sacrificed a lot during his long recovery.

Behram's Comeback from Coma—2009

It was the first weekend of August 2009. The phone rang. Usman was on the phone from Indianapolis. "Abu has gone into a coma. He's in the hospital, and the doctors think he's critical. I'm leaving for Karachi tomorrow."

I wanted to be with my brother. I asked Usman, "Can you book a seat for me as well?"

Usman's travel agent booked me on an Etihad Airlines flight on Monday, the earliest flight from JFK. I was thinking fast. I had no issues or work deadlines to meet in the next two weeks. I could get away for two weeks.

I called Bhaijan in Bethesda about Behram's hospitalization. I told him about my travel plans. I could go for two weeks only since I was to attend a conference in San Diego in the last week of August, where I was presenting a technical paper on pipeline restoration at a conference.

I arrived in Karachi after some twenty hours of flying including a brief stop in Abu Dhabi. I was expecting the worst while I prayed for my brother.

Usman received me at the Quaid-e-Azam Airport and took me straight to South East hospital in Clifton. It was almost midnight; the streets were quiet.

Teeki, Irfan, and Taimoor were there with grim faces. We visited Behram in the intensive care unit. It was a dimly lit room. Behram was unconscious and lying on his back. His face was pale. He was on oxygen. He was in a deep sleep. He did not respond to my greetings.

For the next few days, the routine was to go to the hospital and stay in the waiting room. Family and friends were pouring in. Among my friends, I remember Azhar Ali who came almost daily to the hospital. There was no change in Behram's condition.

Bhaijan also flew from Bethesda and joined us in Karachi.

Ghazli was very expressive; she wanted the "whole" Behram, nothing less. She did not want a disabled husband.

The children, Irfan and Taimoor, were facing their first possible tragedy—losing their father. Usman, being the eldest, was more prepared for the worst scenario.

Behram had no will. He did not have a joint account with Ghazli. The residential properties were in his name only. In case he died, there would be estate issues. He had paid little attention to that. Maybe it was not his time to go.

Usman and I were mentally ready for the worst while Irfan and Taimur were not. We even discussed possible burial arrangements.

Behram was on epilepsy medication. Perhaps he had failed to take the daily dose, which resulted in his coma, which he was in for almost ten days. My sister, Shaheen, was in Rawalpindi. She could not come earlier due to prior commitments. She was really concerned and called every day. A steady stream of family and friends visited the hospital.

On the tenth day, we met with the doctors' team including the heart and kidney specialist, Dr. Nadir Syed, the son of Dr. Shauket Syed, a renowned heart specialist in Karachi. The prognosis was very grim. Behram's heart and kidneys were failing. The doctors wanted us to sign off on a procedure to revive the heart if required. Among the team, only Dr. Nadir was hopeful for a miracle.

Then it happened. Shaheen came from Rawalpindi on the twelfth day. She went to the hospital and went inside the room where Behram lay in a coma. She called out, "Behram, open your eyes!" Behram opened his eyes and woke up. He has been waiting to hear his sister's voice all that time. It was a miracle. Ghazli' s prayers were heard and accepted. Behram lived for ten more years.

Dr. Fareed Baqai (1935–2017) Remembered

After completing their medical education in Pakistan and Great Britain in 1965, Drs. Farid and Zahida Baqai started their practices in Karachi. In the late 1960s, they established a small, 20-bed hospital in Nazimabad that grew to be a 350-bed general hospital in twenty years. Nazimabad Hospital became a center of excellence with modern sophisticated treatment for middle- and low-income patients.

Farid, a surgeon, and Zahida, a gynecologist, joined the Naval Hospital in Karachi. They were married in 1967 and recognized the health care infrastructure issues and the growing need of a health care delivery system for a large population. The concept of community development based on self-reliance without depending on the public sector took root.

In the early 1980s, the construction of a medical college was begun and the first batch of MBBS students was admitted in 1988. In 1992, the

Baqai Foundation established the first dental college in Karachi, which had a population of over 10 million. The medical and dental colleges were accredited by the University of Karachi for MBBS and BDS degrees respectively.

From humble beginning, having been orphaned at early age, Farid was the second oldest son with three younger siblings at the time of the partition who were raised by a young widow, Fatima. She worked hard as a seamstress to run the household in Jacob Lines, Karachi, after emigrating from Delhi in 1947.

By 1952, the eldest brother, Moinuddin Baqai, had graduated from Punjab University, Lahore, with a master's in economics that landed him a job as an officer in the Research Department of the State Bank of Pakistan. That brought immediate financial stability to the family, which moved to Pakistan Chowk and became our neighbors.

By that time, Farid had joined Dow Medical College as a freshman and was studying until late at night. Dr. F. U. Baqai belonged to an illustrious Delhi family. His forefathers emigrated from Iran to Delhi during the Mughal rule. Two brothers, Baqaullah and Zakaullah, rose to eminence in the profession of TIB. The descendants of Hakeem Baqaullah came to be known as Baqais. When Dr. F. U. Baqai was only five, his father, Hakeem Nizamuddin, died. During the communal mass massacre that preceded the partition of India, Dr. Baqai's mother, Fatima, emigrated from Delhi to Karachi with her five sons, indeed a trying time for her. Having lost all she had, she nonetheless took good care of her family. She certainly did a fine job ensuring that each of her sons got higher education with her small earnings from sewing and making dresses for APWA. The brave woman breathed her last in 1992. Dr. Baqai had to face a real hard time to continue his education and maintain the family doing odd jobs.

Dr. F. U. Baqai did his MBBS in 1958 from Dow Medical College, Karachi.

Refer to https://tribune.com.pk/story/1454823/pioneer-private-medical-education-passes-away

He started his career in Ophthalmology at Spencer Eye Hospital, and he moved to Jinnah Postgraduate Medical Centre and got a chance to be attached with Col. Saeed Ahmed who strengthened his roots of Surgery. He obtained his fellowship in Surgery, and FRCS from Edinburgh and FICS in 1965. He was elected as a Fellow of the Pakistan College of Physicians and Surgeons (FCPS) in 1993. He served the Pakistan Navy from 1965 to 1969 as Surgeon Commander at Combined Military Hospital Rawalpindi in 1971. He was elected Secretary of Pakistan chapter of International College of Surgeons in 1965 and the President of the Chapter in 1993. He hosted the Asia Pacific Congress of ICS in 1985. He was the Secretary and a President of Society of Surgeons of Pakistan. He was the Convener of the International Conference of the College of Physicians and Surgeons of Pakistan held in December 1993.

In 1969, he established Baqai Hospital at Nazimabad, and in 1987, he founded Baqai Medical Complex which now consists of Baqai Medical College, Baqai Dental College, Baqai Institute of Health Sciences, Department of Postgraduate Studies, Department of Hematology, Baqai Institute of Medical Technology, Baqai Institute of Oncology and Institute of Nursing. Dr. F. U. Baqai introduced the Community Oriented Medical Education (COME). He was widely travelled, attended a large number of medical conferences. He has number of papers to his credit and is at present Chairman of Baqai Foundation and Chairman, Department of Surgery of Baqai Medical College.

By the turn of the century, the Baqai Medical University was well recognized by the international academic community. The faculty was well qualified and experienced and worked under the guidance of Farid and Zahida Baqai as chancellor and vice chancellor respectively. He considered his achievements a gift of God, and he was always receptive to new ideas and projects including Shehar-e-Baqa, thirty-eight kilometers from Hyderabad, a mega city of health and education.

Dr. Farid Baqai passed away on July 10, 2017. H was buried in the complex compound, a fitting testament to his utmost dedication and immense service to the medical infrastructure of Karachi. The community lost a visionary and a dedicated philanthropist while I lost a compassionate family member and a friend.

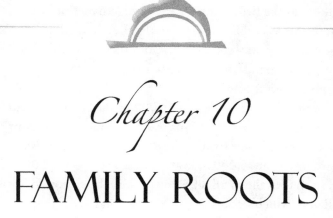

Chapter 10

FAMILY ROOTS

Our family goes back to the reign of Mughal emperor Jehangir and touches two areas of Hoshiarpur and Gurdaspur in the northeastern part of Punjab, India. Our ancestors settled on the eastern and western banks of River Beas, one of the five rivers of Punjab, in the town of Kahnuwan. In the late 1870s, they moved from Kahnuwan to Batala, seventeen miles south.

When Sher Shah Suri conquered Punjab, he ordered a body of Afghans from Roh to settle in Kahnuwan and the adjoining areas of Beas in the district of Hoshiarpur. On his way to India, Emperor Babur, the founder of the Mughal Empire, crossed the Beas opposite Kahnuwan and spent the nights of January 2–3, 1526, very near it. In his memoirs, he called it Kanwahn.

Batala, India

Batala was in the heart of one of the most fertile tracts of Punjab, and its cash crops, vegetables, and fruits provided a flourishing economy. The climate was moderate because of the adjacent hills, and an average rainfall of thirty inches supported the Rabi and Kharif crop seasons. The commodities were sent to Amritsar.

In 1846, as the British took over the governance of Punjab, the tract between the Sutlej and Beas passed to the British. In 1884, the Amritsar-Pathankot railway was completed, a distance of sixty-six miles over a two-year period. Batala and Gurdaspur were twenty-four and forty-four miles from Amritsar respectively.

The population of Batala was 25,000 in the late nineteenth century and consisted of 60 percent Muslims. By comparison, Amritsar was nearly six times as large (165,000 in 1891). The Muslims were nearly the largest group—over 75,000 followed by the Hindus at 65,000 and Sikhs 28,000. In spite of the small Sikh population, the city owed its rise to the Sikh religion, which became known as its religious capital.

Waziruddin (1800–1872)

The recorded history begins when Mian Ahmad and his wife, Sultan Bibi, lived in Kahnuwan. He died in 1820 leaving behind two sons and a number of daughters. With their inheritances, the children lived opulent lives. Waziruddin (1800–1872) was the grandson of Mian Ahmed, a hakim who was fond of traveling. He and his wife produced four sons, Azizuddin, Ghulam Nabi, Ghulam Qadir, and Ghulam Mohammad.

Waziruddin wanted his sons to receive an English education, wear clothing of the new civilization, and change with the times if it did not conflict with their moral values. Waziruddin persuaded his eldest son, Azizuddin, who had received some schooling, to enter the provincial revenue department as a *patwari*, quite contrary to the customs of the landlords. But Waziruddin was a man of strong will and moral courage and broke with traditional thinking at that time.

Waziruddin had a great influence on the social and intellectual growth of the family. He bridged the traditional and modern ways of life. He was ahead of his times in that rural community, and he valued education and the changes happening under British rule. He led a full life and equipped his family with a fuller one.

Ghulam Nabi (1852–1926)

Ghulam Nabi was Waziruddin's second child. He was sent to Batala when he was six for education, and he lived with his uncle Azizuddin and his wife, Sharfu. Ghulam Nabi was a brilliant student. When he was in eighth grade, the divisional inspector of schools visited the school and talked to some the students including Ghulam Nabi. He was impressed with the self-confidence and intelligence Ghulam Nabi exhibited.

Ghulam Nabi was selected by the British authorities to pursue a medical career in the new medical school in Lahore after his graduation from high school. The medical school, opened in 1860, would be later elevated to King Edward Medical College.

Upon his matriculation in 1868, Ghulam Nabi was awarded a scholarship by the Punjab government to cover his tuition, hostel expenses, and monthly pocket money of Rs. 2. The family traveled to Lahore by slow coaches through Batala and Amritsar. A rail link between Batala and Amritsar opened later in 1884.

He excelled academically through his hard work and devotion to learning. He spent the summers in Lahore reading voraciously and experimenting in labs.

Tragedy struck the family when Waziruddin died on August 3, 1872. He was buried the same day next to father in the three-hundred-year-old family graveyard next to his father and forefathers.

Ghulam Nabi graduated with distinction from the medical college in 1873 and placed second in the order of merit out of nine students. He was the thirty-second doctor and the fourth Muslim doctor since the school opened its doors in 1865.

It was ironic that Waziruddin had initiated a similar scholarship to a deserving entry-level student in the medical college in the amount of Rs. 25 per month, and the recipient of that scholarship was Thakur Das, who had been unable to receive a full scholarship upon admission in 1868.

Ghulam Nabi moved to Batala in December 1876. The family was blessed with the birth of several girls including Fatima (my grandmother), who was born on April 13, 1878. The family bought a huge mansion (*haweli*) in Bazaar Kalan (High Street) previously owned by Khundwala, an army commander of Maharaja Ranjit Singh.

At that time, there were more than a score of Kakezai families living in Batala, some of whom were distantly related to Ghulam Nabi. It included families of Mian Husain Baksh (Mian Fazle Husain's father) and Nawab Maula Baksh.

In 1882, Ghulam Nabi joined the Punjab Medical Service and was posted to Peshawar as assistant surgeon. The family was blessed with their first son, Abdul Aziz, born in January 1884, following five girls between the ages of three and eleven. The celebration and festivities lasted several months including a visit to Batala.

A Brief Encounter and a Lifetime Opportunity

While in Peshawar, an incident happened that would change Ghulam Nabi's life and would bring him honor, affluence and fame. On March 28, 1885, Amir Abdul Rahman Khan, the forty-one-year-old ruler of Afghanistan, arrived in Peshawar on an official visit with the viceroy of India. The ruler fell sick and wanted the services of a competent doctor, preferably a Muslim proficient in Persian, to look after him. The British civil surgeon recommended Ghulam Nabi. The young assistant surgeon became the personal physician of the king and a member of the royal party during their nineteen-day travel to India. At the end of his stay, the king thanked Ghulam Nabi for looking after him, presented him with gifts, and even invited him to Kabul. This brief encounter changed the life of Ghulam Nabi and the fortunes of the family some twenty years later.

This episode did not sit well with the British civil surgeon, who fabricated a malicious report on the conduct of Ghulam Nabi during the Afghan ruler's visit. Ghulam Nabi decided to resign from the job due to the conflict with the civil surgeon after serving the government for ten years. The lieutenant governor, Sir Charles Aitchison, accepted his resignation with regret. Aitchison admired the courage of Ghulam Nabi in resigning from a well-sought-after job. In 1896, when an opportunity came, he did not hesitate to recommend him as chief medical officer of

Bahawalpur as well as personal physician to the nawab of Bahawalpur, Sadiq Mohammad IV.

His three daughters married on three consecutive days, November 2–4, 1898, in Batala. Fatima (my grandmother) was married to Shaikh Khairuddin (my grandfather) of Amritsar.

Dr. Ghulam Nabi served as personal physician to the Nawab of Bahawalpur, a princely state in former India (1887–1897). In Bhawalpur, he was responsible for the construction of a new, high-quality jubilee hospital, which opened in 1898.

As a result of his services to the nawab, he was awarded full pension equal to his final salary that continued until his death in 1926.

Personal Physician to King in Afghanistan—1905–1917

In 1905, history repeated itself; the viceroy of India, Lord Curzon, received a request from the Afghan ruler for the services of a Persian-speaking Indian Muslim doctor to act as his permanent personal physician. Lord Curzon sent three names to Amir Habibullah that included Ghulam Nabi's as a strong favorite.

Amir Habibullah, son of the late Abdul Rehman, made the decision quickly after learning that Ghulam Nabi had treated his father in India. Ghulam Nabi was leading a quiet, peaceful, retired life in Batala. All his children except one were married. He was fifty-three. On receiving a communication of his selection from the foreign secretary, he readily accepted the appointment. The family traveled in a special train from Batala to Amritsar, then to Lahore and Rawalpindi, and then to Peshawar and Jamrud. From Jamrud, the family traveled in special coaches to Jalalabad and then to Kabul.

In Kabul, the family consisted of Ghulam Nabi, his mother, Zuhra, his wife, Nur, daughter Sultan, and Zainab, the young wife of their son, Abdul Aziz. It was exclusively a female domain.

Habibullah was thirty-three and exactly twenty years younger than Ghulam Nabi. He liked the doctor and was kind and generous to him. Before long, at the request of Habibullah, Ghulam Nabi's younger brother, Ghulam Muhammad, who was also a doctor, was invited to serve the king's harem.

King Habibullah established Habibyia College, the first secondary school for boys. The teachers were mostly Indian Muslims. During his service, Ghulam Nabi was an instructor of Urdu at the college.

In July 1915, Nur, wife of Ghulam Nabi, died at the age of sixty-one after a short illness in Batala. Until the end, she was in full senses and said a few words of farewell to her eleven children. Ghulam Nabi could not come since Amir had had a minor stroke. For Zuhra, it was a great loss since she had known Nur longer than any of the mourners—almost fifty years. Nur, being the young daughter-in-law, had become indispensable in running the household.

The loss of his beloved wife was inconsolable. Ghulam Nabi thought of committing suicide. In the spring of 1917, he left the service of the amir and returned to Batala. He was lonely without his wife. He was amply rewarded for his service with a lifetime pension equal to his salary of Rs. 1,700 per month. He was sixty-seven when he returned to Batala, and he lived in luxury with two concurrent pensions of over Rs. 2,500 per month.

The life of Dr. Ghulam Nabi and his family story is fully described in a book by his grandson, *A Journey into the Past: Portrait of a Punjabi Family*, by K. K. Aziz (1927–2009).

Ghulam Muhammad (1862–1946)

Ghulam Nabi's brother, Ghulam Qadir, continued to serve Ahabibullah's harem as doctor until 1919, upon which he returned to Peshawar. His son, Hakim Jan, set up a business in Kabul and a office in Peshawar that exported Afghan goods to India and imported Indian goods to Afghanistan. He developed intimate relations with the new king, Amanullah, and Nadir Khan, the future king. His business prospered under Amanullah and even more under Nadir Shah. Nadir Shah granted a pension of Rs. 1,000 to Ghulam Muhammad and his seven successive generations. The pension was received by Hakim Jan till his death in 1963, his son, Asghar, till his death in 1972, and his brother, Azhar Ali, till Zahir Shah (1914-2007) was dethroned in 1973. In December 1933, he closed his trading business and moved to Lahore. The small role that our extended family played in Afghanistan was well rewarded.

Abba ji's Maternal Uncles

Abdul Aziz and Abdul Hamid, maternal uncles of my father, had different tracks in life.

Abdul Aziz (1884–1970)

Abdul Aziz was born on January 24, 1884, in Peshawar thirteen years after the marriage of Ghulam Nabi and Nurunnisa; he followed five daughters born in succession.

Abdul Aziz had his early education at Lady of England High School in Batala. Since there was no college in Batala, he went to Amritsar for further studies followed by studies at Foreman Christian College of Lahore. The college enrollment totaled 329, of which 173 were Hindus, 96 were Muslims, 32 were Sikhs, and 28 were Christians. He lived at the Muslim hostel. He graduated with a BA and married Zainab in 1903.

Ghulam Nabi decided to send his son to England. In September 1904, Abdul Aziz bade goodbye to his family including his young wife, Zainab, left for Bombay, and sailed to England. Upon arrival in London, he lived at 69 Shepherds Bush Road in Western London having been admitted to the Lincoln Inn.

Lincoln Inn was the oldest inn of court having been established in the thirteenth century. The bar curriculum was flexible and imposed hardly a burden on the students; it required some lectures, debates, and some training in elocution and argumentation of a case. The student barristers had to be present for formal dinners and comply with various customs and regulations.

He was joined by Shaikh Abdul Qadir and Mohammad Iqbal to read for the bar. They shared accommodation at the Shepherds Bush Road and then at 40 Dewhurst Road in London. It was rather a coincidence that three Shaikhs shared the same roof—Shaikh from Kahnuwan, a Kakezai Shaikh, and a Kashmiri Shaikh. Abdul Qadir was storyteller, and Iqbal was good listener and poet.

In addition to preparing for the bar, Abdul Aziz attended classes at Oxford and Cambridge universities learning French and German. He also traveled to European cities including Berlin, Heidelberg, Vienna, and Geneva. There were literary gatherings at Sayyid Ameer Ali's residence, where British men of letters and scholars imparted wisdom and knowledge.

He became a friend of Abdullah Yousaf Ali, who was another source of inspiration. He came to England for a year's furlough from the Indian civil service. (That friendship lasted until the death of Yousaf Ali in 1953.) Abdul Aziz returned to Batala in September 1908. Ghulam Nabi's family was in Afghanistan. He rejoined his parents and his wife. He was very happy to be home.

He initially started his practice in Rangoon, which was not successful, and he returned to Hassar. There were additions to the family—a daughter, Akhtar, followed by a son born in 1912 but who died within a year. He moved to Lahore and continued his law practice.

There was a story concerning the end of Abdul Aziz's legal career. While arguing a case in a Punjab Court before an English judge, he interrupted the judge thinking that the judge had uttered a word that was wrong; he suggested its substitution with the appropriate word. To resolve the question, an Oxford Dictionary was brought in and the word in dispute was looked up. The dictionary supported Abdul Aziz's reading. He came home and announced to Zainab, "Today, I have given a lesson in English language to an Englishman or rather tried to. But he does not understand anything. Anyway, I have said farewell to the legal practice." The real reason as later events showed was that his heart was not in the legal practice; it lay elsewhere. He confided in his wife that he wanted to live his own life and pursue his literary passion. Money was not an issue. Ghulam Nabi had granted him a permanent monthly allowance of Rs. 500, a large sum in those days, from the income of the estate.

Abdul Aziz taught English and economics at Islamia College, which was run by Anjaman-e- Hamayat-i-Islam. He was appointed as a professor and offered a salary of Rs. 400 per month. There were fifteen teachers and 555 students. The teachers were burdened with a heavy load, but he taught there for four years.

Upon the death of Ghulam Nabi in 1926, his estate was divided among the heirs. With an ample inheritance and income, Abdul Aziz could pursue his literary and scholarly pursuits. His father's generous allowances throughout his life had supported his extravagant habits and carefree lifestyle.

A third child, a son, was born in 1927. He was named Khurshid Kamal Aziz.

While in England, Abdullah Yousaf Ali had planted seeds in Abdul Aziz of becoming a Mughal historian, and he began to pursue that dream. He began a concentrated study of the Mughal period of Indian history. He chose Emperor Shahjahan. He produced three chapters on "The Mughal Court and Camp" and "The Mughal Army" that were published in 1930 and 1932.

Abdullah Yousaf Ali translated the Qur'an from Arabic to English in 1934. My uncle remembered that when Yousaf Ali published the translation of first chapter of the Qur'an in English, there were riots and he received death threats; people were not ready for translations of the Qur'an for fear of misinterpretation.

Another literary passion of his was Punjabi poetry. A classical crown jewel of this poetry was Waris Shah's "Hir," which was recited by the *fakirs* and *dervishes* in the countryside. One day, a dervish showed up and sang several stanzas of "Hir" that were so melodious that it enlightened his heart, brought extreme pleasure to him, and cast a spell on the gathering. It seemed that Abdul Aziz was born again. That experience changed his life and work for the next several decades.

He began by collecting copies of "Hir" in Lyallpur and Lahore. After two years of study, he discovered there were different versions of the poem, which led him to prepare a true and correct text of the poem. In 1928–29, with the help of his friends, he collected fifty to sixty manuscripts some of which for very high prices. Finally, "Hir" was printed in 1960; it included a fifty-page introduction touching on Waris Shah's life and uncovering the underlying depth of Sufi thought and granting him proper place in the history of Punjabi literature. He drew parallels between "Hir" and poems by Chaucer, Goethe, Dante, and others. He wrote to his son, K. K. Aziz, the following.

I know I told you this many years ago. But I want to say it again because it is important. I gave every ounce of my talent and health to my work on "Hir." But all my exertions would have been wasted without the encouragement your mother gave, and the suffering she bore. She was, in every sense, my co-author. The "Hir" was as much hers as mine.

I visited his home on Poonch Road in Lahore in the early 1960s. He was then a frail man in his seventies. We all affectionately called him Aghaji out of respect. He was of medium build with thin hair. He used to wear reading glasses and wore Western clothes. His daily routine was regimented. He was taken care of by his daughters Razia and Kishwar. He loved afternoon tea with toast. He let the tea brew for exactly three minutes in the pot. He would pour milk first before pouring tea into it. Then sugar was added. He followed this routing meticulously. He ate dinner early that consisted of one meat dish and one dish of lentils with home-made *rotis* followed by a dessert. I am told that he was a cigarette and cigar smoker but limited his smoking to once a day only.

His life partner, Zainab, preceded his death by twenty-two years, in 1948. He died on December 14, 1970, at age eighty-two. His son, K. K. Aziz, wrote memoirs of his family a quarter-century later entitled *Portraits of a Punjabi Family, 1800–1970, A Journey into the Past*. The book cover included a photo taken in 1939 of the family gathering in Batala. The photo included Abdul Aziz and his wife, children, grandchildren, and great-grandchildren including the Fatima-Khairuddin grandchildren.

Abdul Hamid (1889–1943)

He was the younger son of Ghulam Nabi. After graduating from Aligarh University with a MA in English, he taught English for a year at Islamia College. He then joined the Punjab Civil Service and became a successful civil servant in the British Government.

He was married to Sardar Begum in 1916. It was a big celebration in the family. The wedding party consisting of nearly three hundred traveled from Batala to Wazirabad by a special train and returned with the newly married couple to Batala via that train.

Sardar Begum bore him four children, Bilquis, Zubair, Shamim and Nasim. He was a deputy commissioner in Montgomery for many years. His wife died at a young age during childbirth in 1931.

On March 25, 1932, he married a young Pathan girl, Farrukh, domicled in Kashmir. He took her to London on a honeymoon. Farrokh (Bobo Gul) also bore him four children, Salman, Tariq, Riffat, and Farida.

Abdul Hamid died of a sudden heart attack on September 13, 1943. Coincidently, it was the thirteenth of Ramadan. He had been trransferred a few months from Montgomery (Sahiwal) as chief executive officer of Lahore Corporation, the first Indian to get this appointment.

Abdul Hamid contrasted with his older brother, Abdul Aziz. He was over six feet tall with a broad frame; he was a sportsman and was more like his dad and grandfather in personality, temperament, and outlook. He was a practicing Muslim observing fasts during Ramadan and prayers; he was a humble person with an extraordinary sense of loyalty to the family including relatives and their children. Since his home was near the Data Darbar, he visited the shrine and offered Nafal prayers regularly. His funeral procession had over 20,000 people headed by the British governor of Punjab, Sir Bertrand Glancy (1882–1953); he was buried in Miani Sahib graveyard.

He was held in high esteem by my father, being eleven years his junior.

Bobogul (1911–2009)

Bobo became a very young widow when her husband passed away in 1943. She became responsible for seven children ranging in age from three to sixteen. The youngest was Farida, and the oldest was Zubair. Only one daughter, Bilquis, was married at that time.

Bobo had her roots in Afghanistan, and she spoke Persian fluently. She always wore a *saree* and a smile. My father, though older than her, treated her with tremendous respect and affection. She had great charm. She was strong and had a steel interior that allowed her to face the roller-coaster of life with fortitude and certainty.

At a minimum, she was responsible for getting all her children educated and arranging for their marriages. She single-handedly played the role of both parents for over sixty years. She would consult my father on important occasions since she respected his unadulterated advice. She would affectionately call him by his full name, Mohammed Hasan, while no other member of the family dared to address him with his name.

Bobogul's younger sister, Qamar, married M. Z. Babar, from a nawab family, in 1939. She was the family's matriarch. She was graced with sevenfold happiness of her grandchildren being married. She became a great-great-grandmother several times over.

She outlived several of her children, Bilquis (1921–82), Nasim (1930–73), and Zubair (1926–71) as well as sons-in-law Tariq Hameed (1930–2008) and Ghulam Hasan (1912–2006).

She saw the burial of her younger brother, Sarwar, and sister, Qamar, as well as her husband, Babar. She never saw her husband in her dreams until a few days before her death. Her husband was called Sheikh Sahib. He told her, "Bobo, get up and offer the Fajr prayer!"

She woke up and mentioned her dream to the attendant. The attendant asked, "Who is Sheikh Sahib?"

She was then told that Sheikh Sahib was her husband.

Bobo had waited to dream about her husband for sixty-six years. He had finally come to get her. That was her last dream. She died on November 16, 2009, the same day Owais's son, Omer, was getting married. Both her daughters were in Lahore when she passed away. Farida, the younger daughter, lived in London and was visiting the family. She and her sister, Riffat, were able to fulfill the last wishes of their mother—washing her body before burial.

It was more than a coincidence that Farida and her husband, Sallo, were in Lahore. Originally, they were scheduled to depart for London from Karachi. Sallo had changed the flight itinerary for health reasons and was back in Lahore. Salman and Tariq came from Karachi. All her children were present for the farewell and the last rites of the family's matriarch. It was really a sad day in our lives. She had graced us with her presence at my wedding as well and gave us a silver tray that we treasure. Sonia and I were happy when she visited us on Staten Island.

She was also a world traveler too. She drove via land from London to Peshawar along with my uncle, Ghulam Hasan, in 1961.

I saw some of her pictures shown by her son, Rikki, of her visit to England with her husband on an official visit in the early 1940s. She looked very graceful, almost royal, which she claimed to be through personal connections to the king of Afghanistan. Her presence is felt in all the children and their grandchildren. She was truly one of a kind.

The following is a remembrance of Bobogul by her granddaughter, Farezeh.

"I don't know where the name came from. In fact, the only person who didn't call her Bobo was her youngest child, the baby of the family, Farida, my mother.

"Bobo was a force to be reckoned with. She was a beautiful, strong woman who sadly became a widow at a young age at a time when remarriage never even felt like an option. She lived for her children, but she was in charge—the boss. She rode horses bareback in Kashmir, pulled a snake from around someone's neck with her own hands, and was fearless when a thief broke into her house. She made decisions that others followed. She married young and became a widow very young. She lost her oldest daughter, Shireen, at age eight. She faced many tragedies, but she always survived and had a zest for life like no other. I loved that about her. Always smiling and curious and opiniated. She was funny and creative. We were taken on Roman holidays, albeit the pretend holiday was in Lahore, but we loved it. Having ice cream on Mall Road.

"As a child, she would go out in the snow in Kashmir and fill her mug with snow and mix it with honey and drink it. She loved the sound of water. Her dream was to have a cottage, called Garambus cottage, by the waterfall. She loved playing cards even if was solitaire. Her memory was incredible.

"Bobo's smile that won a thousand hearts exhibited the most perfect set of teeth that lasted a lifetime. I often said to her that they were so perfect that people would think they were false. She said, "Stop telling everyone my teeth are real. I'm not a horse!" She always used a *miswak*. She taught us to use it and how I hated it and the taste of it.

"She was way beyond her time. She once said that she told people in Pakistan that they should give the money to the poor instead of sacrificing a lamb at Eid. She received such a backlash—haram, haram! But I was so proud of her thinking.

"She loved Britain and the royal family. She came to London on her honeymoon in 1932 and stayed at the Savoy. She remembered her husband as the greatest love story. She said she adored him and vice versa. I said no one could be that perfect, but she said he was. He made her very happy. She said that when she wore perfume, he would tell her not to stray too far. When on honeymoon in London she looked outside the window and screamed. Her husband was in the middle of prayer. He came running worried about her. She said, 'Look! A white man cleaning the street!' She had never seen that before.

"She was my protector and strength. If my governess was unkind to me, I knew Bobo was my refuge, my soft place to land.

"She would come to London every summer. She walked every morning for five kilometers at least, did grocery shopping if needed, and laid the table for breakfast. After breakfast, we all headed to my parents' restaurant. She was always helpful and pitched in. She was delegated a stool in the corner, and she peeled a ton of garlic. She would tell us the secret of peeling garlic easily was to soak them in water overnight. After the restaurant service, she would come home and water the lawn.

"She would glamorize marriage: 'Marry him, Farizeh. You will travel the world and wear jewels.' On my wedding day, Bobo was so happy and said she had longed for this day. In my wedding day speech, I told everyone how amazing she was and how I hoped that one day I would be as strong, amazing, and loving as she was.

"Bobo hated to cook. She made it clear that cooking was something she never learned and wasn't interested in. She had a long-standing cook named Majeed; he was with her for four decades. However, in her later years, she taught me how to make *kishmish pulao*. She said it was the only dish she knew how to make.

"She was independent and forward thinking. She gave her children their inheritances when they were young. She was broad minded; she would listen to us and never belittle us. She encouraged us to listen to our parents and respect people. If there was a place to go, people to meet, or a travel opportunity, Bobo was the first in line. Her energy was contagious; it spread across the four generations she lived to see.

"Bobo was ninety-three when she came for my youngest sister's wedding. She always walked unaided. Never a dull moment, never a complaint.

"Bobo spoke Farsi. It was her choice of language, and she delved into it when having secret conversations with her children or getting angry. The most common phrase she used was *Bala be shaklatay*. I still use this phrase, and it's been picked up by my six-year-old daughter.

"I remember her with a smile—a beautiful smile."

Khurshid Kamal Aziz (1927–2009)

Khursheed Kamal Aziz, better known as K. K. Aziz, was born in December 1927 in a village, Ballamabad, near Faisalabad. He was educated at the M. B. High School, Batala, Forman Christian College, Government College, Lahore, and Victoria University of Manchester. He had been on the academic staff of the Government College, Lahore, and of the Universities of Punjab, London, Cambridge, Khartoum, and Heidelberg. During intervals from teaching, he served as deputy official historian to the government of Pakistan, chairman of the National

Commission on Historical and Cultural Research, and special policy adviser to Prime Minister Zulfiqar Ali Bhutto.

He was an author of over dozen books and a historian of rank with an international reputation.

K. K. Aziz was the only son of Abdul Aziz, my father's maternal uncle. Thus he was a first cousin even though he was twenty-seven years junior to him.

His autobiography detailed the family history and genealogy.

I last met him in 2005. He acknowledged his appreciation and satisfaction for our deep affection for him. That was our last meeting. He remembered our parents fondly and talked about their hospitality. He was still writing though he was in frail health. He was aided by his wife, Zarina, in collecting the research material that facilitated his writing. He died in 2009 and was buried in Johar Town, Lahore.

General Khalid Mahmood Arif (1930–2020)

General Arif is a relation on the paternal side. His father, Akbar Hussain, was the son of Azizuddin (1835–1924), the older brother of Dr. Ghulam Nabi (1852–1926). The latter was my father's maternal grandfather. The genealogical is presented in the Roots Chart.

General Khalid Mahmud Arif was born in 1930. He entered the First Officers Training Course at Kohat and joined the Pakistan army in 1949 as a lieutenant in the armored branch. He held important positions during two main martial-law administrations. He was a prisoner of war during the 1971 war with India. Upon repatriation, he became the director general of military intelligence. He was promoted to a four-star general and was vice chief of Army Staff in 1984 until his retirement in 1987. He played a critical role in stabilizing the administration of President Zia-ul-Haq.

He was a professional soldier who served the country with integrity and loyalty. Upon retiring, he became a military historian and wrote several books.

In 1995, he authored a book on the political and military history of Pakistan, *Working with Zia: Pakistan's Power Politics.* In 2001, he published *Khaki Shadows: Pakistan 1947–1997,* about the politics, government, and armed forces of Pakistan. In this book, he wrote about the Pakistan army having changed much during his service.

The changes transformed the army from an ill-equipped colonial force to a well-chiseled, hard-hitting and fairly modern war machine capable of defending the motherland, The army also tasted political power-intoxicating and bitter- and in the process learnt a lesson or two, the most important being that politics and soldiering are full time professions each requiring undivided attention. The military interventions in Pakistan bore heavy price tags for the country and for the army itself. The cost is best avoided in the greater interests of both. The army faces a great responsibility and a bright future. The future of the country is inseparably linked with democracy.

In 2010, he authored another book, *Estranged Neighbours: India, Pakistan (1947–2010)* on relations between India and Pakistan.

He had moved from Rawalpindi to Lahore to be near his family. Unfortunately, the move did not end on a happy note. In 2015, he lost his younger brother, Ahmed Tabussam (1934–2015), and his life partner, Khalida, after sixty years of blissful marriage. Then in 2017, he lost his daughter, Humera Aamir.

In January 2018, Sonia and I met him in his Lahore home for condolences. He was always a quiet person but had become lonely. I remember him saying that he regretted coming to Lahore. He passed away on March 6, 2020, as his kidneys failed.

I first met him in the 1950s when he was stationed in Lahore. Later, when I was at Northwestern University, he attended an officer's career course at Fort Knox, Kentucky (1963–64). Abba ji wrote to me with his address in Fort Knox, but I was too busy with my studies to reach out to him.

During his active duty in Rawalpindi, General Arif's family was close to my sister, Shaheen, and her husband, Brigadier Ahsan, who were stationed there. Ahsan was posted there as brigade commander, engineers. Shaheen remembers one incident of support. We had arrived in Rawalpindi the previous night from Lahore when we learned that my brother Jamshed had been rushed to the hospital and was in critical condition. We needed immediate plane tickets. General Arif intervened to assure that seats were available on the next flight for our return.

I had met General Arif's brother, Ahmed Tabussum, through my cousin, Javed, in 1979. He was then working at Columbia University in New York and lived in Brooklyn with his wife, Nasreen, and their children. The family was fond of cooking gourmet dishes, and they entertained us often. Sonia and I met General Arif several times during his visits to New York on occasions when Ahmed's children were married.

My Father's Family

My paternal grandmother, Fatima (1874–1922), was the second eldest daughter of Dr. Ghulam Nabi and Nur. She was married at age fourteen to Shaikh Khairuddin (1857–1928), who hailed from Amritsar. I don't know much about my dada (paternal grandfather) except that he was a pious and respected person. He had been a minor government functionary (*numerdar*) and later served as the imam (*mutwalli*) of a mosque in Amritsar. They had two girls and five boys.

My father, Mohammed Hasan, was the fourth child following the two girls, Habeeb (1890–1900) and Iqbal (1891–1914), and son, Ahmed Hasan 1 (1893–1900). He was born in December 1900 in Batala. By the time my father was born, two older siblings, Habeeb and Ahmed Hasan 1, had died.

My father's younger brothers were Ahmed Hasan, Jamil Hasan, and Ghulam Hasan. They and my father were married at the same time in December 1930, with one day between each wedding. It was perhaps a repeat of the joint weddings of their mother and her sisters held in 1888. It was also a pragmatic decision minimizing wedding expenditure by combining three events. While my father chose his wife, Rashida, outside the immediate family, Ahmed Hasan married his first cousin Akhtar, daughter of Abdul Aziz, and Jamil Hasan married Hanifa, daughter of Amir and Zuhurul Haq. Amir was another granddaughter of Dr. Ghulam Nabi from daughter Barkat (married to Muhammed Husain).

Chacha Ahmad Hasan (1903–1979)

I visited his family when he was employed as a civilian for the Army Ordnance Depot in Quetta. After retiring, he moved to Lahore.

Chacha had five children: Javed, Nasreen, Asad, Naveed, and Najam. All his children except Nasreen were married and had successful lives.

I became friendly with Asad and Naveed when I used to visit them at their home on Elgin Road (later named Sarwar Road after the 1965 war) in Lahore Cantt.

During the summer nights, the whole family would sleep on cots in the back. That was totally novel for me as I was used to always sleeping inside in Karachi.

Asad joined the civil service of Pakistan upon completing his master's degree at Government College, Lahore. He married his love, Talat, in 1966. My cousin, Bilal, remembers the wedding.

Being the youngest family member, I was the groom's surbala; I had to be fitted with the same sherwani as the groom on a very short notice. The tailor was summoned and was told that my sherwani took precedence over all other clothes. I got a matching sherwani to all my cousins who got married. I was the surbala and made a lot of money.

Chacha Jamil Hasan (1908–2006)

He was the hardest working person I ever met. He had held a position in the Pakistan railway from which he retired when he was fifty-five.

As he was growing up, he felt a spiritual vacuum and turned to religion. There were rumors that that he ran away to Darul-Uloom, Deoband, for a short while before he was persuaded to continue his railway training. The Sunni Deobandi Islamic movement began at

Deoband, a town in Saharanpur district, Uttar Pradesh. The school was founded in 1866.

In 1930, he married his first cousin, Hanifa. It was an arranged marriage at the behest of my father. The couple raised five children: Asif, Seerat, Nasima, Farhat, and Rukhsana.

Chacha Jamil and the children came to Karachi often during our early years. He accompanied my father to the Boy Scouts Jamboree in Malir Cantt. He brought me some biscuits too.

He started a poultry farm, Al-Khair, after his retirement, which he ran for twenty years. The farm was named after his father, Khairuddin. He stayed at the farm full time to supervise the feeding of the chicks and assure cleanliness. It was a successful enterprise and a source of income for the entire family.

He was deeply religious. He carried a Qur'an during his travels. He was curious as to our family origins. He was happy when a mystic told him that our family had originated from Gazni and come with the well-known Sufi saint Syed Ali Hajveri (1009–1072) from Afghanistan in the eleventh century. During one of my regular visits, he gave me a copy of a paper that included over a hundred names of family elders who were deceased. He told me that that he would individually include all those names as part of his daily prayers for forgiveness (*mughfarat*) and supplication.

He died on March 16, 2006. We were in Manchester, UK, for our son's wedding having breakfast when I had the urge to call Behram in Karachi, who was unable to attend the wedding. The moment we were connected, he mentioned that Chacha Jamil has passed away that morning.

"Inna Lillahe Wa Inna Ilahe Rajeoon," "We belong to God and we shall be returned to Him."

Refer to https:// en..wikipedia.org/Ali_Hujwiri

Abu 'l-Ḥasan 'Alī b. 'Uthmān b. 'Alī al-Ghaznawī al-Jullābī al-Hujwīrī (c. 1009-1072/77), known as 'Alī al-Hujwīrī or al-Hujwīrī (also spelt Hajweri, Hajveri, or Hajvery) for short, or reverentially as Shaykh Syed ʿAlī al-Hujwīrī or as Dātā Ganj Bakhsh by Muslims of the Indian subcontinent, was an 11th-century Iranian Sunni Muslim mystic, theologian, and preacher from Ghazna, who became famous for composing the Kashf al-maḥjūb (Unveiling of the Hidden), which is considered the "earliest formal treatise" on Sufism in Persian.

Bilal remembers the following.

"He would visit us at our apartment in Lahore while I was in school. He was very strict, but somehow, that never transferred to me. I was his favorite (at least I thought so). He would come to lunch and always separated his two rotis so he would keep track of how much he ate. I would always mess up his count and he would say, "Yar phir hasab kharab kar dia," "You have again upset my counting."

He would not let my dad drive him back in the afternoon; he would insist that I do that. When we got on the road, he would insist that I drop him off at the bus stop. Even though it would only take me another ten to fifteen minutes to drop him off at the farm, he did not want to get used to that luxury."

Chacha Ghulam Hasan (1912–2006)

He was the youngest brother and a teenager when his parents passed away. He became the responsibility of my father, who provided for his college education and financial support. He was married to his cousin Shamim at the behest of my father in 1944.

Chacha Ghulam Hasan joined the Indian air force in 1945 and immigrated to Pakistan in 1947 after the partition.

He was the only brother who learned to drive. He was fond of traveling and visited the UK every three to four years. He would buy a new car, a Vauxhall or Opel, and drive back to Pakistan, about five thousand miles. He would usually be the only driver with his wife and/or kids on board. He did it in 1955, 1958, and last in 1965. He narrated stories of his journey through Europe and Asia through Turkey, Iran, and Afghanistan. Those days, travel was generally safe and without any incident.

His two children, Mussarat and Bilal, were dear to my father. Both were the youngest grandchildren in our family at that time.

My father always wished that his youngest brother would earn the rank of air commodore, a wish that was fulfilled after his death. Chacha was a group captain when he was selected to represent the air force for the Armed Services Payroll Commission appointed by General Yayha in 1969. The representatives from the army and navy had ranks of general and commodore. For balance and equality of the team, he was promoted to air commodore. He retired from the air force upon completing the Pay Commission Report in 1974. He lived in London for two years with his family including his children.

Being a religious person, he followed the dietary restrictions for Muslim *halal* food and regularly performed mandatory and voluntary prayers daily. As an elder, he was a role model and spiritual guide for the entire family. Chacha and Aunty Shamim moved to Athens, Alabama, in the 1980s to be with their daughter's family.

He was the Hasan family patriarch and an inspiration for his nephews, nieces, and grandchildren. His grandson Azam recalled that he learned to drive at his behest. Later, he named his son Hasan in honor of the great-grandfather.

He died on August 11, 2006, and was buried in Huntsville, Alabama. He left behind a legacy of hard work, affection, and family bonds.

Dr. Muhammad Sharif Family

Iqbal, my father's sister (1891–1914) was the second wife of Dr. Mohammed Sharif, a successful physician in Batala. Upon marriage in 1908, she bore him two sons, Najmuddin Yousaf (1910–1986) and Latif. She died soon after Latif was born. Dr. Sharif was married for the third time to Khurshid Begum. Four more children were born from this marriage: Shamsa (1917–2011), Misbahuddin (M. D.) Ariff (1919–2003), Salahuddin (S. D.) Asif (1921–2001), and Najma (1929–).

All the children of Dr. Mohammad Sharif had successful lives. N. D. Yousaf became a scientist with a degree from Cambridge University, UK. He later became dean of the Agricultural University, Lyallpur. His research on sugarcane was appreciated so much so that he was awarded the President's Pride and Performance Medal in the 1960s.

Shamsa (1920–2012) was married to B. A. Khan (1908–1982), an engineer with the Pakistan railways. They had five daughters followed by a son, Sikandar.

Najma was married to Anwar Haq, an attorney. They had two daughters.

M. D. Ariff obtained a law degree, while S. D. Asif became a surgeon, obtaining a FRCS from UK; he worked at Wah Hospital until his death. Both had successful careers. M. D. became a successful businessman, a director of Ispahani Company in East Pakistan, and he moved to West Pakistan in 1971. Ariff was married to Duroo and had two children, Sonia and Aamir. Ariff and Duroo moved to the US in their final years. S. D. was married to Dr. Sugra and had two girls. They moved from England to Pakistan in 1972. They worked for an army hospital in Wah Cantt until the very end.

Dr Ghulam Nabi: 1905

Dr. Ghulam Nabi (1905)

Abdul Aziz (1937)

Dr. Ghulam Mohammad's Family Sittig (L-R): Salamatullah, Hakim
Jan, Ghafur; Standing (L to R): Fazle Elahi, Rahim Jan and GA Gul

A Group Photo at Batala (1917) Sitting (L to R): Abdul Hamid, Abdul Aziz, Muhammad Hussain, Akbar Husain, Abdul Hamid; Floor (L to R): Ghulam Hasan (Chacha), Sadiq, Hakim Jan, and Muhammad Hasan (Abba ji)

Abdul Hamid (1942)

Abba ji with Chaudhri Mohammad Ali

My Dada -Shaikh Khairuddin

Dr. Mohammad Sharif

Family Group 1939

Standing (L-R): Hanifa, Anwar, Fahmida, Abdul Majid, Jamil
Hasan with Farhat, Mohammad Hasan (abba ji), Ahmed Hasan,
Ghulam Hasan, Khurshid, Irshad, Kishwar, and Razia
Middle row (L-R): Nasima, Muhammad Hayat, Akhtar, Abdul
Aziz, Khurshid, Muhammad Husain, Zainab, Akbar Husain, Amna,
Rashida(Apa ji) with Behram, Abdul Hamid with Nargis
Bottom (L-R): Shafaq, Khaleeq, Jamshed, Nasreen, Asif, Ahmed Tabassum,
Khalid Arif, Waheed, Parvez, Javed, Parveen, Seerat and servant

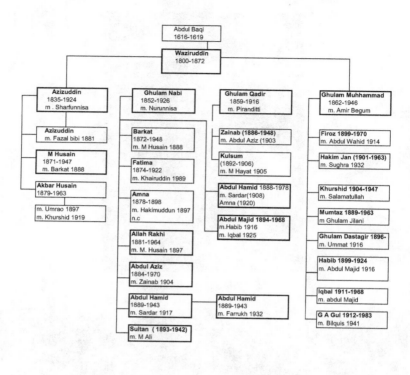

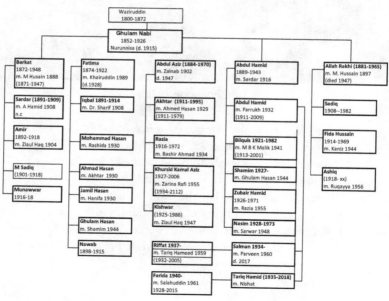

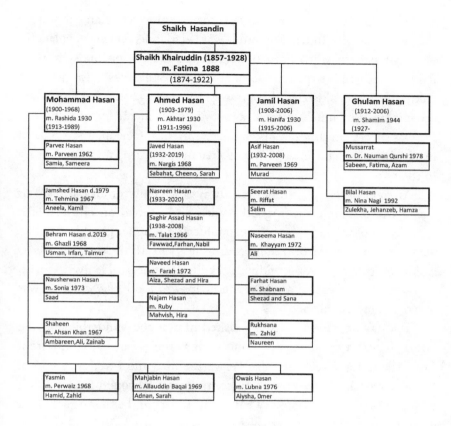

Misbahuddin Ariff (1919–2003)

He joined MM Ispahani Co. in Calcutta, India, and immigrated to East Pakistan in 1947. Ariff became a well-established businessman working with MM Ispahani Co. East Pakistan until 1971.

During the 1971 riots, he sent away his family, including Duroo and Aamir, to Lahore, anticipating unrest by the militant Mukti Bahini. He was alone at home when his home, perched on a hill, was raided. The rioters were firing their weapons as they came up the hill. He was really scared. He called Zakir Hussain, then governor of East Pakistan, for help. He was rescued just before his home was overtaken. He had had a close call.

After the Pakistan army restored order, he moved to Karachi prior to the proxy war with India. That proxy war led to independent Bangladesh.

Ariff had to work hard to reestablish the tea business in West Pakistan. There were no imports from the Bangladesh (former East Pakistan). West Pakistan did not possess the sloping hill tracts like Sylhet accompanied by much-wanted rain, two key elements for growing tea. He was successful through his contacts in Africa, Ceylon, and England in reviving his tea business in West Pakistan and setting up a new factory in the north.

An avid bridge player, he was always the center of all parties. His was a worldly man and a good reader, and he had an encyclopedic knowledge of cricket. His broad shoulders, physique, good looks, and gentle manners made him quite charming. Beneath the surface, he was a hardworking and serious individual with a soft heart. He lived a lavish lifestyle. He always had a great appetite for *desi* food; *shuljam ghost* was one of his favorite dishes.

The day he passed away, we visited him at the Vanderbilt nursing home. It was a Sunday afternoon. Sonia's aunt, Lilu, had come from Long Island for a weekend. She, Perwaiz, Sonia, and I went to see him. He was awake. He was trying to communicate through his eyes as if saying, *Don't go* or *Goodbye*. We did not understand either signal. That evening, his soul passed on to heaven. It was August 3, 2003. He left behind a darling wife after sharing fifty-three years of endless love with her.

Chapter 11

LESSONS IN THE PURSUIT OF HAPPINESS

As I reflect on the years that have passed by at a rather amazing speed, I realize the journey had been a lot of fun. I could have not planned it better. I must confess there were some anxious moments, but mostly the bumps were trivial and easily forgotten. It is time to share the lessons I have learned before they fade away.

I remember my first love in New York City the year after the Beatles had run over and conquered the hearts of young Americans. The presidential election had been won by a liberal Democrat from Texas, who defeated the Republican maverick from Arizona. It was a cool and refreshing autumn in Manhattan. It was my first meeting with the only daughter of Thomas Edison, named Ebasco, in the shadows of the Trinity Church in the Financial District. It was love at first sight. The love affair lasted nearly half a century and granted me the opportunity to travel from the California highlands to the New York islands, from the Northwest to the Southeast, and across the plains of the Midwest—nearly all the states. My love affair's high points were many.

I faced engineering challenges—harnessing the Mississippi River for the Vidalia Hydro power plant and the Missouri River for the Rainbow Redevelopment Project; I did forensic engineering on North Dakota and South Dakota dams. The advent of the nuclear era in the seventies provided me an opportunity to work on the Shearon Harris Plant in the Carolinas, St. Lucie Plant in Florida, and the WPPSS Project in Washington State. The successful surge of nuclear power stations in the 1980s was marred by the Three Mile Island and the Chernobyl accidents followed by backlash that killed the nuclear industry.

The high point was working in the World Trade Center Complex for over twenty-one years. The New York skyline was at my feet. The sunrise over the East River and the Brooklyn Bridge was breathtaking. The glow of the Empire State Building in the waning light of the winter sun was romantic. On a clear day, one could see as far as West Point on the Hudson River.

I survived the WTC bombing in 1993 and the 9/11 tragedy in 2001. I even survived a heart attack. I must say I have been resilient.

The 2020 coronavirus has descended on the world with powerful economic disruption and loss of human lives. Its emotional and economic impact may last for several years and perhaps become the biggest story for years to come, but it will pass. Humanity's pursuit of happiness will continue.

I share with my readers my lessons in pursuit of happiness, some of which are universal values we ignore until we learn them through real-life experiences.

Here are a few of the lessons of my journey.

Be a Dreamer

Dreams can be real. Follow your dreams. God will open doors to fulfill your dreams. The possibilities are immense. Rewards will be coming, and your destiny awaits you.

Be Prepared

Follow the Boy Scout motto. The world is changing fast with disruptions taking place constantly and more rapidly. Be prepared to face each adversity calmly and with dignity and resolve. Focus on the present, do not look back, and act to the best of your ability.

Be Patient

Every adversity becomes an opportunity. Do not complain. No pain, no gain—that is true. The pain prepares you to be stronger. Difficulties are a part of life. God knows the outcome. God is testing you. It may be a while, but your blessings await you.

Be a Team Player and Share

Realize the power of teamwork. Have a clean and receiving heart. Share with others, and be a team player. It will bring you happiness and goodwill from others and few regrets.

Hug Others

Experience the power of hugging particularly family and friends during sad and happy occasions alike. For sad occasions in particular, hugging provides therapeutic benefits and comfort and reduces anguish and stress.

Prophet Mohammed (pbuh) was hugged by Angel Gabriel during their first encounter during the revelation of the Qur'an. Being unable to read or write, he was asked to recite the first revelation of the Qur'an. When he failed to do so, the angel hugged him; he was then able to recite the first verses of the revelation. It was the hug that did it.

Believe in Yourself

Be yourself, and know who you are. You were created in the best mold by God. You eat the fruits of your words. Say it and it will come true. Do not despair; success awaits you. The possibilities are immense. Remain positive. Follow good thoughts—They are real. Listen to the voices within. Success await you.

God has a plan for you.

Author's Photo

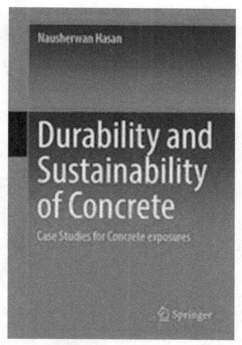

Author's Book Cover "Durability and Sustainability of Concrete" (2020)

Staten Island Sunset

Appendices

1. Letter from Abba ji to son, Sheri, dated September 8, 1964 congratulating him on his MSCE degree.
2. Letter from Abba ji to daughter Shaheen after her marriage to Maj. A. Y. Khan in 1967.
3. Letter from Abba ji to son, Behram, who was posted in East Pakistan in 1968. The letter talks of consulting a heart specialist and insomnia. Behram had a dream about Abba ji's illness/death during this time. Part of the letter is written by Yasmin.
4. Apa ji letters to Yasmin

Abba ji Letter (1964)

Typed Version of Abba ji letter dated September 8. 1964 *6/B SMHS, Karachi 3*

My dear Sheri,

I was delighted to learn the good news that you have with the Grace of

God got your MS Degree. Please accept the heartiest congratulations for your brilliant success which you deserve/ I remained worried about your exam and had been praying for your success. Thank God that you completed your education and now free from worries. Inshallah you will get a good job very soon. You need not worry on that score.

You will be surprised to know that Shaheen and Pollah (Yasmin) left for Jeddah on 29th August. They gave a surprise to Parvez. Your mother was keen to send them, and everything was arranged in a few day's time. They got foreign exchange of Pounds76 each. I think by this time they must have written to you. They are enjoying their best and must have performed Umra by this time.

Mr. Anwar Ali reached Karachi the same night and has gone to Tokyo to attend IMF Conference. He came to see us and promised that he will have dinner with us on his return about 20th instant.

Parvez has been offered the post of Chief Economist of West Pakistan and Mr. Shoaib called A. Ali to relieve Parvez. Mr. Ali cabled back that Parvez could be relieved latest December. I have written to Parvez to come by the end of the month to discuss other matter with him. The post carries a salary of Rs 2300 with a status of Secretary of the Province and equivalent to Joint Secretary of the Centre. Anyhow he will be here to stay in Lahore and can pay us frequent visits.

Ghulam Hasan, Shamim and children paid us a visit for 4 days. Shamim and children left on Saturday by freighter and Ghulam Hasan left on Sunday.

I think I have written to you that Allaudin left for USA for his MS. His brother Mohiyudin has been engaged with a daughter of a Hakim, who is a relative.

Behram could not be successful in securing a job so far. He can join Habib Bank at Rs 400 but I told him to wait for some time till he gets a good job. In the meantime, he has got admission to Law and may be appearing for Ist. LLB in December.

Gigli and Muna have started college. We sometime feel very lonely.

You must have a job in USA so you may be able to bring a car on your return. In the meantime, Parvez would be here and you may get a senior scale in WAPDA.

I just got a call from Mani that Bobo is reaching here by air tonight.

The weather is quite pleasant these days.

Jamshed is perfectly well. He had a mind to pay us a visit in October, but I told him to take leave in December when Parvez will be here, inshallah.

Sometime back, I was not getting good sleep., but now I am quite well and get regular sleep. I close this letter because your mother has to write to you.

I once again congratulate you on your (success) and am proud of your achievement. With love from all us

Yours affectionately

Mohammad Hasan

My dear Shaheen,

Thank you for your loving letter of the 24th inst. Rehotta did not get your letter so far. If you had written from Karat then there is a possibility of getting that, otherwise it had been misplaced or lost.

We are all happy to learn that you enjoyed your travel trip & are keeping fit. I hope you will continue writing to us regularly or give us a ring.

These days we are feeling very lonely, as you, Rohan & gigli left suddenly.

I get letter from jawhid regularly & he was disappointed very much as Rohan cancelled his visit to Chittagong at the last moment.

I received a call from Perez just now. They are all well & Rohan is in perfect health. He told me that Rohan will get promotion in grade III with retrospective effect; it means that he would get arrears for the last 2 years. He may also be transferred to Head Office when he joins.

I hope inshallah gigli will get through. We may get to know about him from Ghulam Hasan this evening. Ghulam Hasan may come to Pindi in a day or two.

I was sorry to learn the plight of your room. I hope you will renovate it in time. Generally very few people know how to keep the room clean & tidy.

Hillman is still lying in the same condition. It is to be towed by lifting the front wheels, so far there has been hurry & so nothing could be done. I think it will be required on gigli's return.

Eneeba left for jebal last evening. Your brother gave Rs. 50/- to Anika & 2 almonds for Nanita, to Eneeba.

I hope you must have written to Rohilla young khan

Abba ji Letter (1967)

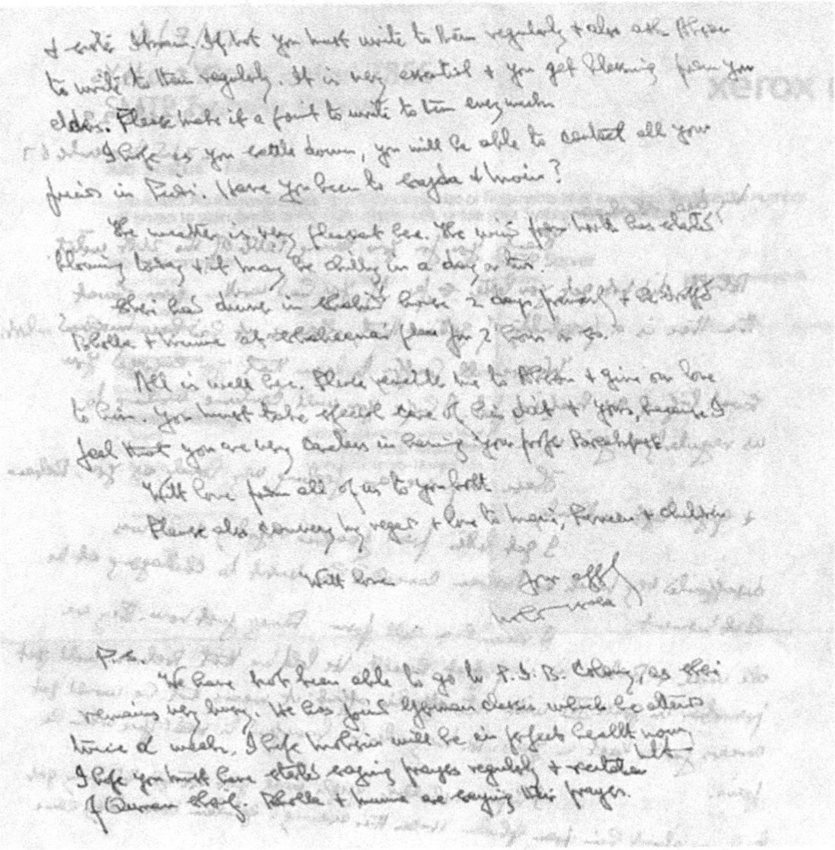

Abba ji Letter (1968)

338

Abba ji Letter to Behram (1968)

Apaji's letter (Karachi, Pakistan) To Yasmin (Staten Island, NY
(Undated)

ASA- Yasmin!

I received your letter. Thanks. I feel happy to receive your letter. I do indulge sometimes. Two months ago, the blood sugar was 165. I felt weak. It was very cold also. I am more careful with the diet now. I eat at home only. I am afraid of the eye operation. Please pray for success of my operation. Eyes are quite week. May Allah Bless Sonia and Sheri, who are taking care of you. It is their duty as well. But it is difficult in a foreign country.

I am happy you like your job. I thank Allah. I pray for all the children. Please pray after, especially Fajr, every prayer with sincerity for Hamid's success, Inshallah.

How is sweet Zahid?

It's cold here. Perwaiz was here yesterday and is well. He awaits your letter.

Everybody in Pindi is well. I have conveyed your regards to Tehmina. She is reciprocating the same to you. Kakub's son is getting engaged in April. She is the daughter of Wajid Mirza, family friend. She was studying with Shezy in USA.

Riffat and Tariq are in London for treatment.

Aneela is growing well and tall. I pray for her happiness and good fortune. Both the kids are doing well in studies.

Khala (Fatima) is better now. But she was pretty sick. I went to see Naz with Perwaiz last week.

Tell Sonia to bring a face lotion when she visits next time.

After my operation, I intend to renew my passport. I may visit if God wills.

Salam to Sheri and Sonia. Love to saad. Salam to Munna and Allauddin. Love to Eddie and Sarah.

My job is to pray. It is up to God to accept it, who is Qadir and Karim.

We remember God in difficulty, and not otherwise.

With the Grace of God, all my children are good. Good habits, hard work are essential.

My dear Yasmin, you should encourage and support Perwaiz. He misses you and the children. He is waiting for your letter. He received letters from the kids.

You must provide Islamic education to your children.

Perwaiz is staying with Baqai, since we do not have a spare bedroom. He joins us for lunch sometimes.

Yesterday we went to Canteen with him. I like his company. Otherwise I am all alone in my bedroom.

Lease has been renewed for one year. Behram receives Rs 2700 rent. I receive Rs 500.I give Rs 100 to Mali, and Rs 200 to two Ayas, rest for fruits etc. Pervez sent me $450, which was deposited in the bank. I will use the funds for my operation.

Rashida, sister of Farida, who taught Zahid came to see me.

Irfan is in Public School in Clifton. Taimur is at Haider Ali Rd School and goes in a school van. He is quite bright. He brings your mail from outside and says its letter from Phophu. Yasmin. He reads Quran. Make sure Zahid and Hamid read Quran regularly, whenever they find time, lest they forget it.

Baqai is sincere and wise. May God keep him happy and grant him good health. Parwaiz praises him.

I will get operated after the sugar is in control. It's in God's hand.

Ask Sheri and Sonia if they need anything, I will send thru Moin Baqai. Behram and Ghazli send salam.

Love to children. Take care of your health and leave the matter in the hand of Almighty.

Love to all the grandchildren (by name).

With prayers,

Yours Mother

Karachi – January 16, 1984

ASA- I received your letter. Thanks.

Congratulations on your job. Inshallah Tala, you will be confirmed as well.

I am always praying for you. He is all powerful and listens to prayers made with true and sincere heart. He is the Provider, Creator, and Maa'lik.

My dear- there is time for everything. Our job is to ask. To Him belong the Universe, and He is the Controller and knows our intentions and actions. Be patient.

Perwaiz Ahmed is perfectly fine and lives with Baqai. Every Friday he comes to Nazi or Iftikhar, or our home. He misses the children, as I do. He is after all the father of the children.

He is happy with Baqai with his own bedroom and bath, as well servant Ask Bhaijan to call me. I will wait for his phone.

I repeat Perwaiz is fine and earing well. He will come when he gets leave.

I am sending a readymade suit for you on your birthday, and one for Zahid and Hamid.

Shaheen is fine. Owais is at Tufail Rd, Lahore. Ambareen and Ali are fine too.

Many happy New Year to you all, with peace, and good health. May god protect from every evil. Amin.

I feel satisfied when I receive your letters.

With prayers and love
Yours Mother

CPSIA information can be obtained
at www.ICGtesting.com
Printed in the USA
BVHW031946050121
597053BV00010B/52